Good grief, more PEANUTS!®

Other Titan Facsimile Editions by Charles M. Schulz

On sale now:

Peanuts

More Peanuts

Good Ol' Charlie Brown

Coming soon:

Snoopy

You're Out of Your Mind, Charlie Brown!

But We Love You, Charlie Brown

Peanuts Revisited

Go Fly a Kite, Charlie Brown

Peanuts Every Sunday

Good grief, more PEANUTS!

By CHARLES M. SCHULZ

TITAN COMICS

GOOD GRIEF, MORE PEANUTS!

ISBN: 9781782761570

PUBLISHED BY TITAN COMICS, A DIVISION OF TITAN PUBLISHING GROUP LTD,

144 SOUTHWARK ST, LONDON SE1 0UP. TCN 302.

COPYRIGHT © 2015 BY PEANUTS WORLDWIDE LLC.

PRINTED IN INDIA.

10 9 8 7 6 5 4 3 2 1

WWW.TITAN-COMICS.COM

WWW.PEANUTS.COM

ORIGINALLY PUBLISHED IN OCTOBER 1956 BY RINEHART & WINSTON

NEW YORK & TORONTO

A CIP CATALOGUE RECORD FOR THIS TITLE

IS AVAILABLE FROM THE BRITISH LIBRARY.

THIS EDITION FIRST PUBLISHED: SEPTEMBER 2015

CHARLIE BROWN

VIOLET

SNOOPY

PATTY

SHERMY

LUCY

SCHROEDER

BEETHOVEN

'PIG-PEN'

LINUS

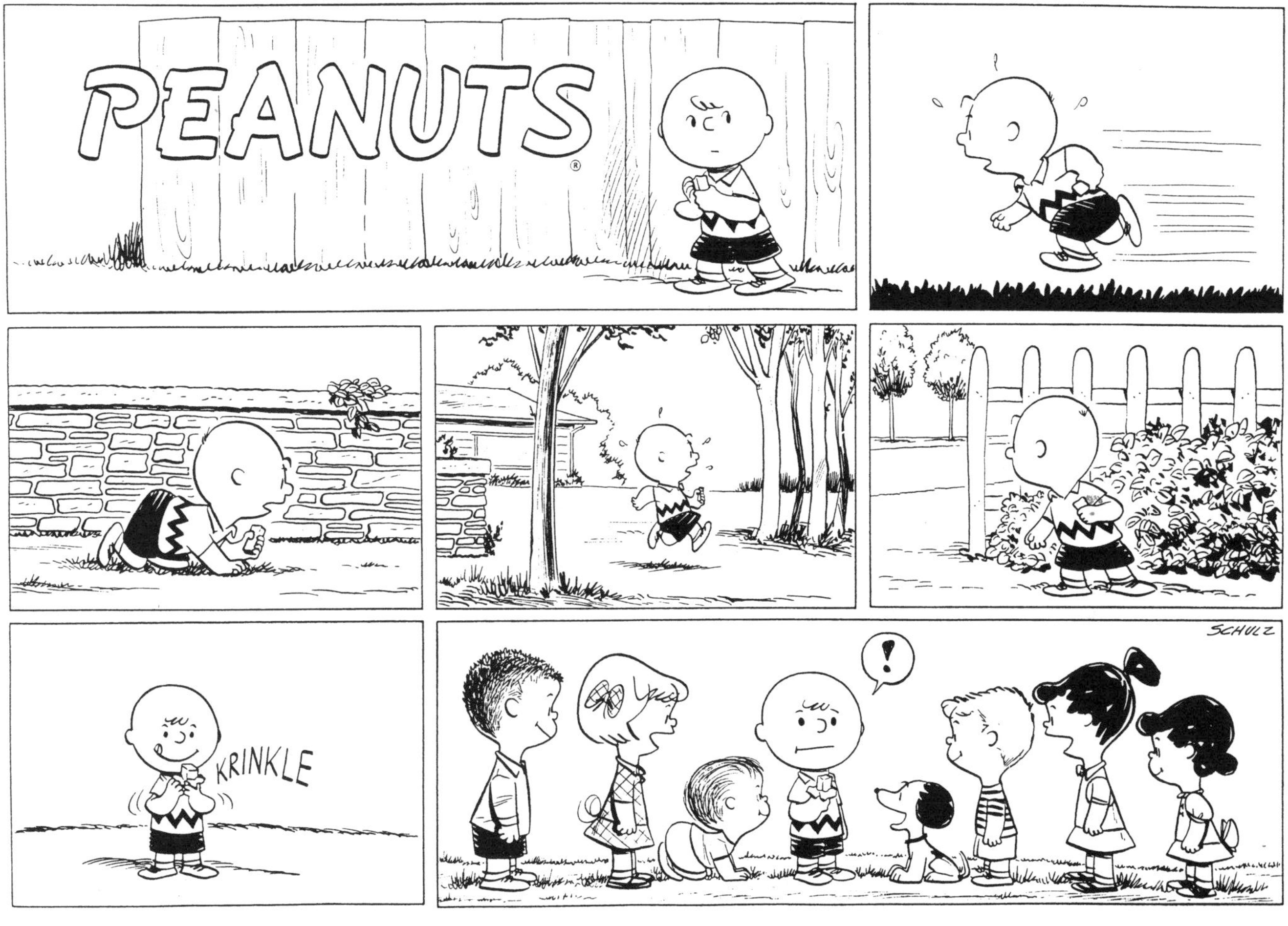
PEANUTS®
KRINKLE
SCHULZ
!

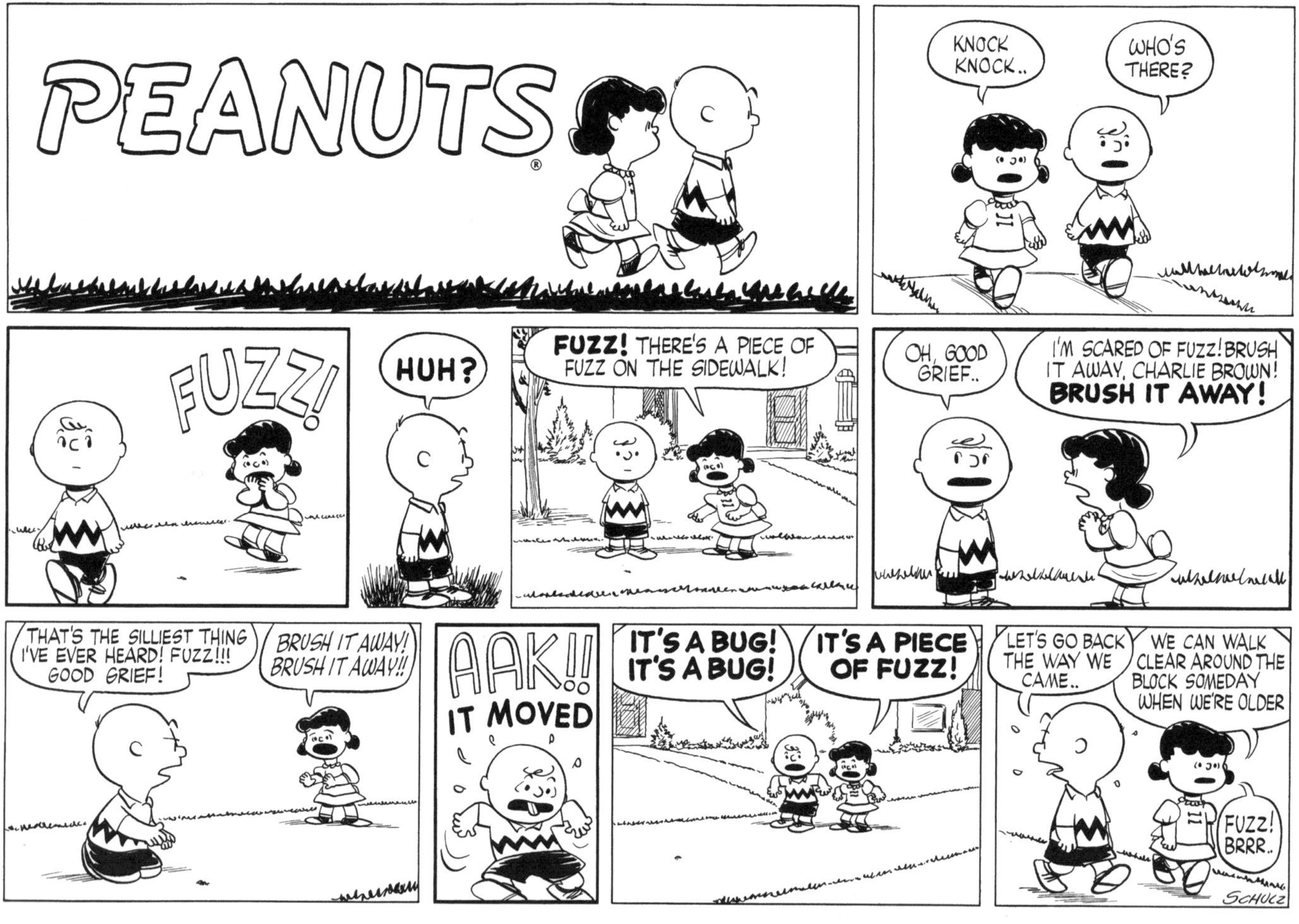
PEANUTS®
KNOCK KNOCK..
WHO'S THERE?
FUZZ!
HUH?
FUZZ! THERE'S A PIECE OF FUZZ ON THE SIDEWALK!
OH, GOOD GRIEF..
I'M SCARED OF FUZZ! BRUSH IT AWAY, CHARLIE BROWN! BRUSH IT AWAY!
THAT'S THE SILLIEST THING I'VE EVER HEARD! FUZZ!!! GOOD GRIEF!
BRUSH IT AWAY! BRUSH IT AWAY!!
AAK!!
IT MOVED
IT'S A BUG! IT'S A BUG!
IT'S A PIECE OF FUZZ!
LET'S GO BACK THE WAY WE CAME..
WE CAN WALK CLEAR AROUND THE BLOCK SOMEDAY WHEN WE'RE OLDER
FUZZ! BRRR..
SCHULZ

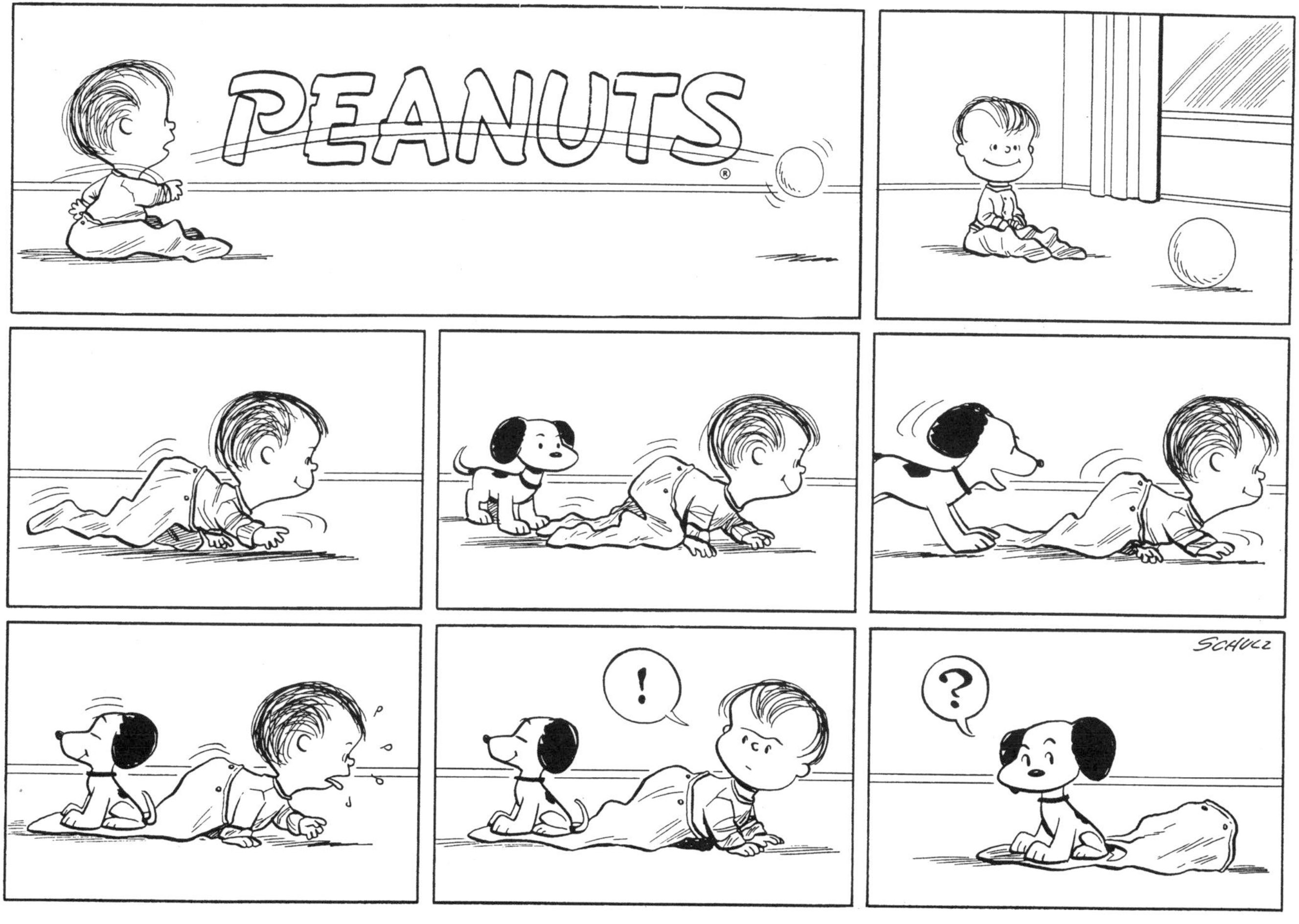
PEANUTS
!
?
SCHULZ

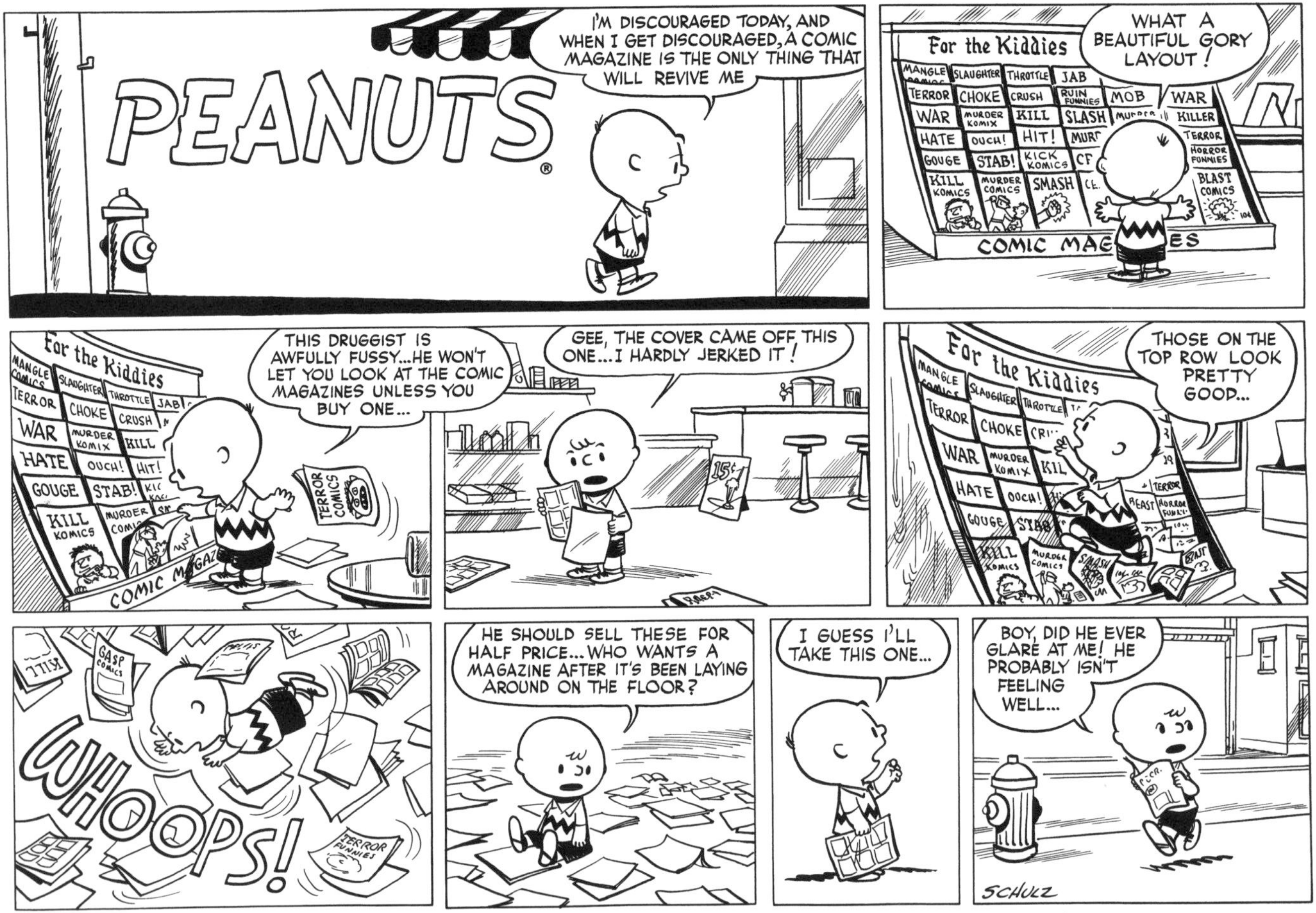
PEANUTS®
I'M DISCOURAGED TODAY, AND WHEN I GET DISCOURAGED, A COMIC MAGAZINE IS THE ONLY THING THAT WILL REVIVE ME
For the Kiddies
WHAT A BEAUTIFUL GORY LAYOUT!
THIS DRUGGIST IS AWFULLY FUSSY...HE WON'T LET YOU LOOK AT THE COMIC MAGAZINES UNLESS YOU BUY ONE...
GEE, THE COVER CAME OFF THIS ONE...I HARDLY JERKED IT!
THOSE ON THE TOP ROW LOOK PRETTY GOOD...
WHOOPS!
HE SHOULD SELL THESE FOR HALF PRICE...WHO WANTS A MAGAZINE AFTER IT'S BEEN LAYING AROUND ON THE FLOOR?
I GUESS I'LL TAKE THIS ONE...
BOY, DID HE EVER GLARE AT ME! HE PROBABLY ISN'T FEELING WELL...
SCHULZ

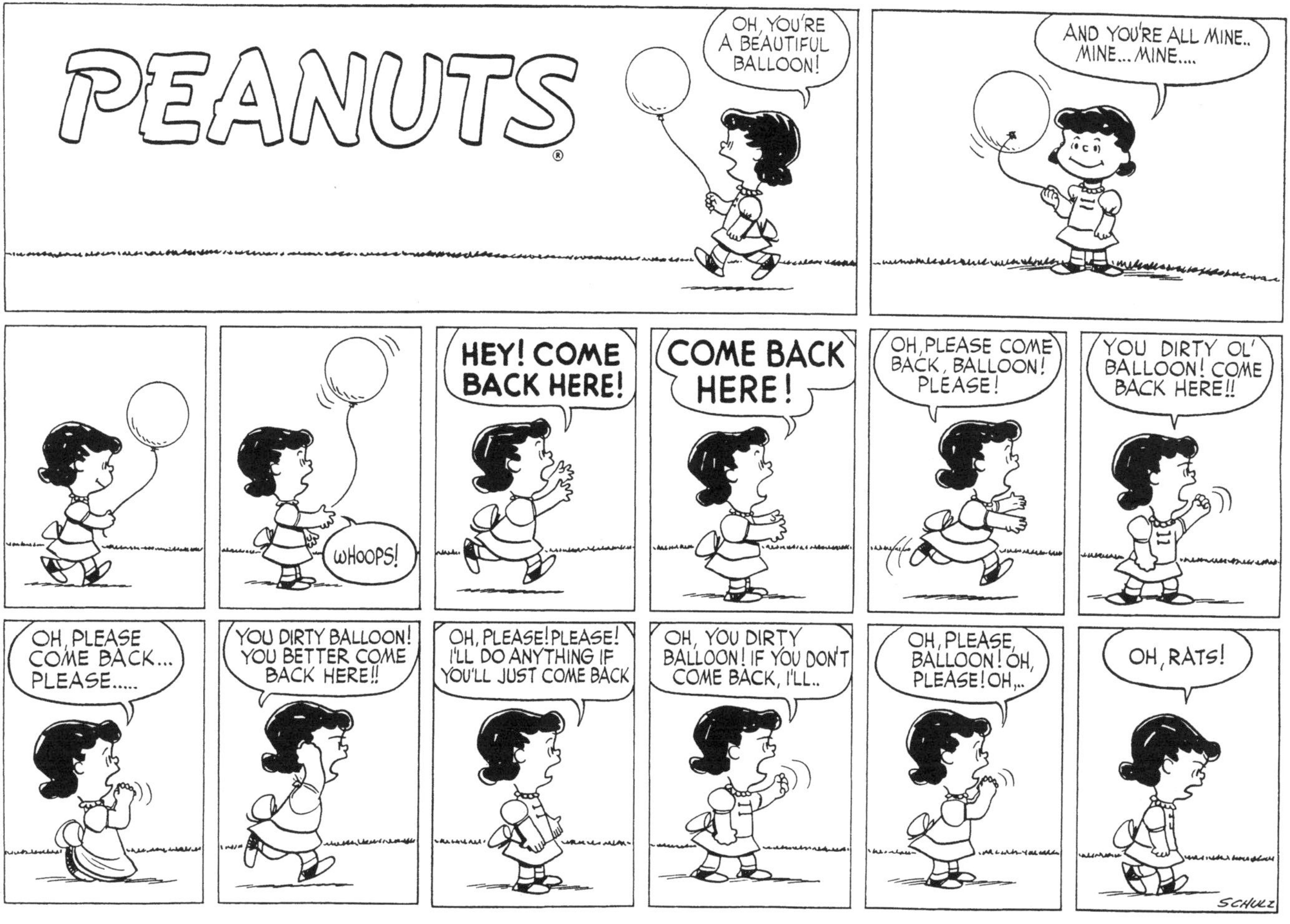
PEANUTS®
OH, YOU'RE A BEAUTIFUL BALLOON!
AND YOU'RE ALL MINE.. MINE... MINE....
WHOOPS!
HEY! COME BACK HERE!
COME BACK HERE!
OH, PLEASE COME BACK, BALLOON! PLEASE!
YOU DIRTY OL' BALLOON! COME BACK HERE!!
OH, PLEASE COME BACK... PLEASE.....
YOU DIRTY BALLOON! YOU BETTER COME BACK HERE!!
OH, PLEASE! PLEASE! I'LL DO ANYTHING IF YOU'LL JUST COME BACK
OH, YOU DIRTY BALLOON! IF YOU DON'T COME BACK, I'LL..
OH, PLEASE, BALLOON! OH, PLEASE! OH,..
OH, RATS!
SCHULZ

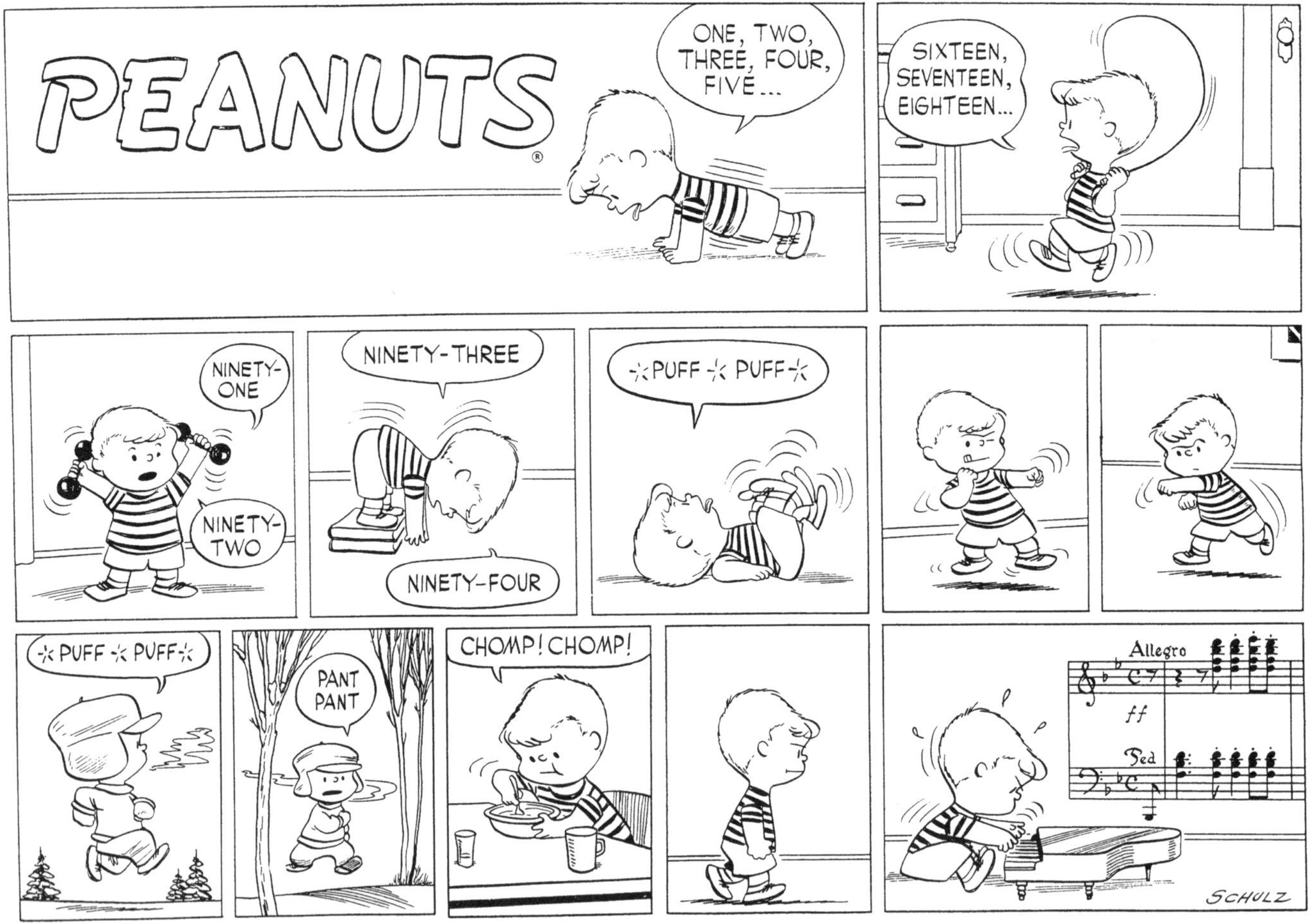
PEANUTS®
ONE, TWO, THREE, FOUR, FIVE...
SIXTEEN, SEVENTEEN, EIGHTEEN...
NINETY-ONE
NINETY-TWO
NINETY-THREE
NINETY-FOUR
PUFF PUFF
PUFF PUFF
PANT PANT
CHOMP! CHOMP!
Allegro
ff
Ped
SCHULZ

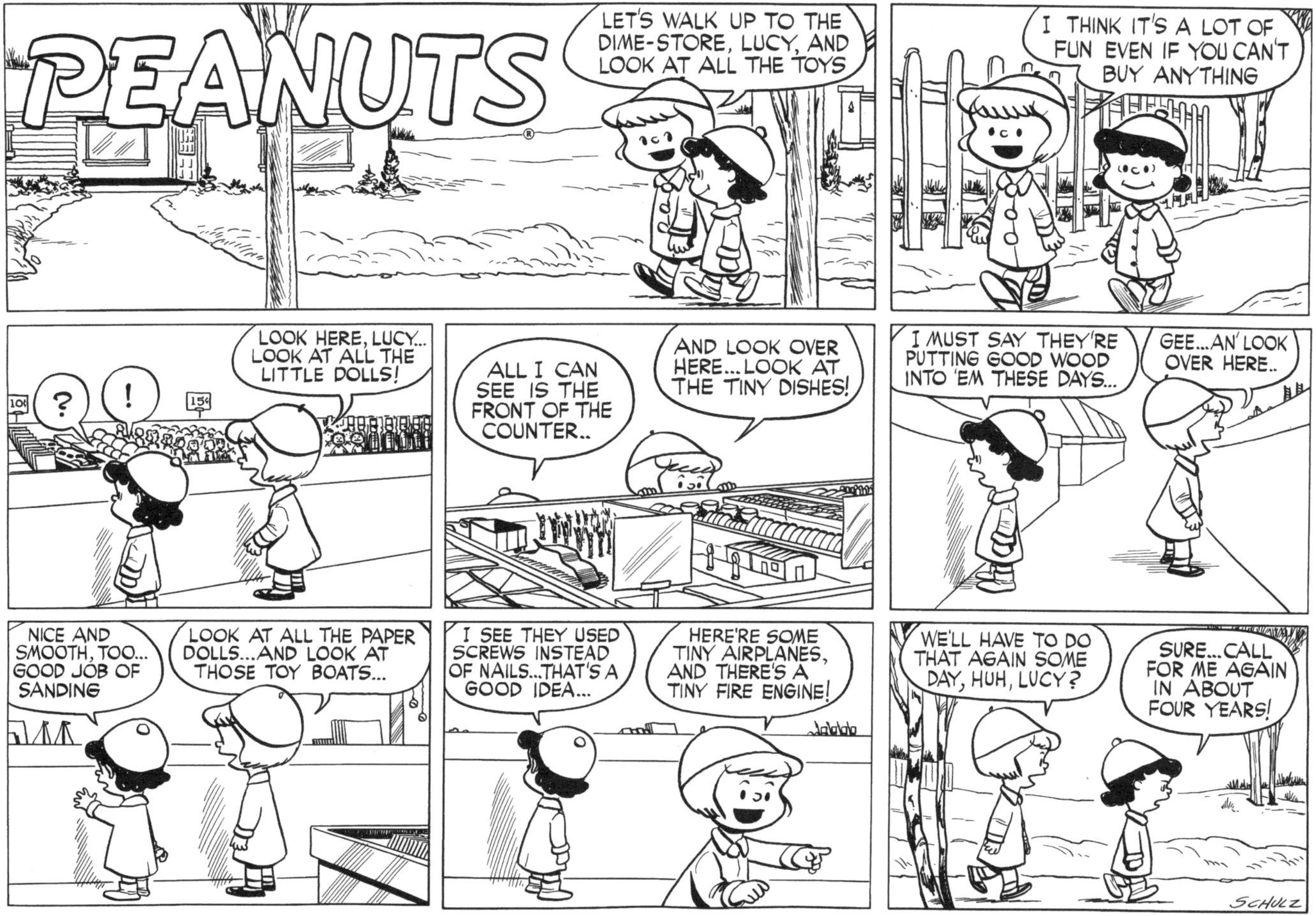
PEANUTS
LET'S WALK UP TO THE DIME-STORE, LUCY, AND LOOK AT ALL THE TOYS
I THINK IT'S A LOT OF FUN EVEN IF YOU CAN'T BUY ANYTHING
LOOK HERE, LUCY... LOOK AT ALL THE LITTLE DOLLS!
10¢
?
!
15¢
ALL I CAN SEE IS THE FRONT OF THE COUNTER..
AND LOOK OVER HERE... LOOK AT THE TINY DISHES!
I MUST SAY THEY'RE PUTTING GOOD WOOD INTO 'EM THESE DAYS...
GEE... AN' LOOK OVER HERE..
NICE AND SMOOTH, TOO... GOOD JOB OF SANDING
LOOK AT ALL THE PAPER DOLLS... AND LOOK AT THOSE TOY BOATS...
I SEE THEY USED SCREWS INSTEAD OF NAILS... THAT'S A GOOD IDEA...
HERE'RE SOME TINY AIRPLANES, AND THERE'S A TINY FIRE ENGINE!
WE'LL HAVE TO DO THAT AGAIN SOME DAY, HUH, LUCY?
SURE... CALL FOR ME AGAIN IN ABOUT FOUR YEARS!
SCHULZ

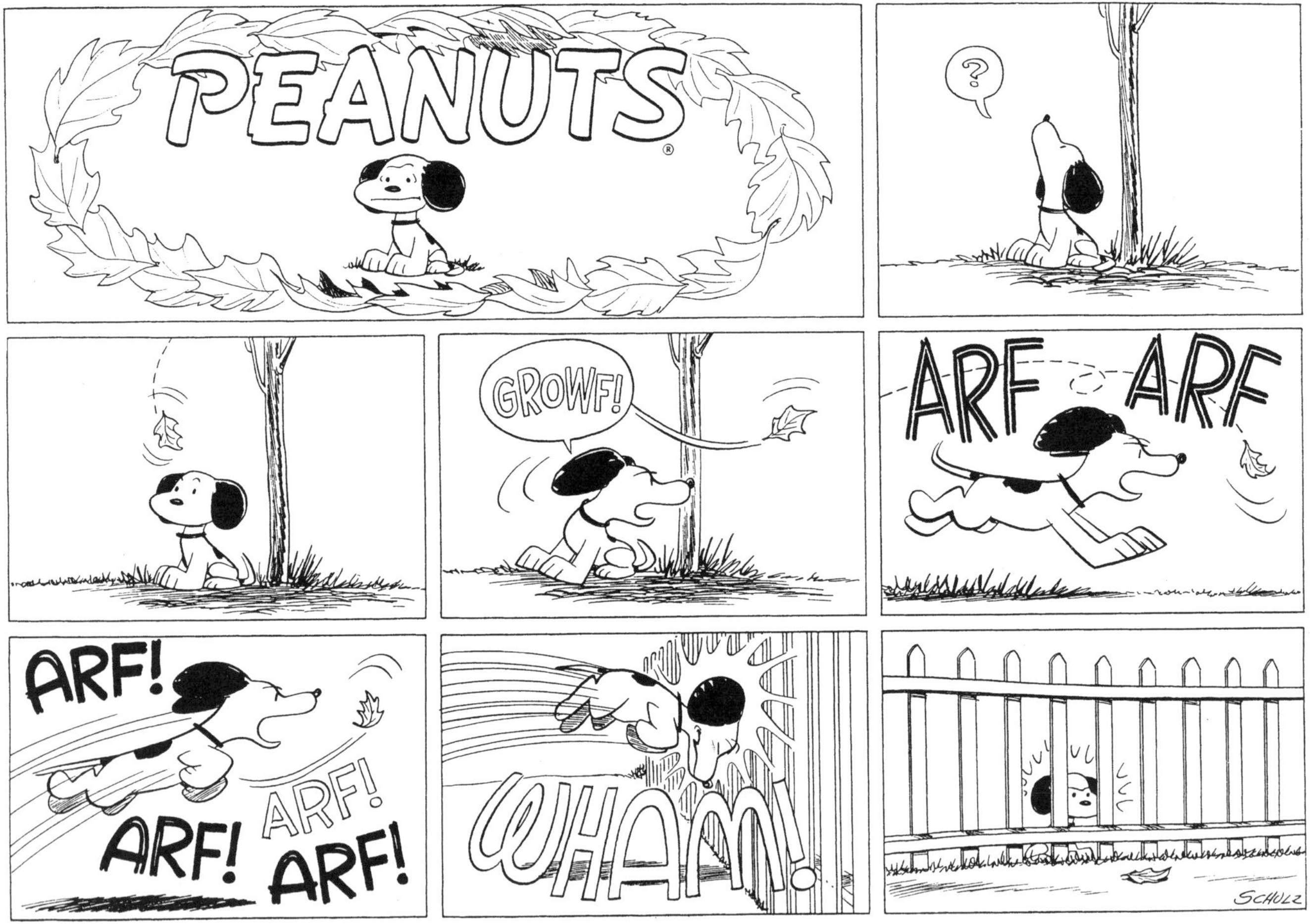

PEANUTS®
?
GROWF!
ARF ARF
ARF!
ARF!
ARF!
ARF!
WHAM!
SCHULZ

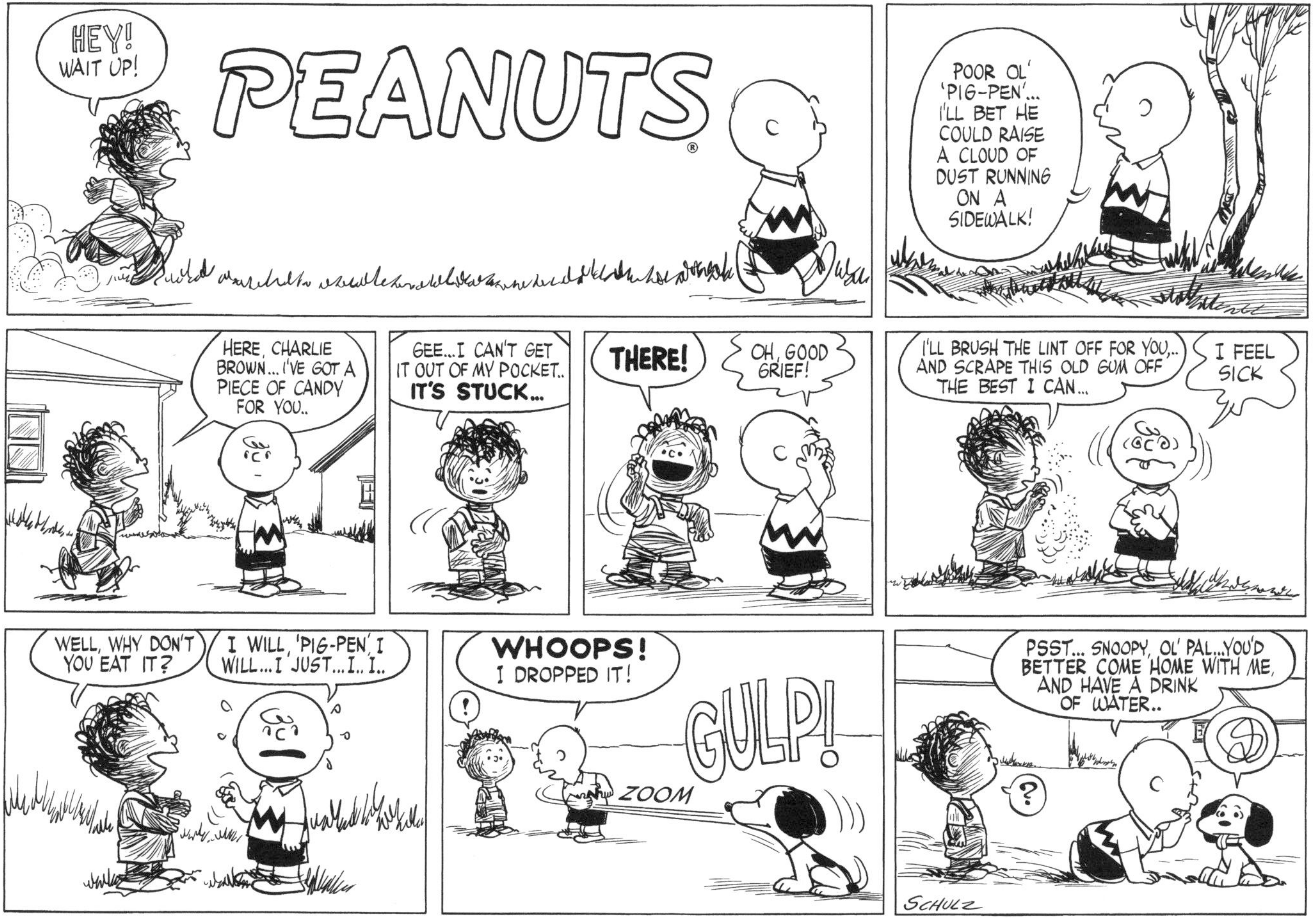
HEY! WAIT UP!
PEANUTS®
POOR OL' 'PIG-PEN'... I'LL BET HE COULD RAISE A CLOUD OF DUST RUNNING ON A SIDEWALK!
HERE, CHARLIE BROWN... I'VE GOT A PIECE OF CANDY FOR YOU..
GEE...I CAN'T GET IT OUT OF MY POCKET.. IT'S STUCK...
THERE!
OH, GOOD GRIEF!
I'LL BRUSH THE LINT OFF FOR YOU,.. AND SCRAPE THIS OLD GUM OFF THE BEST I CAN...
I FEEL SICK
WELL, WHY DON'T YOU EAT IT?
I WILL, 'PIG-PEN', I WILL...I JUST...I.. I..
!
WHOOPS! I DROPPED IT!
GULP!
ZOOM
PSST... SNOOPY, OL' PAL...YOU'D BETTER COME HOME WITH ME, AND HAVE A DRINK OF WATER..
?
SCHULZ

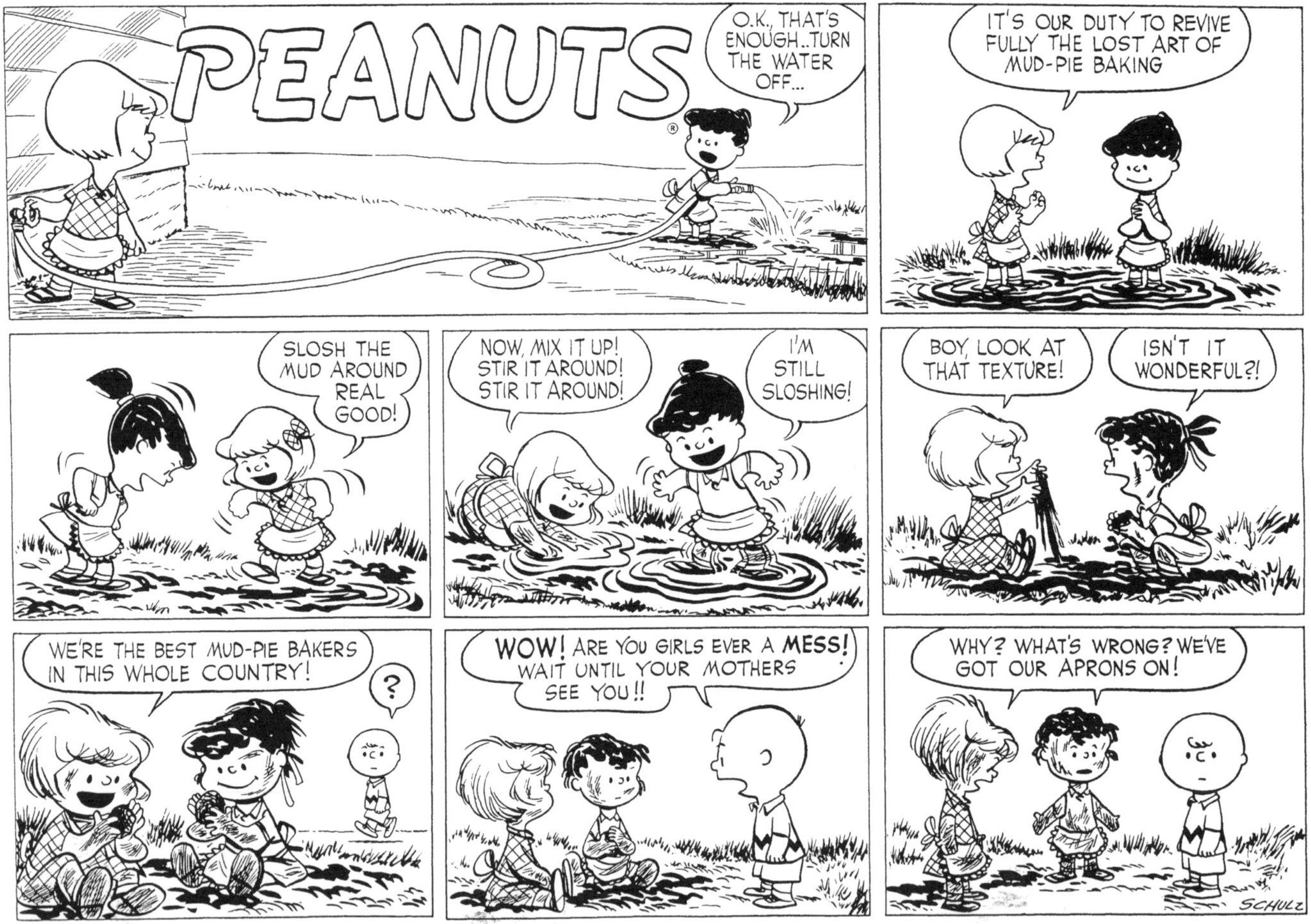
PEANUTS®
O.K., THAT'S ENOUGH..TURN THE WATER OFF...
IT'S OUR DUTY TO REVIVE FULLY THE LOST ART OF MUD-PIE BAKING
SLOSH THE MUD AROUND REAL GOOD!
NOW, MIX IT UP! STIR IT AROUND! STIR IT AROUND!
I'M STILL SLOSHING!
BOY, LOOK AT THAT TEXTURE!
ISN'T IT WONDERFUL?!
WE'RE THE BEST MUD-PIE BAKERS IN THIS WHOLE COUNTRY!
?
WOW! ARE YOU GIRLS EVER A MESS! WAIT UNTIL YOUR MOTHERS SEE YOU!!
WHY? WHAT'S WRONG? WE'VE GOT OUR APRONS ON!
SCHULZ

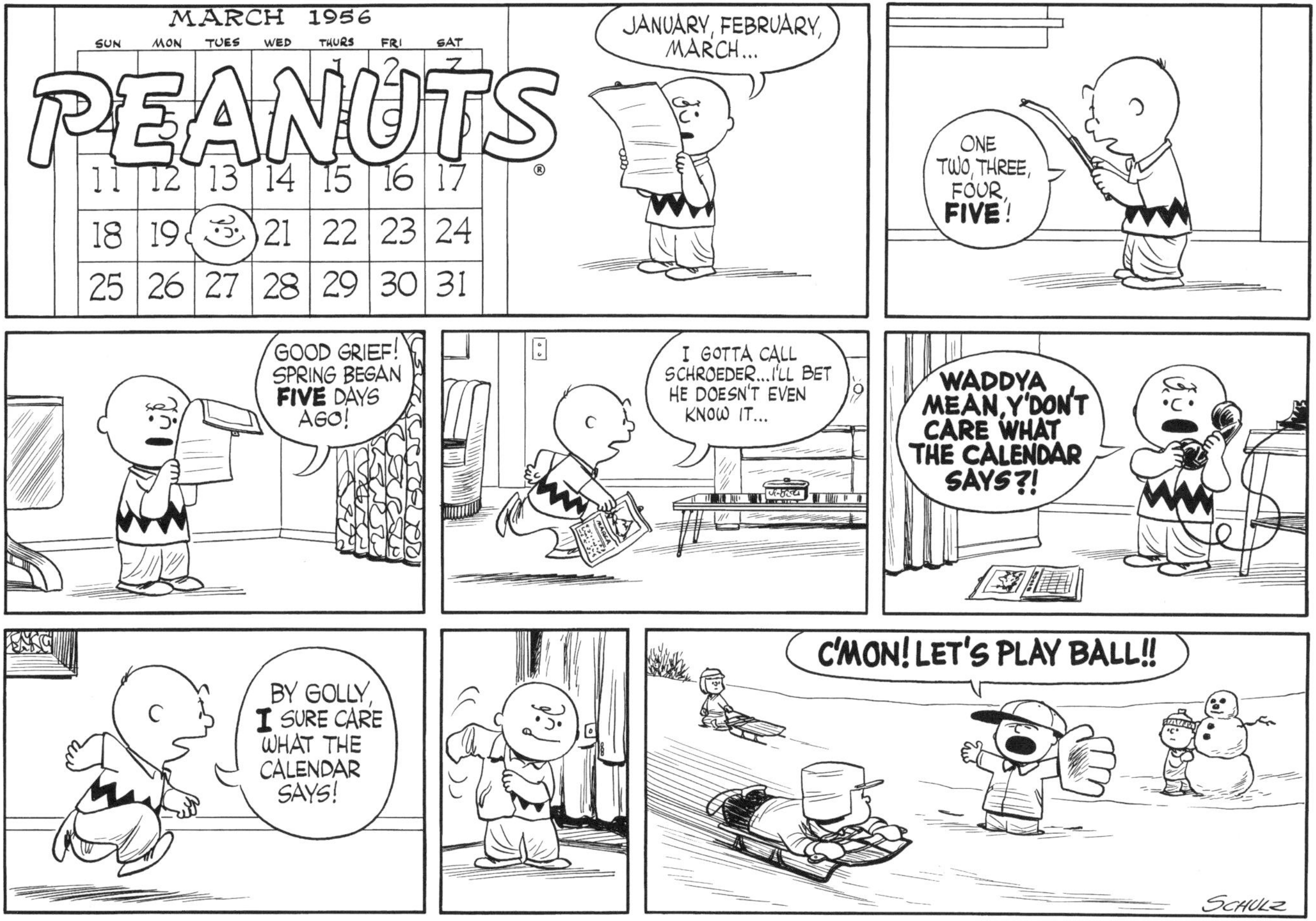
PEANUTS
MARCH 1956
JANUARY, FEBRUARY, MARCH...
ONE TWO, THREE, FOUR, **FIVE**!
GOOD GRIEF! SPRING BEGAN **FIVE** DAYS AGO!
I GOTTA CALL SCHROEDER...I'LL BET HE DOESN'T EVEN KNOW IT...
WADDYA MEAN, Y'DON'T CARE WHAT THE CALENDAR SAYS?!
BY GOLLY, **I** SURE CARE WHAT THE CALENDAR SAYS!
C'MON! LET'S PLAY BALL!!
SCHULZ

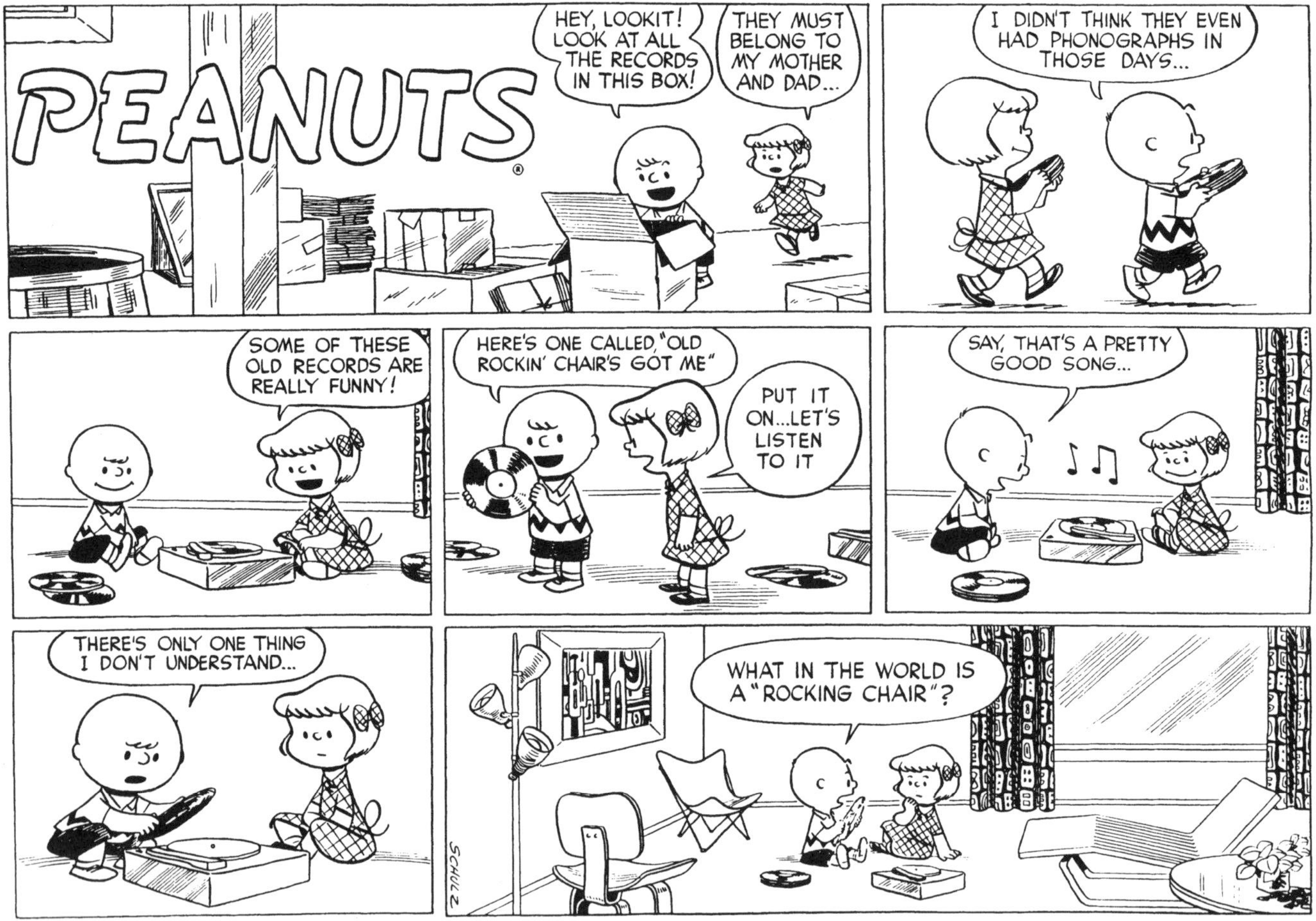
PEANUTS
HEY, LOOKIT! LOOK AT ALL THE RECORDS IN THIS BOX!
THEY MUST BELONG TO MY MOTHER AND DAD...
I DIDN'T THINK THEY EVEN HAD PHONOGRAPHS IN THOSE DAYS...
SOME OF THESE OLD RECORDS ARE REALLY FUNNY!
HERE'S ONE CALLED, "OLD ROCKIN' CHAIR'S GOT ME"
PUT IT ON...LET'S LISTEN TO IT
SAY, THAT'S A PRETTY GOOD SONG...
THERE'S ONLY ONE THING I DON'T UNDERSTAND...
WHAT IN THE WORLD IS A "ROCKING CHAIR"?
SCHULZ

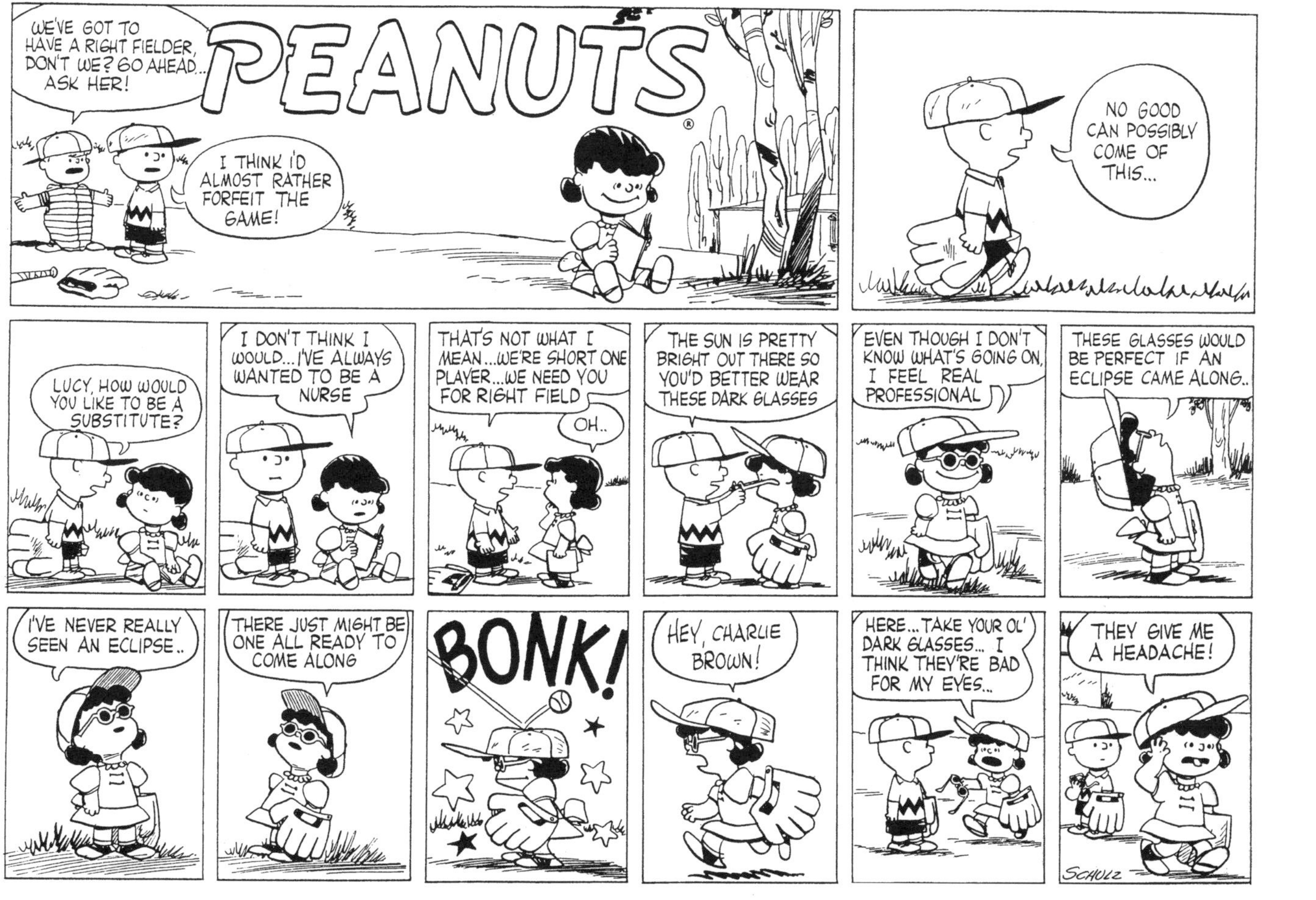
WE'VE GOT TO HAVE A RIGHT FIELDER, DON'T WE? GO AHEAD... ASK HER!
PEANUTS
I THINK I'D ALMOST RATHER FORFEIT THE GAME!
NO GOOD CAN POSSIBLY COME OF THIS...
LUCY, HOW WOULD YOU LIKE TO BE A SUBSTITUTE?
I DON'T THINK I WOULD... I'VE ALWAYS WANTED TO BE A NURSE
THAT'S NOT WHAT I MEAN... WE'RE SHORT ONE PLAYER... WE NEED YOU FOR RIGHT FIELD
OH..
THE SUN IS PRETTY BRIGHT OUT THERE SO YOU'D BETTER WEAR THESE DARK GLASSES
EVEN THOUGH I DON'T KNOW WHAT'S GOING ON, I FEEL REAL PROFESSIONAL
THESE GLASSES WOULD BE PERFECT IF AN ECLIPSE CAME ALONG..
I'VE NEVER REALLY SEEN AN ECLIPSE..
THERE JUST MIGHT BE ONE ALL READY TO COME ALONG
BONK!
HEY, CHARLIE BROWN!
HERE... TAKE YOUR OL' DARK GLASSES... I THINK THEY'RE BAD FOR MY EYES...
THEY GIVE ME A HEADACHE!
SCHULZ

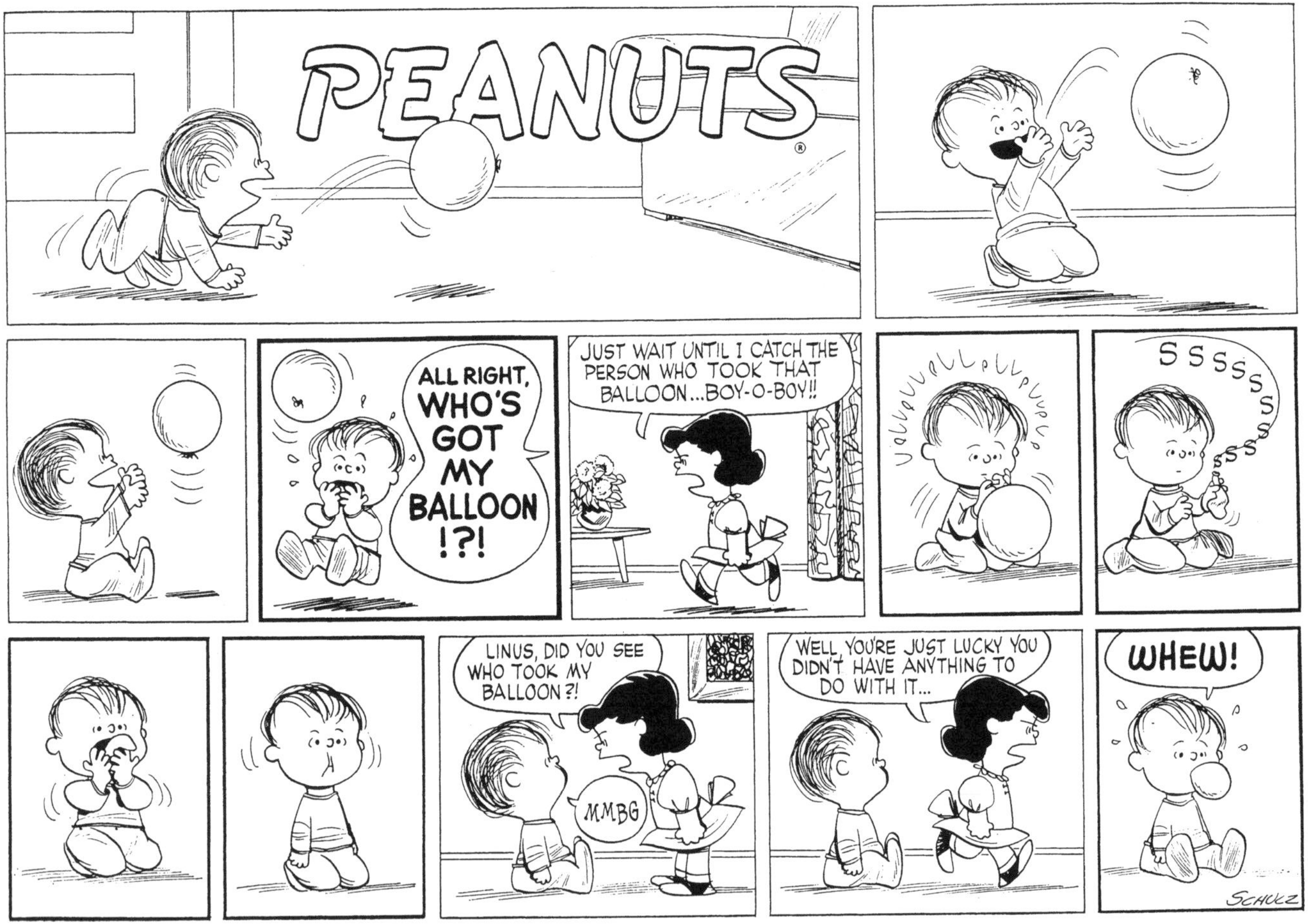
PEANUTS
ALL RIGHT, WHO'S GOT MY BALLOON !?!
JUST WAIT UNTIL I CATCH THE PERSON WHO TOOK THAT BALLOON...BOY-O-BOY!!
SSSSSSSSSS
LINUS, DID YOU SEE WHO TOOK MY BALLOON?!
MMBG
WELL, YOU'RE JUST LUCKY YOU DIDN'T HAVE ANYTHING TO DO WITH IT...
WHEW!
SCHULZ

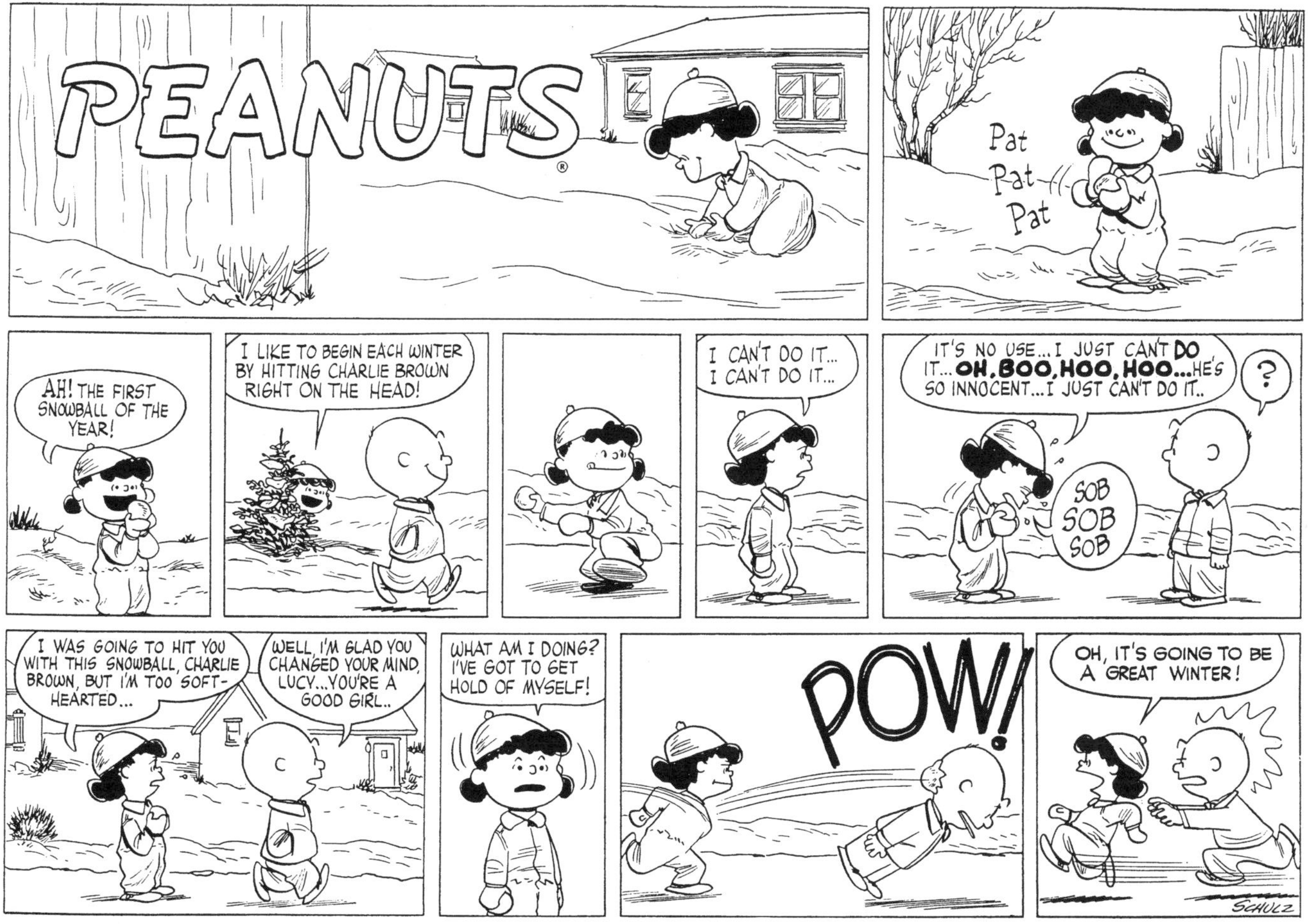
PEANUTS
Pat
Pat
Pat
AH! THE FIRST SNOWBALL OF THE YEAR!
I LIKE TO BEGIN EACH WINTER BY HITTING CHARLIE BROWN RIGHT ON THE HEAD!
I CAN'T DO IT... I CAN'T DO IT...
IT'S NO USE...I JUST CAN'T DO IT...OH, BOO, HOO, HOO...HE'S SO INNOCENT...I JUST CAN'T DO IT..
SOB SOB SOB
?
I WAS GOING TO HIT YOU WITH THIS SNOWBALL, CHARLIE BROWN, BUT I'M TOO SOFT-HEARTED...
WELL, I'M GLAD YOU CHANGED YOUR MIND, LUCY...YOU'RE A GOOD GIRL..
WHAT AM I DOING? I'VE GOT TO GET HOLD OF MYSELF!
POW!
OH, IT'S GOING TO BE A GREAT WINTER!
SCHULZ

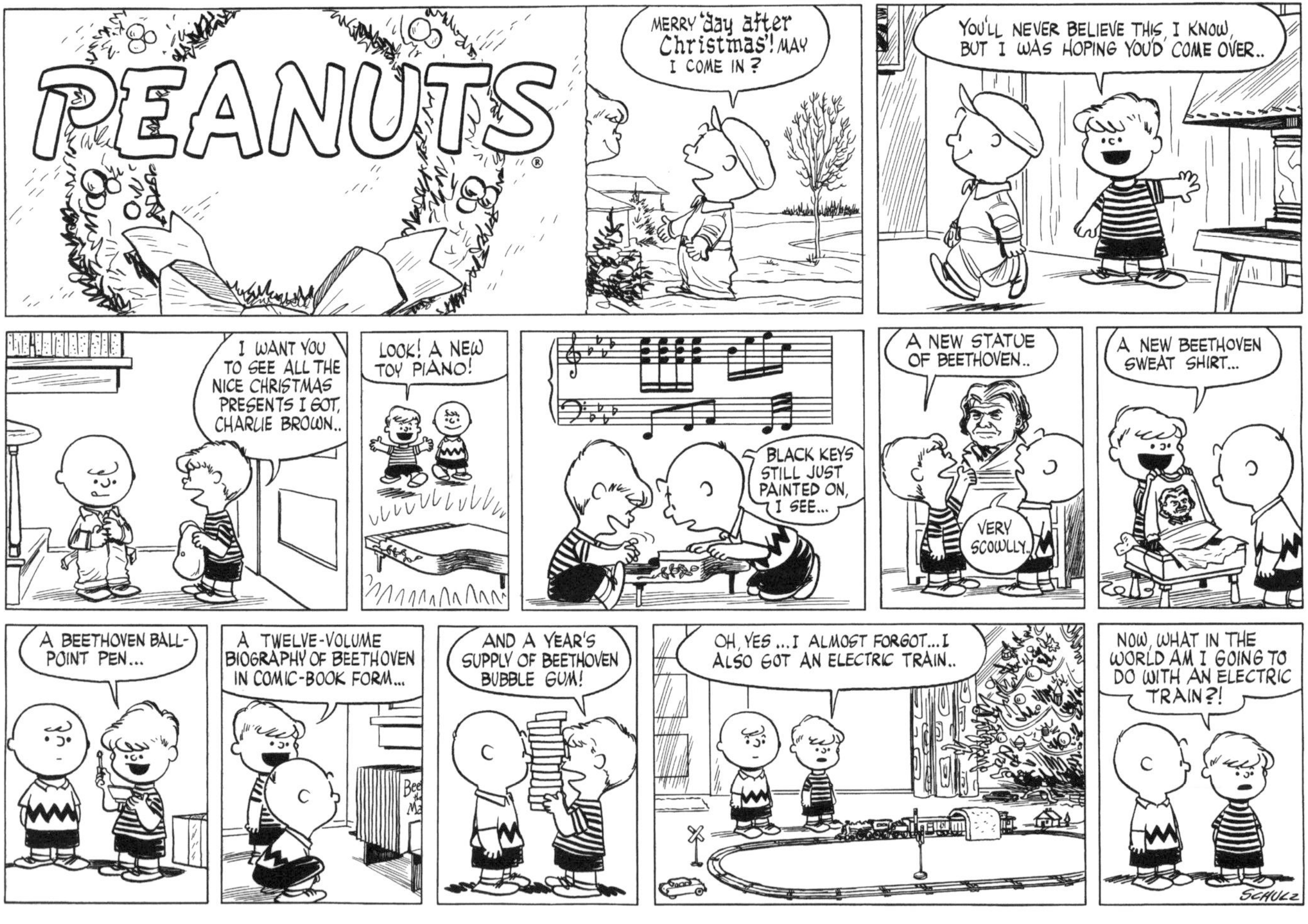
PEANUTS®
MERRY 'day after Christmas'! MAY I COME IN?
YOU'LL NEVER BELIEVE THIS, I KNOW, BUT I WAS HOPING YOU'D COME OVER..
I WANT YOU TO SEE ALL THE NICE CHRISTMAS PRESENTS I GOT, CHARLIE BROWN..
LOOK! A NEW TOY PIANO!
BLACK KEYS STILL JUST PAINTED ON, I SEE...
A NEW STATUE OF BEETHOVEN..
VERY SCOWLLY..
A NEW BEETHOVEN SWEAT SHIRT...
A BEETHOVEN BALL-POINT PEN...
A TWELVE-VOLUME BIOGRAPHY OF BEETHOVEN IN COMIC-BOOK FORM...
AND A YEAR'S SUPPLY OF BEETHOVEN BUBBLE GUM!
OH, YES ... I ALMOST FORGOT ... I ALSO GOT AN ELECTRIC TRAIN..
NOW, WHAT IN THE WORLD AM I GOING TO DO WITH AN ELECTRIC TRAIN?!
SCHULZ

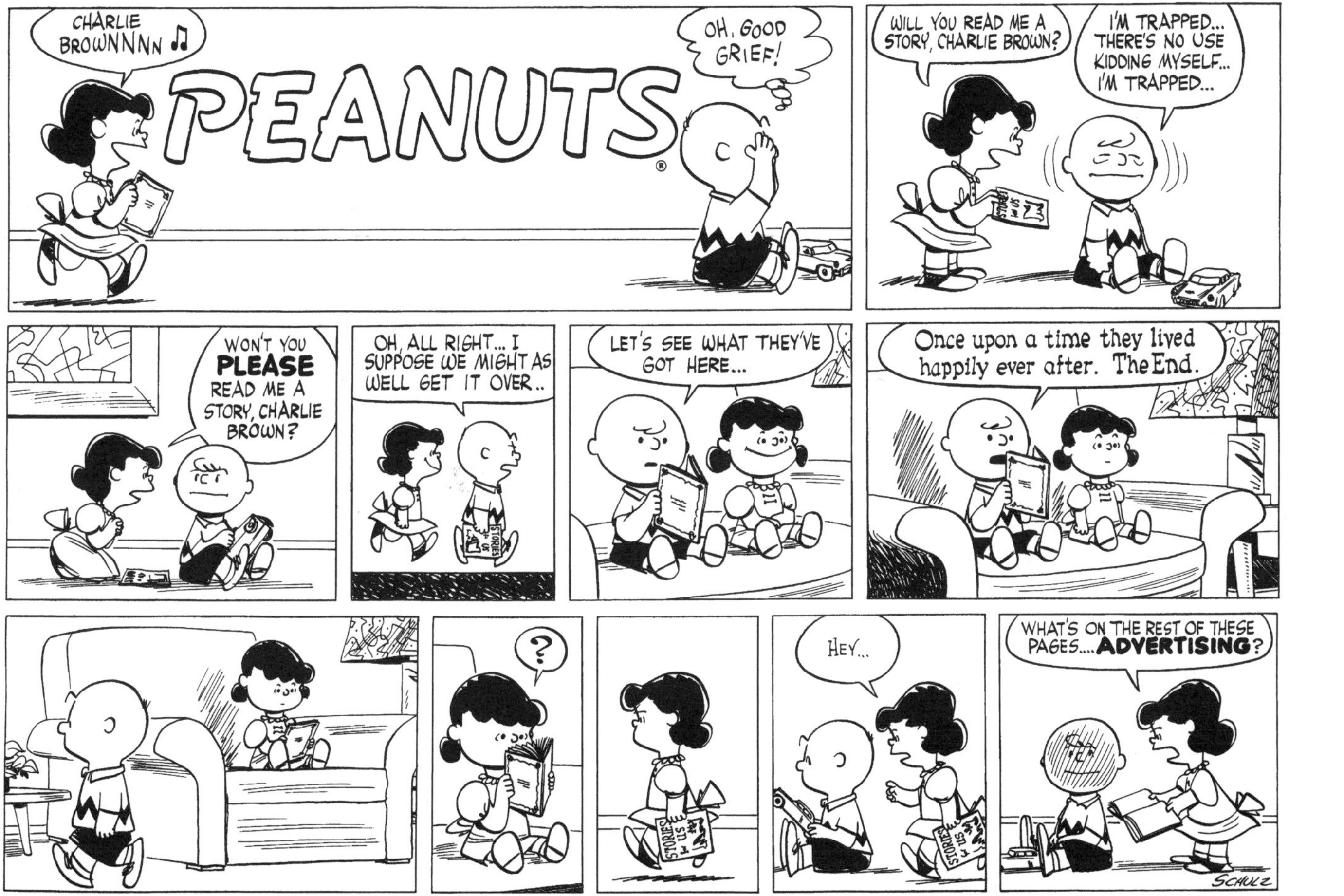
CHARLIE BROWNNNN ♫
PEANUTS®
OH, GOOD GRIEF!
WILL YOU READ ME A STORY, CHARLIE BROWN?
I'M TRAPPED... THERE'S NO USE KIDDING MYSELF... I'M TRAPPED...
WON'T YOU **PLEASE** READ ME A STORY, CHARLIE BROWN?
OH, ALL RIGHT... I SUPPOSE WE MIGHT AS WELL GET IT OVER..
LET'S SEE WHAT THEY'VE GOT HERE...
Once upon a time they lived happily ever after. The End.
?
HEY...
WHAT'S ON THE REST OF THESE PAGES.... **ADVERTISING**?
SCHULZ

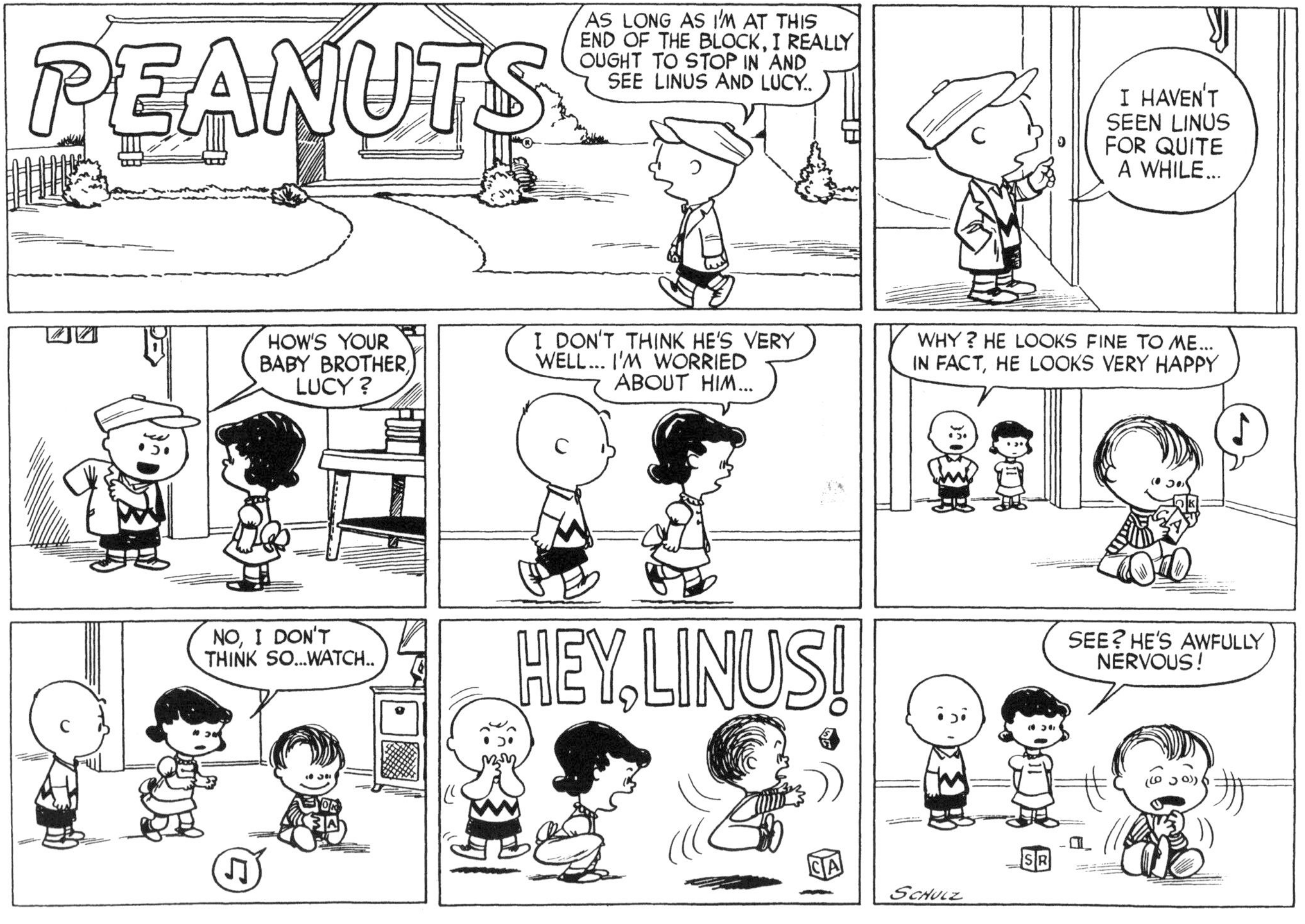
PEANUTS
AS LONG AS I'M AT THIS END OF THE BLOCK, I REALLY OUGHT TO STOP IN AND SEE LINUS AND LUCY..
I HAVEN'T SEEN LINUS FOR QUITE A WHILE...
HOW'S YOUR BABY BROTHER, LUCY ?
I DON'T THINK HE'S VERY WELL... I'M WORRIED ABOUT HIM...
WHY ? HE LOOKS FINE TO ME... IN FACT, HE LOOKS VERY HAPPY
NO, I DON'T THINK SO...WATCH..
HEY, LINUS!
SEE? HE'S AWFULLY NERVOUS!
SCHULZ

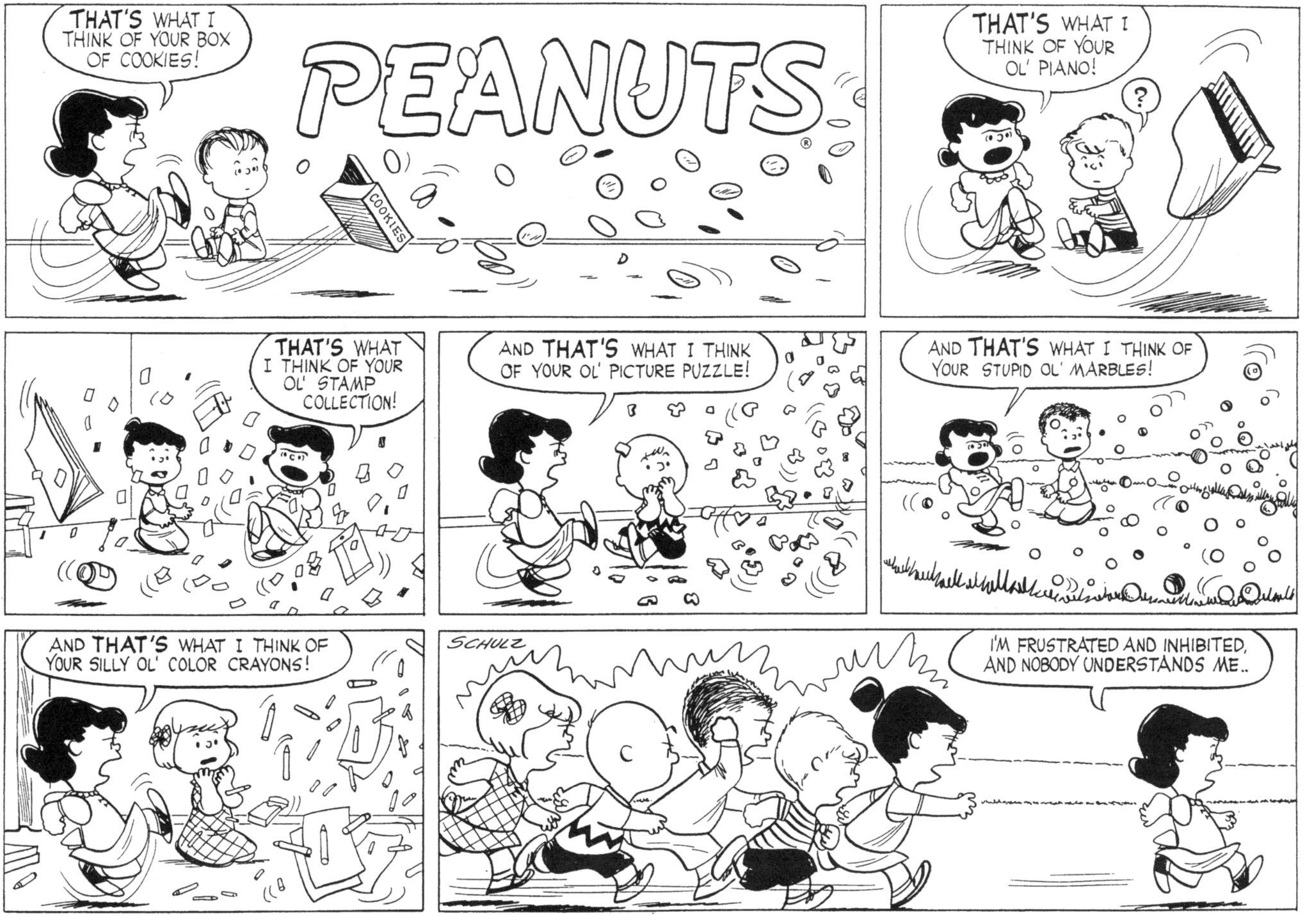
THAT'S WHAT I THINK OF YOUR BOX OF COOKIES!
PEANUTS
COOKIES
THAT'S WHAT I THINK OF YOUR OL' PIANO!
?
THAT'S WHAT I THINK OF YOUR OL' STAMP COLLECTION!
AND THAT'S WHAT I THINK OF YOUR OL' PICTURE PUZZLE!
AND THAT'S WHAT I THINK OF YOUR STUPID OL' MARBLES!
AND THAT'S WHAT I THINK OF YOUR SILLY OL' COLOR CRAYONS!
SCHULZ
I'M FRUSTRATED AND INHIBITED, AND NOBODY UNDERSTANDS ME..

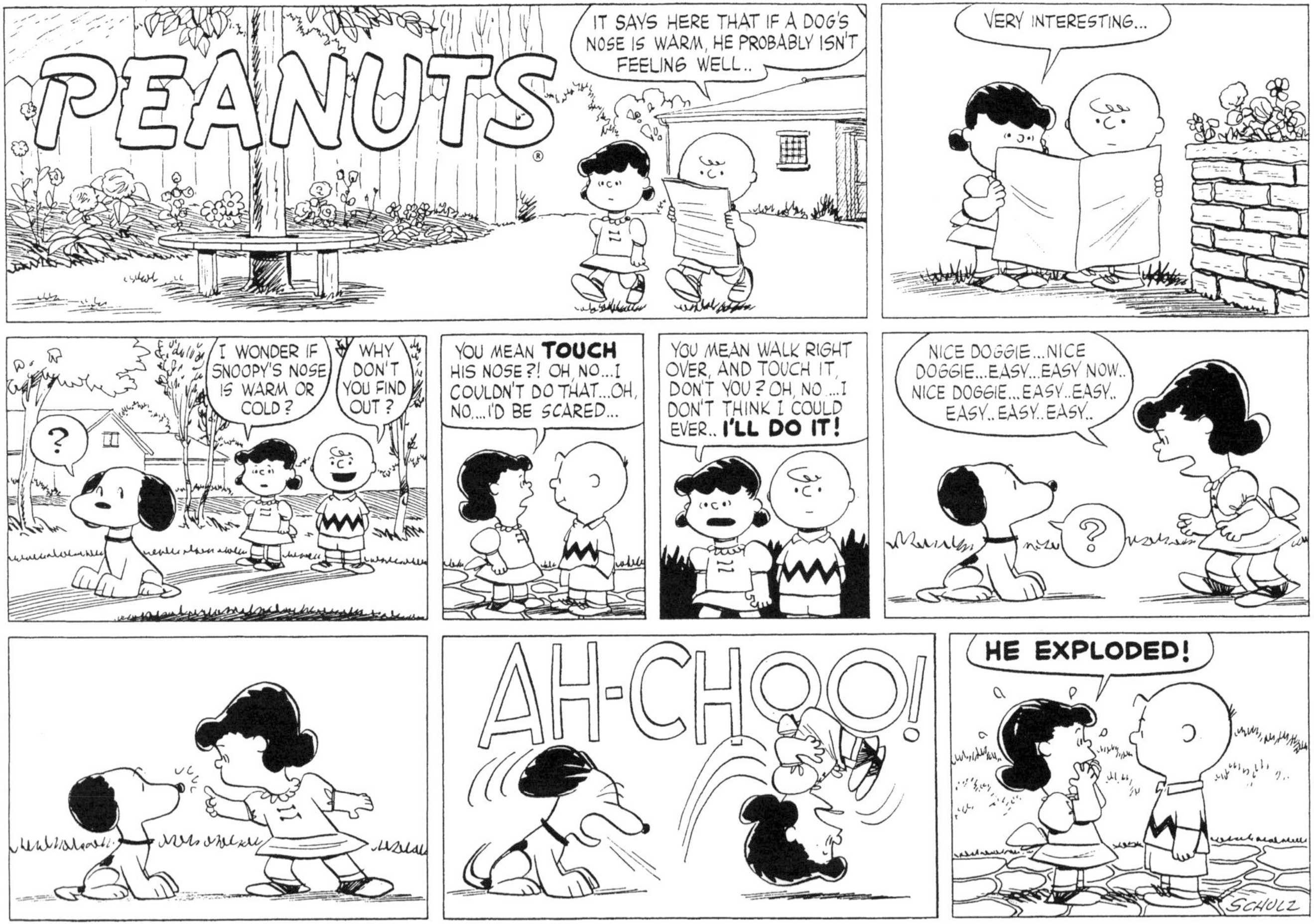
PEANUTS
IT SAYS HERE THAT IF A DOG'S NOSE IS WARM, HE PROBABLY ISN'T FEELING WELL..
VERY INTERESTING...
?
I WONDER IF SNOOPY'S NOSE IS WARM OR COLD?
WHY DON'T YOU FIND OUT?
YOU MEAN **TOUCH** HIS NOSE?! OH, NO...I COULDN'T DO THAT...OH, NO....I'D BE SCARED...
YOU MEAN WALK RIGHT OVER, AND TOUCH IT, DON'T YOU? OH, NO ...I DON'T THINK I COULD EVER.. **I'LL DO IT!**
NICE DOGGIE...NICE DOGGIE...EASY...EASY NOW.. NICE DOGGIE...EASY..EASY.. EASY..EASY..EASY..
?
AH-CHOO!
HE EXPLODED!
SCHULZ

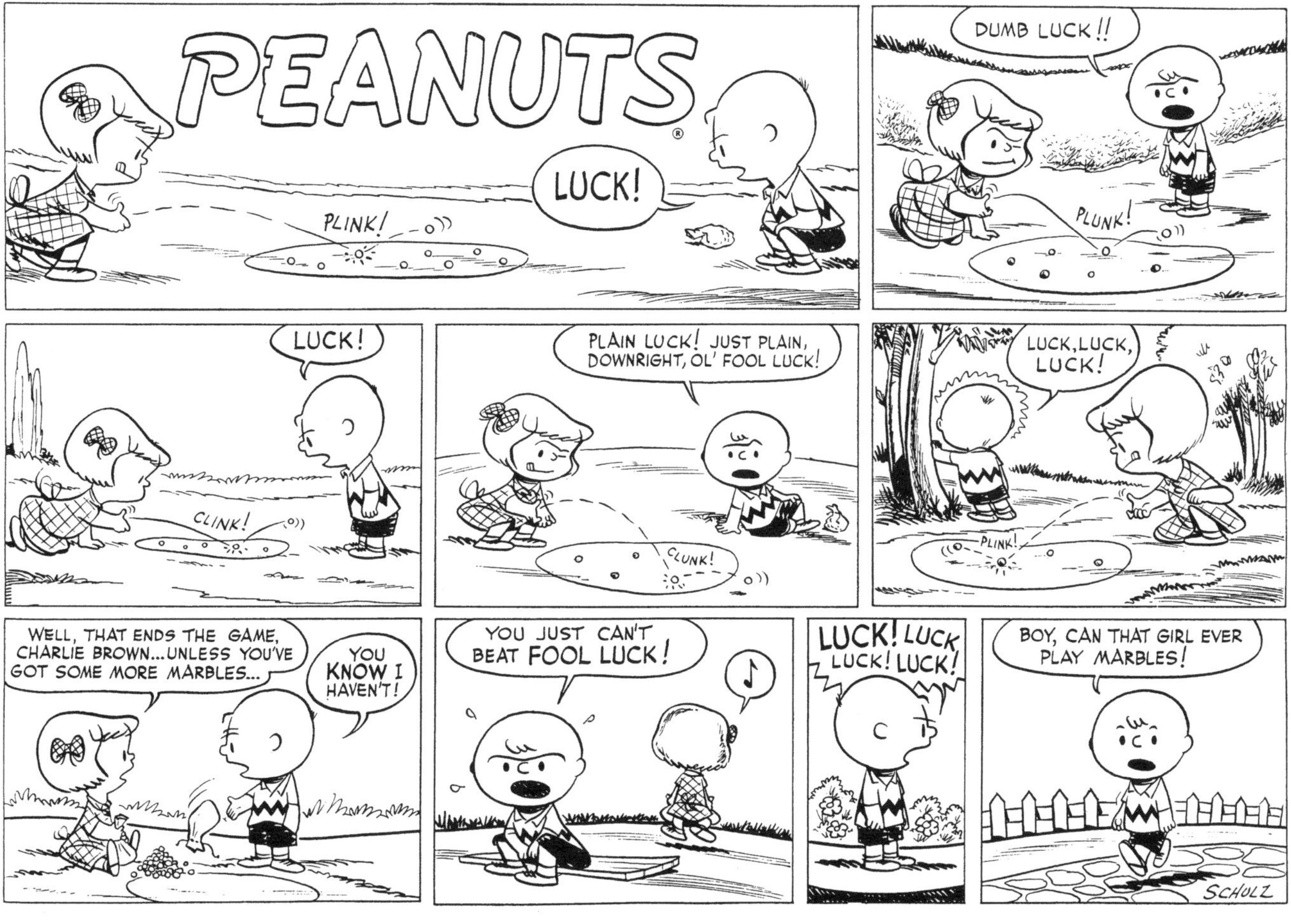
PEANUTS®
PLINK!
LUCK!
DUMB LUCK!!
PLUNK!
LUCK!
CLINK!
PLAIN LUCK! JUST PLAIN, DOWNRIGHT, OL' FOOL LUCK!
CLUNK!
LUCK, LUCK, LUCK!
PLINK!
WELL, THAT ENDS THE GAME, CHARLIE BROWN...UNLESS YOU'VE GOT SOME MORE MARBLES...
YOU KNOW I HAVEN'T!
YOU JUST CAN'T BEAT FOOL LUCK!
♪
LUCK! LUCK LUCK! LUCK!
BOY, CAN THAT GIRL EVER PLAY MARBLES!
SCHULZ

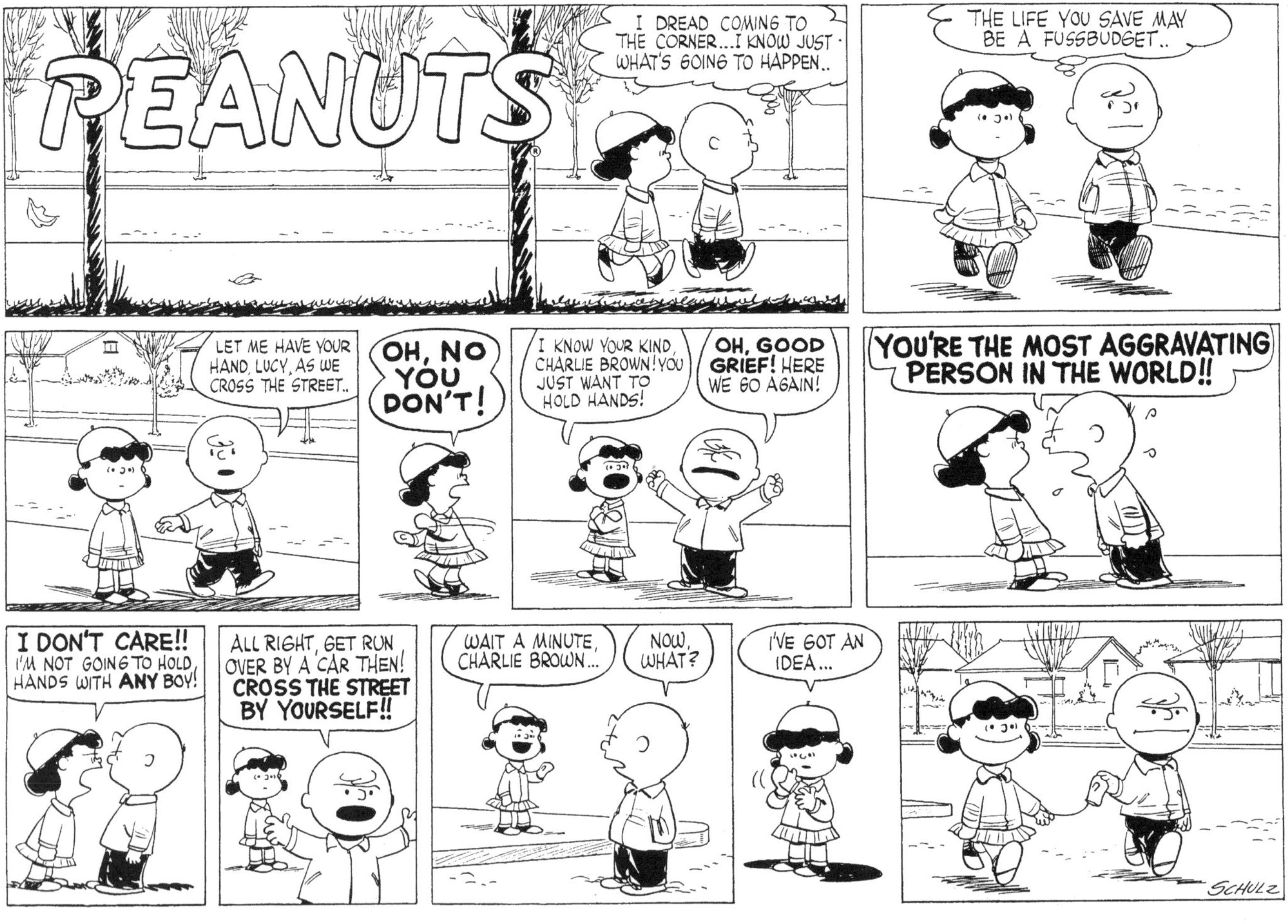
PEANUTS
I DREAD COMING TO THE CORNER...I KNOW JUST WHAT'S GOING TO HAPPEN..
THE LIFE YOU SAVE MAY BE A FUSSBUDGET..
LET ME HAVE YOUR HAND, LUCY, AS WE CROSS THE STREET..
OH, NO YOU DON'T!
I KNOW YOUR KIND, CHARLIE BROWN! YOU JUST WANT TO HOLD HANDS!
OH, GOOD GRIEF! HERE WE GO AGAIN!
YOU'RE THE MOST AGGRAVATING PERSON IN THE WORLD!!
I DON'T CARE!! I'M NOT GOING TO HOLD HANDS WITH ANY BOY!
ALL RIGHT, GET RUN OVER BY A CAR THEN! CROSS THE STREET BY YOURSELF!!
WAIT A MINUTE, CHARLIE BROWN...
NOW, WHAT?
I'VE GOT AN IDEA...
SCHULZ

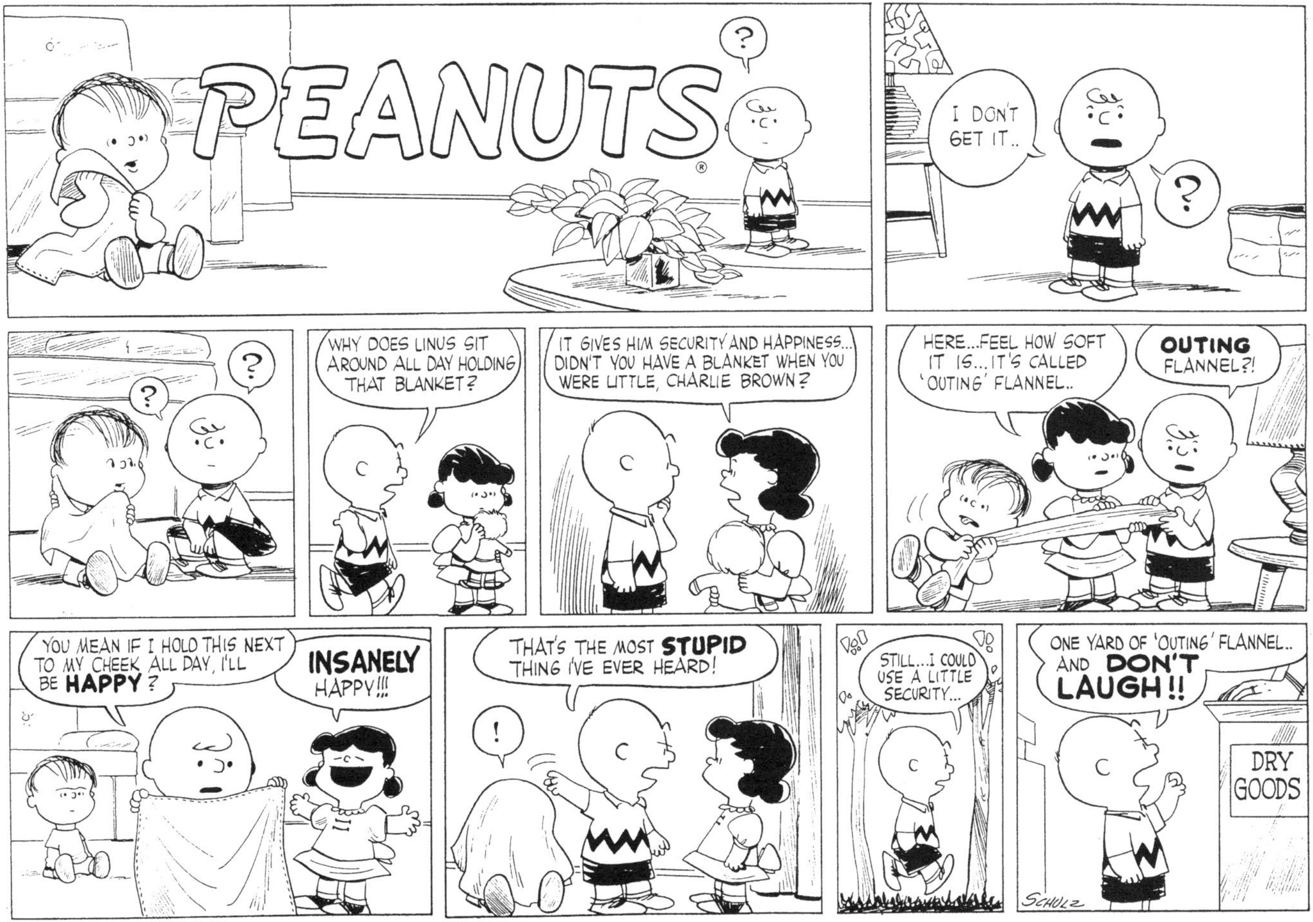
PEANUTS
?
I DON'T GET IT..
?
?
?
WHY DOES LINUS SIT AROUND ALL DAY HOLDING THAT BLANKET?
IT GIVES HIM SECURITY AND HAPPINESS... DIDN'T YOU HAVE A BLANKET WHEN YOU WERE LITTLE, CHARLIE BROWN?
HERE...FEEL HOW SOFT IT IS...IT'S CALLED 'OUTING' FLANNEL..
OUTING FLANNEL?!
YOU MEAN IF I HOLD THIS NEXT TO MY CHEEK ALL DAY, I'LL BE **HAPPY**?
INSANELY HAPPY!!!
THAT'S THE MOST **STUPID** THING I'VE EVER HEARD!
!
STILL...I COULD USE A LITTLE SECURITY...
ONE YARD OF 'OUTING' FLANNEL.. AND **DON'T LAUGH!!**
DRY GOODS
SCHULZ

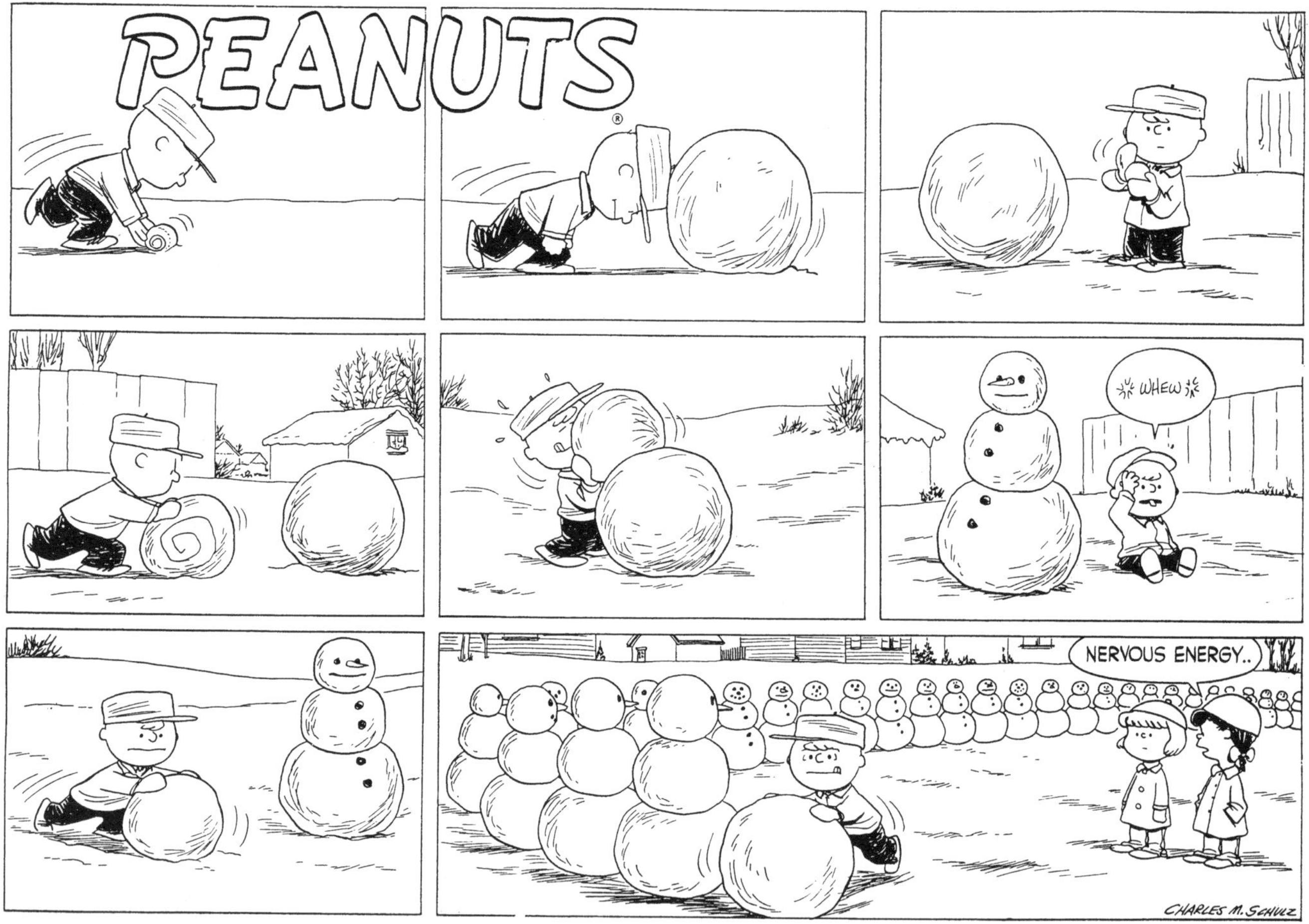
PEANUTS
WHEW
NERVOUS ENERGY..
CHARLES M. SCHULZ

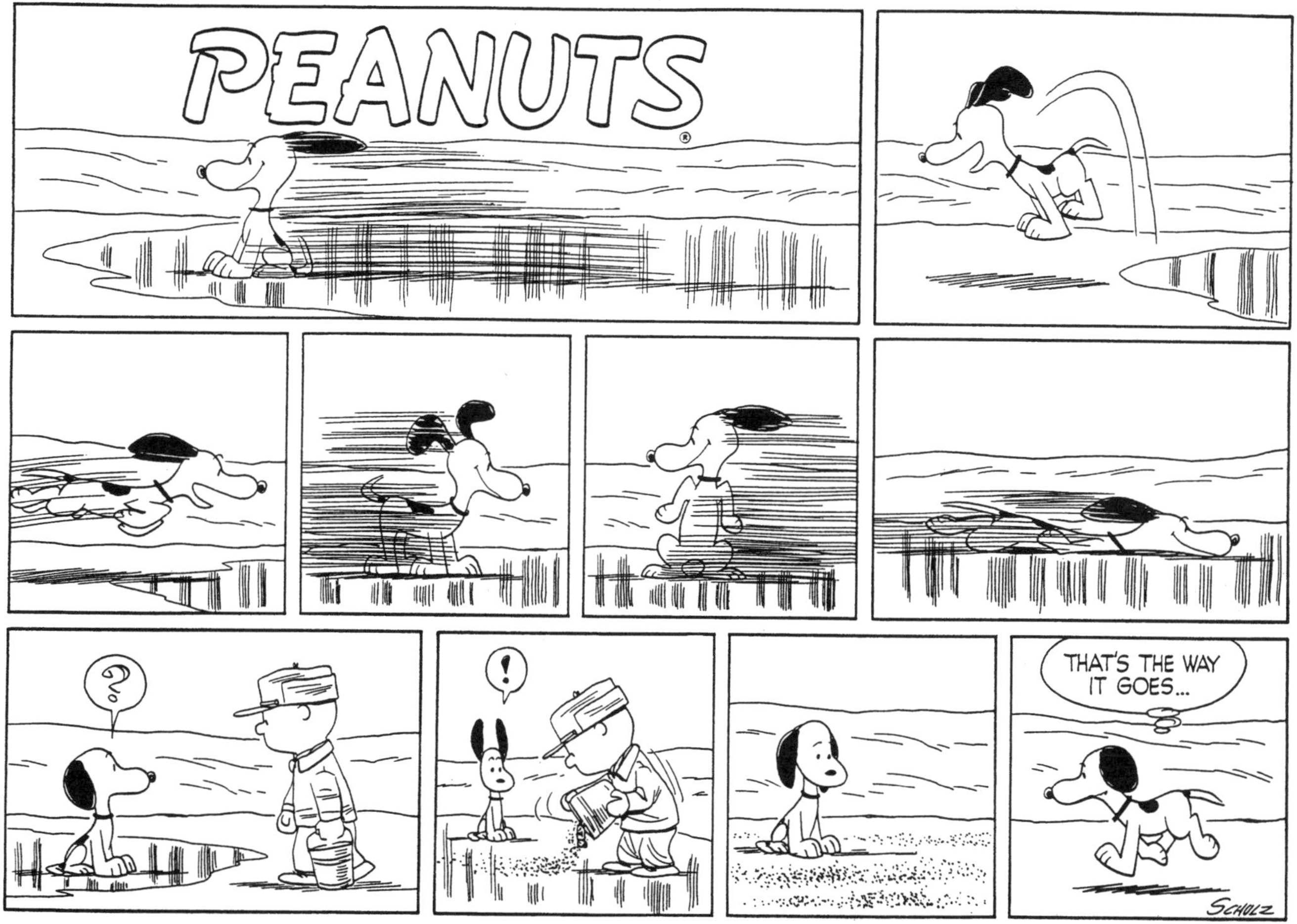
PEANUTS
?
!
THAT'S THE WAY IT GOES...
SCHULZ

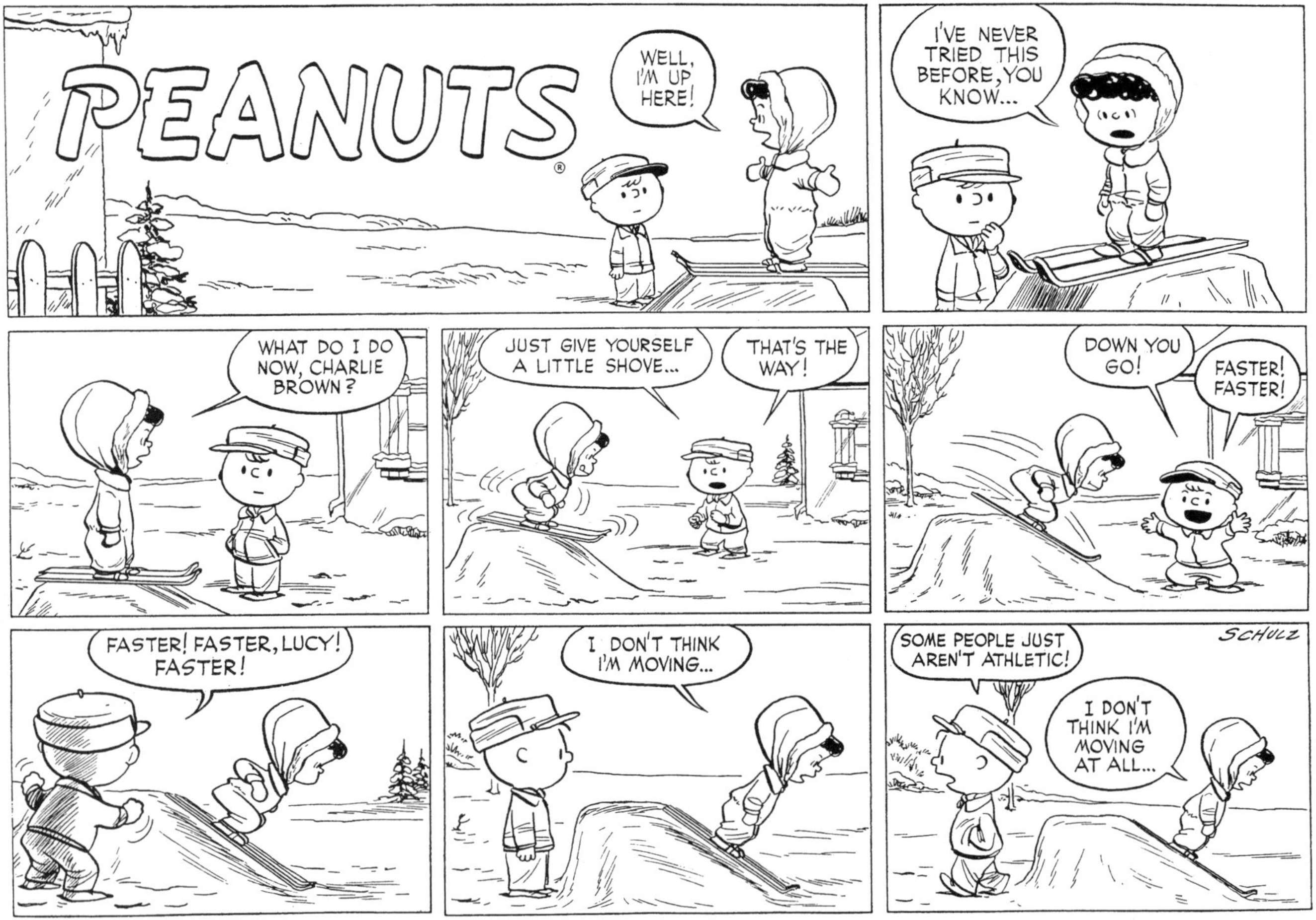
PEANUTS®
WELL, I'M UP HERE!
I'VE NEVER TRIED THIS BEFORE, YOU KNOW...
WHAT DO I DO NOW, CHARLIE BROWN?
JUST GIVE YOURSELF A LITTLE SHOVE...
THAT'S THE WAY!
DOWN YOU GO!
FASTER! FASTER!
FASTER! FASTER, LUCY! FASTER!
I DON'T THINK I'M MOVING...
SOME PEOPLE JUST AREN'T ATHLETIC!
I DON'T THINK I'M MOVING AT ALL...
SCHULZ

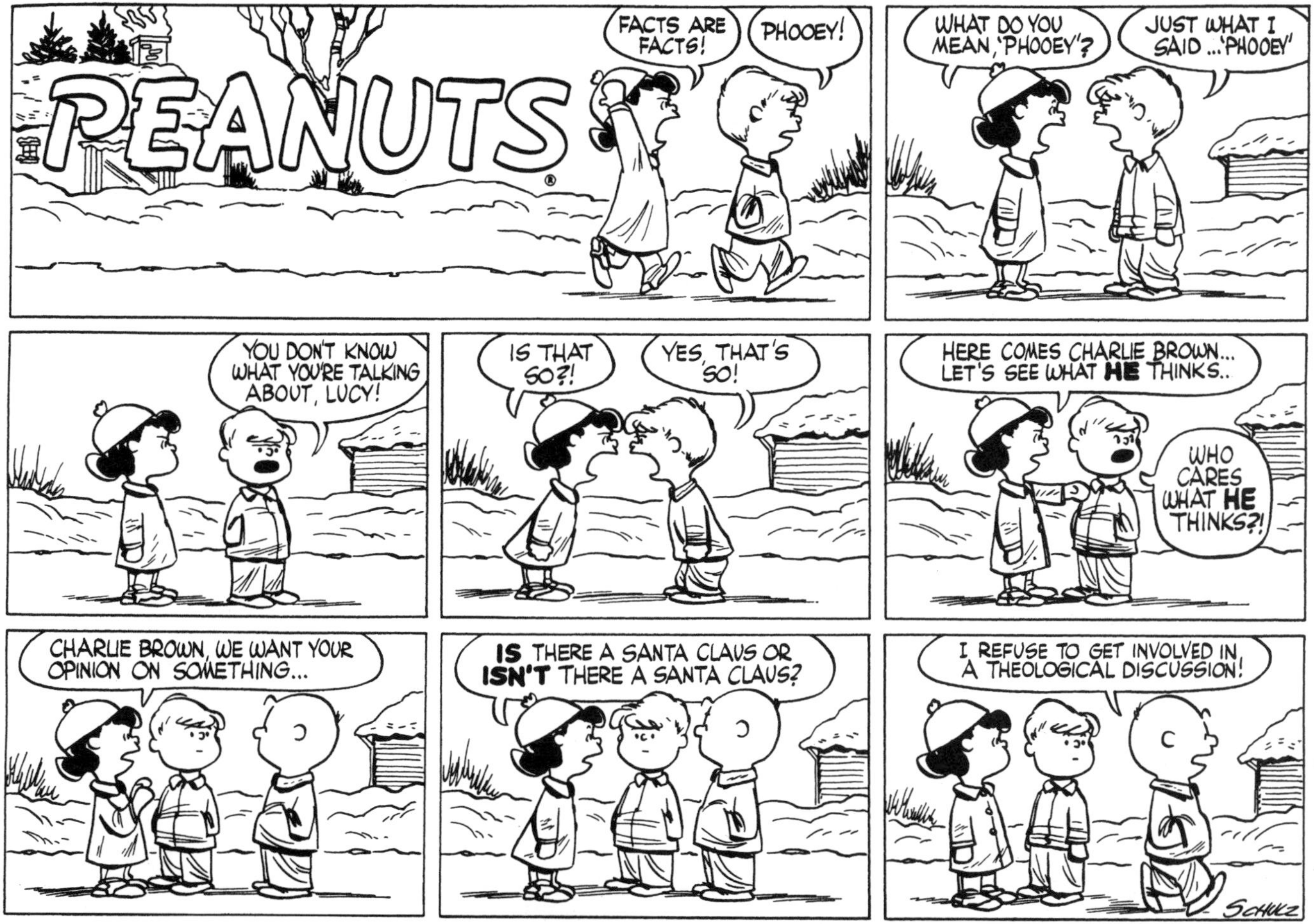
PEANUTS
FACTS ARE FACTS!
PHOOEY!
WHAT DO YOU MEAN, 'PHOOEY'?
JUST WHAT I SAID ...'PHOOEY'
YOU DON'T KNOW WHAT YOU'RE TALKING ABOUT, LUCY!
IS THAT SO?!
YES, THAT'S SO!
HERE COMES CHARLIE BROWN... LET'S SEE WHAT HE THINKS..
WHO CARES WHAT HE THINKS?!
CHARLIE BROWN, WE WANT YOUR OPINION ON SOMETHING...
IS THERE A SANTA CLAUS OR ISN'T THERE A SANTA CLAUS?
I REFUSE TO GET INVOLVED IN A THEOLOGICAL DISCUSSION!
SCHULZ

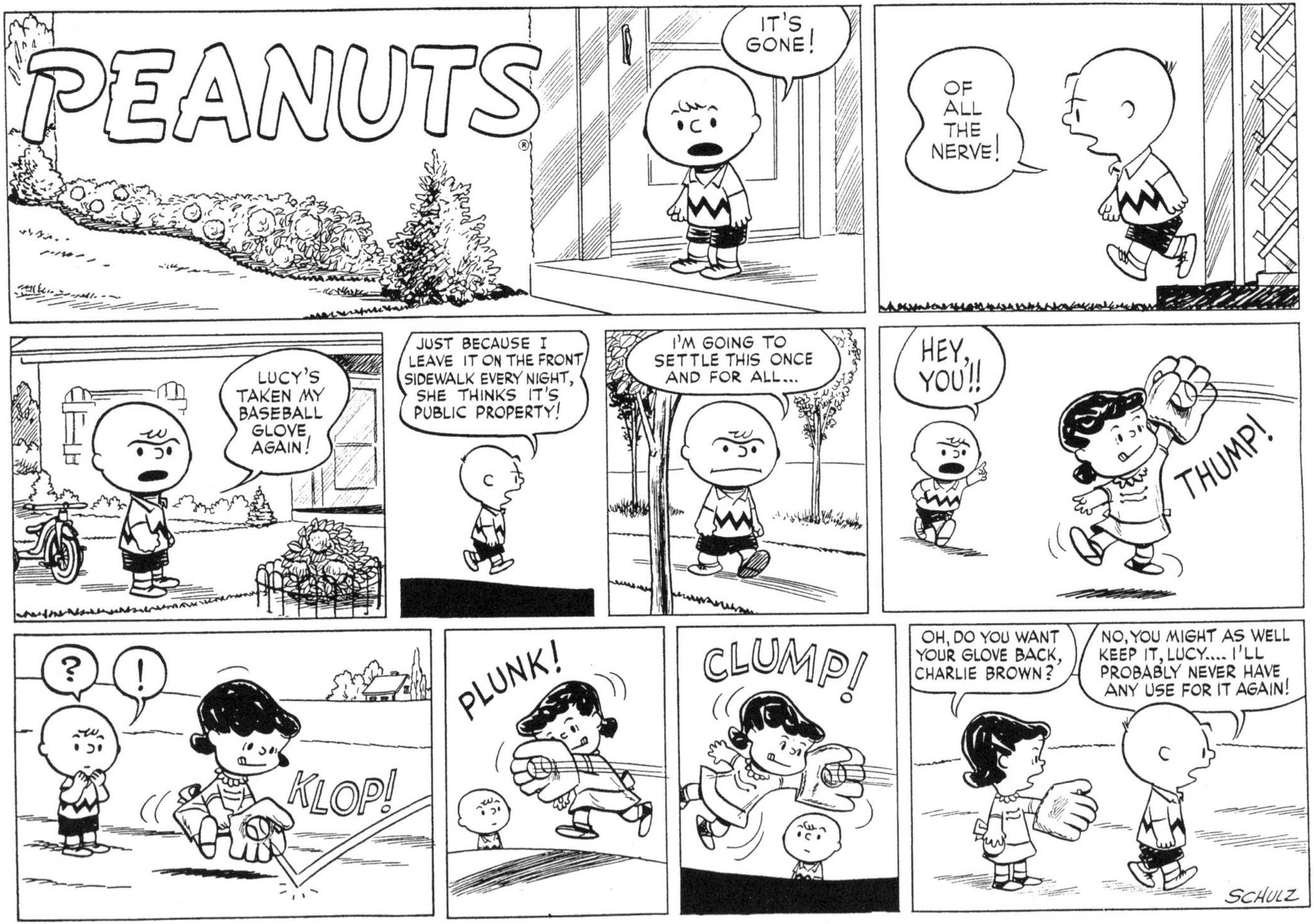
PEANUTS®
IT'S GONE!
OF ALL THE NERVE!
LUCY'S TAKEN MY BASEBALL GLOVE AGAIN!
JUST BECAUSE I LEAVE IT ON THE FRONT SIDEWALK EVERY NIGHT, SHE THINKS IT'S PUBLIC PROPERTY!
I'M GOING TO SETTLE THIS ONCE AND FOR ALL...
HEY, YOU!!
THUMP!
?
!
KLOP!
PLUNK!
CLUMP!
OH, DO YOU WANT YOUR GLOVE BACK, CHARLIE BROWN?
NO, YOU MIGHT AS WELL KEEP IT, LUCY.... I'LL PROBABLY NEVER HAVE ANY USE FOR IT AGAIN!
SCHULZ

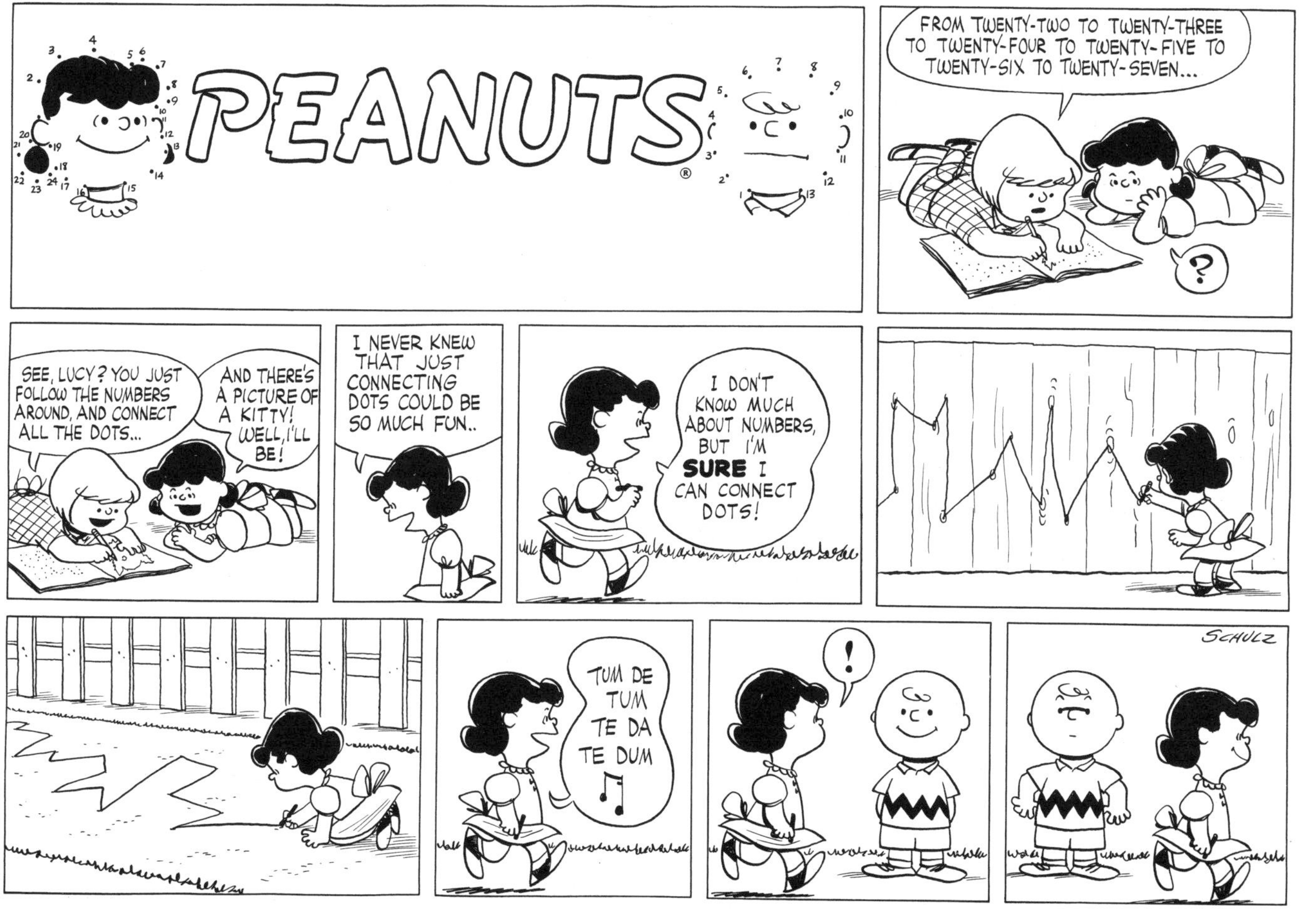
PEANUTS
FROM TWENTY-TWO TO TWENTY-THREE TO TWENTY-FOUR TO TWENTY-FIVE TO TWENTY-SIX TO TWENTY-SEVEN...
?
SEE, LUCY? YOU JUST FOLLOW THE NUMBERS AROUND, AND CONNECT ALL THE DOTS...
AND THERE'S A PICTURE OF A KITTY! WELL, I'LL BE!
I NEVER KNEW THAT JUST CONNECTING DOTS COULD BE SO MUCH FUN..
I DON'T KNOW MUCH ABOUT NUMBERS, BUT I'M **SURE** I CAN CONNECT DOTS!
TUM DE TUM TE DA TE DUM
!
SCHULZ

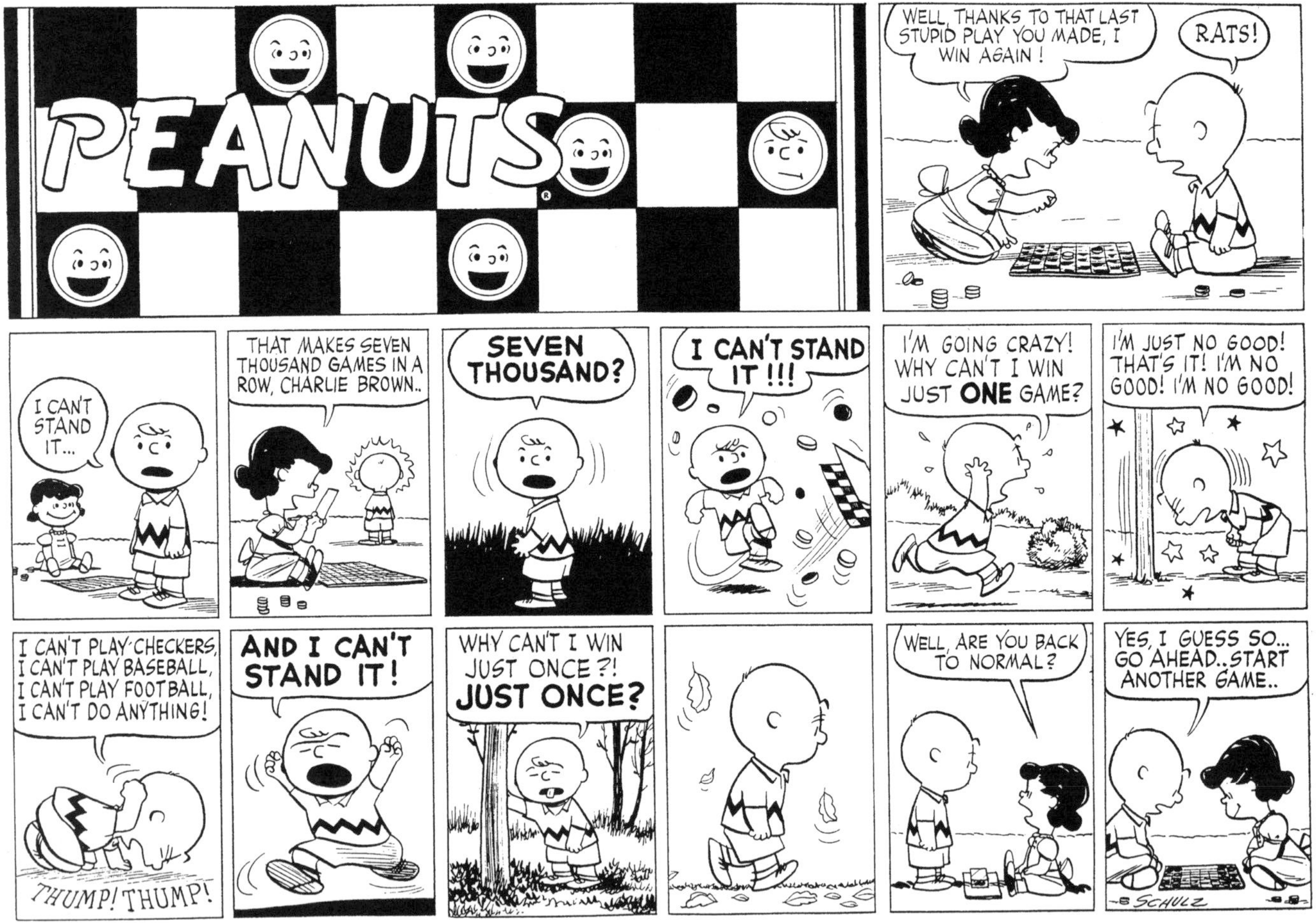
PEANUTS
WELL, THANKS TO THAT LAST STUPID PLAY YOU MADE, I WIN AGAIN!
RATS!
I CAN'T STAND IT...
THAT MAKES SEVEN THOUSAND GAMES IN A ROW, CHARLIE BROWN..
SEVEN THOUSAND?
I CAN'T STAND IT!!!
I'M GOING CRAZY! WHY CAN'T I WIN JUST ONE GAME?
I'M JUST NO GOOD! THAT'S IT! I'M NO GOOD! I'M NO GOOD!
I CAN'T PLAY CHECKERS, I CAN'T PLAY BASEBALL, I CAN'T PLAY FOOTBALL, I CAN'T DO ANYTHING!
THUMP! THUMP!
AND I CAN'T STAND IT!
WHY CAN'T I WIN JUST ONCE?! JUST ONCE?
WELL, ARE YOU BACK TO NORMAL?
YES, I GUESS SO... GO AHEAD..START ANOTHER GAME..
SCHULZ

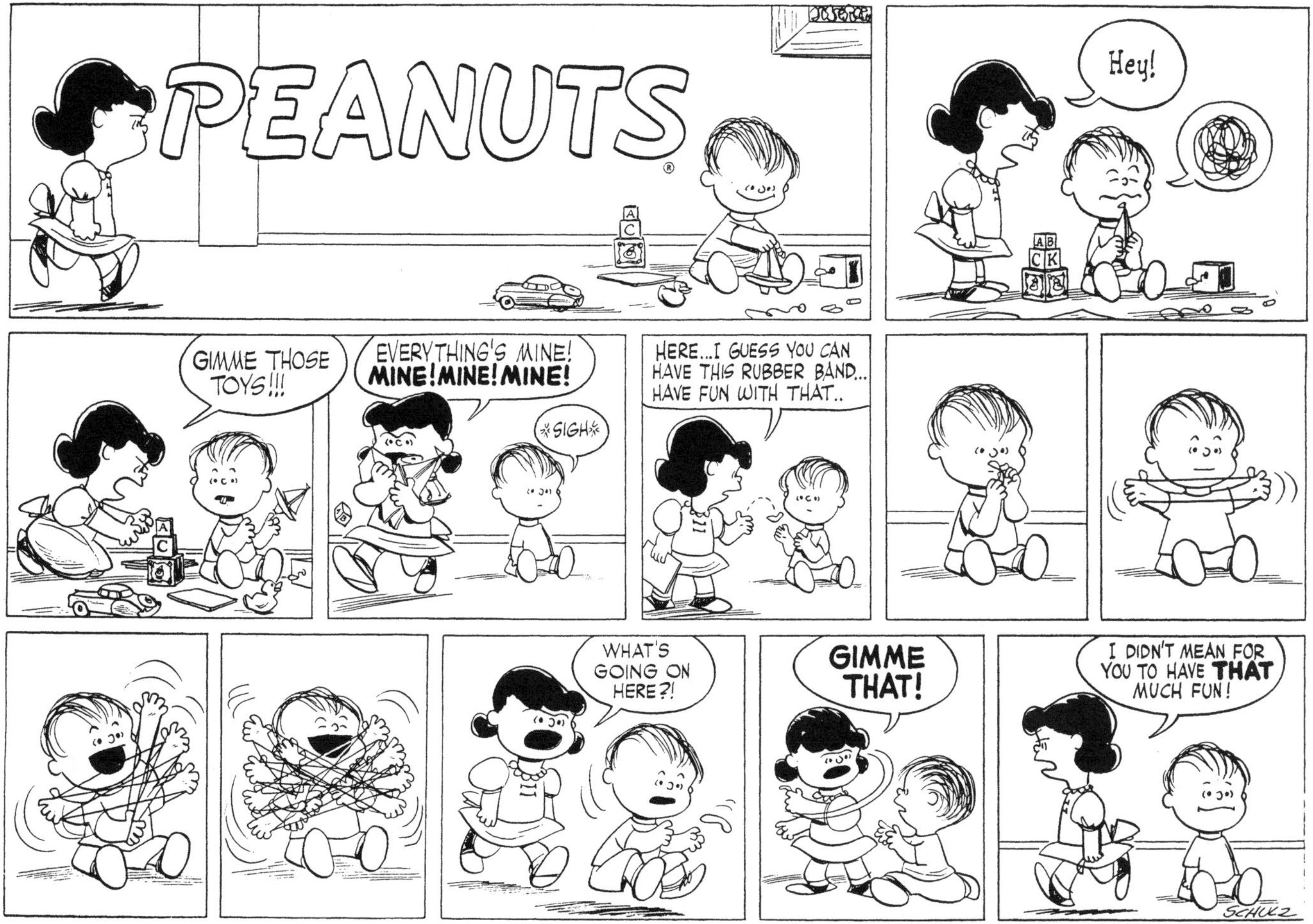
PEANUTS
Hey!
GIMME THOSE TOYS!!!
EVERYTHING'S MINE! MINE! MINE! MINE!
SIGH
HERE...I GUESS YOU CAN HAVE THIS RUBBER BAND... HAVE FUN WITH THAT..
WHAT'S GOING ON HERE?!
GIMME THAT!
I DIDN'T MEAN FOR YOU TO HAVE THAT MUCH FUN!
SCHULZ

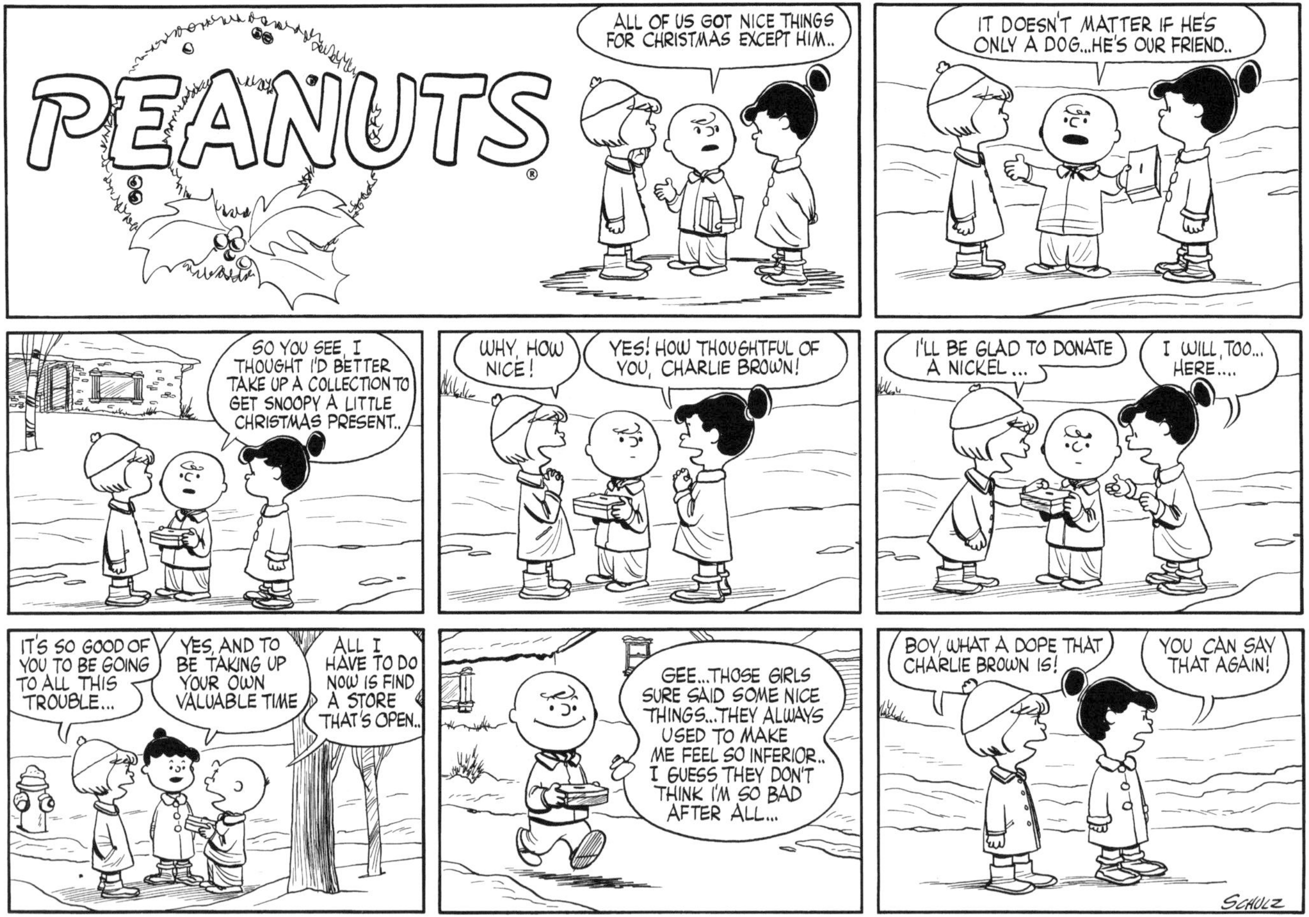
PEANUTS
ALL OF US GOT NICE THINGS FOR CHRISTMAS EXCEPT HIM..
IT DOESN'T MATTER IF HE'S ONLY A DOG...HE'S OUR FRIEND..
SO YOU SEE, I THOUGHT I'D BETTER TAKE UP A COLLECTION TO GET SNOOPY A LITTLE CHRISTMAS PRESENT..
WHY, HOW NICE!
YES! HOW THOUGHTFUL OF YOU, CHARLIE BROWN!
I'LL BE GLAD TO DONATE A NICKEL...
I WILL, TOO... HERE....
IT'S SO GOOD OF YOU TO BE GOING TO ALL THIS TROUBLE...
YES, AND TO BE TAKING UP YOUR OWN VALUABLE TIME
ALL I HAVE TO DO NOW IS FIND A STORE THAT'S OPEN..
GEE...THOSE GIRLS SURE SAID SOME NICE THINGS...THEY ALWAYS USED TO MAKE ME FEEL SO INFERIOR.. I GUESS THEY DON'T THINK I'M SO BAD AFTER ALL...
BOY, WHAT A DOPE THAT CHARLIE BROWN IS!
YOU CAN SAY THAT AGAIN!
SCHULZ

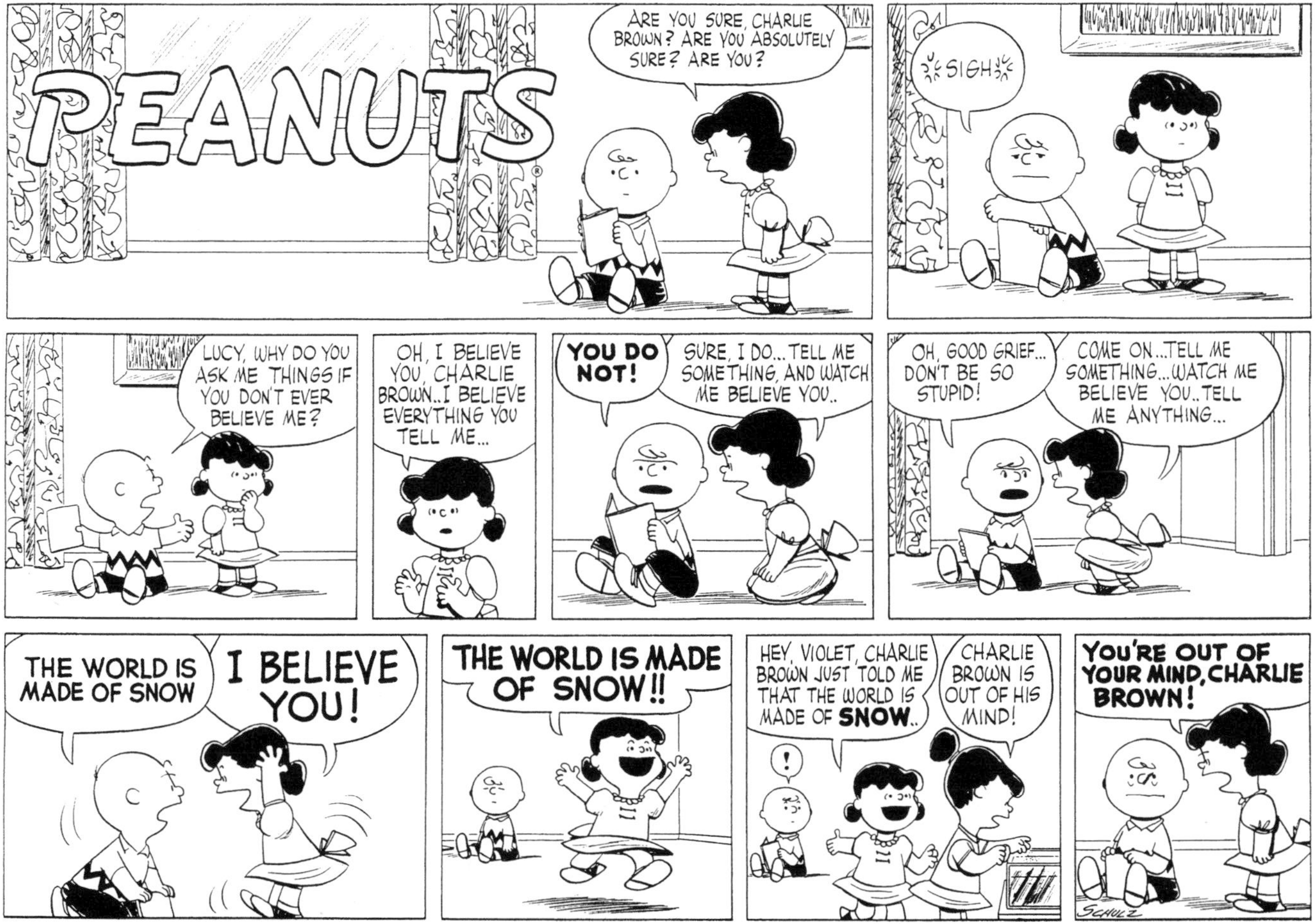
PEANUTS®
ARE YOU SURE, CHARLIE BROWN? ARE YOU ABSOLUTELY SURE? ARE YOU?
SIGH
LUCY, WHY DO YOU ASK ME THINGS IF YOU DON'T EVER BELIEVE ME?
OH, I BELIEVE YOU, CHARLIE BROWN..I BELIEVE EVERYTHING YOU TELL ME...
YOU DO NOT!
SURE, I DO... TELL ME SOMETHING, AND WATCH ME BELIEVE YOU..
OH, GOOD GRIEF... DON'T BE SO STUPID!
COME ON...TELL ME SOMETHING...WATCH ME BELIEVE YOU..TELL ME ANYTHING...
THE WORLD IS MADE OF SNOW
I BELIEVE YOU!
THE WORLD IS MADE OF SNOW!!
HEY, VIOLET, CHARLIE BROWN JUST TOLD ME THAT THE WORLD IS MADE OF SNOW..
!
CHARLIE BROWN IS OUT OF HIS MIND!
YOU'RE OUT OF YOUR MIND, CHARLIE BROWN!
SCHULZ

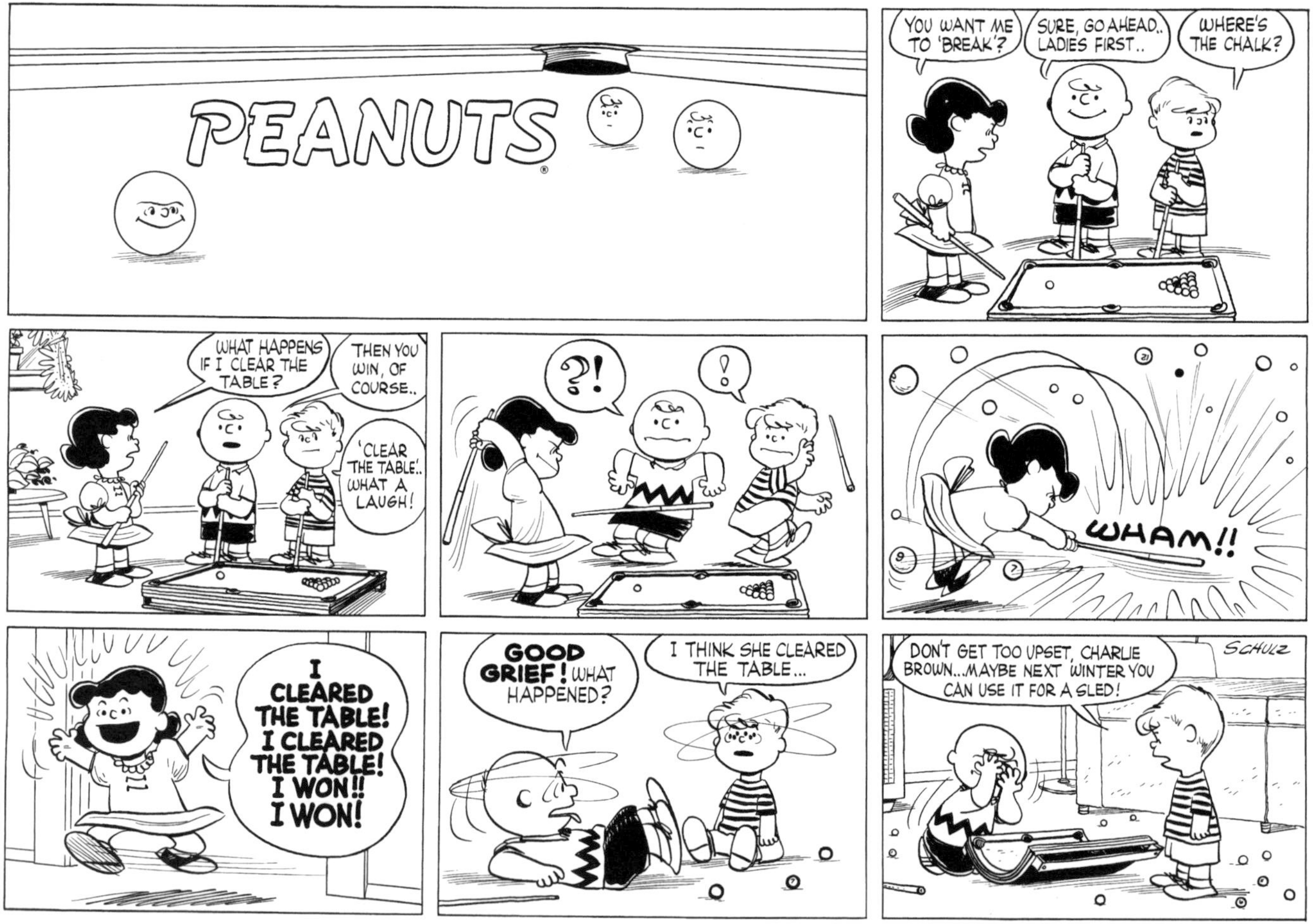
PEANUTS®
YOU WANT ME TO 'BREAK'?
SURE, GO AHEAD.. LADIES FIRST..
WHERE'S THE CHALK?
WHAT HAPPENS IF I CLEAR THE TABLE?
THEN YOU WIN, OF COURSE..
'CLEAR THE TABLE'.. WHAT A LAUGH!
?!
!
WHAM!!
I CLEARED THE TABLE! I CLEARED THE TABLE! I WON!! I WON!
GOOD GRIEF! WHAT HAPPENED?
I THINK SHE CLEARED THE TABLE...
SCHULZ
DON'T GET TOO UPSET, CHARLIE BROWN...MAYBE NEXT WINTER YOU CAN USE IT FOR A SLED!

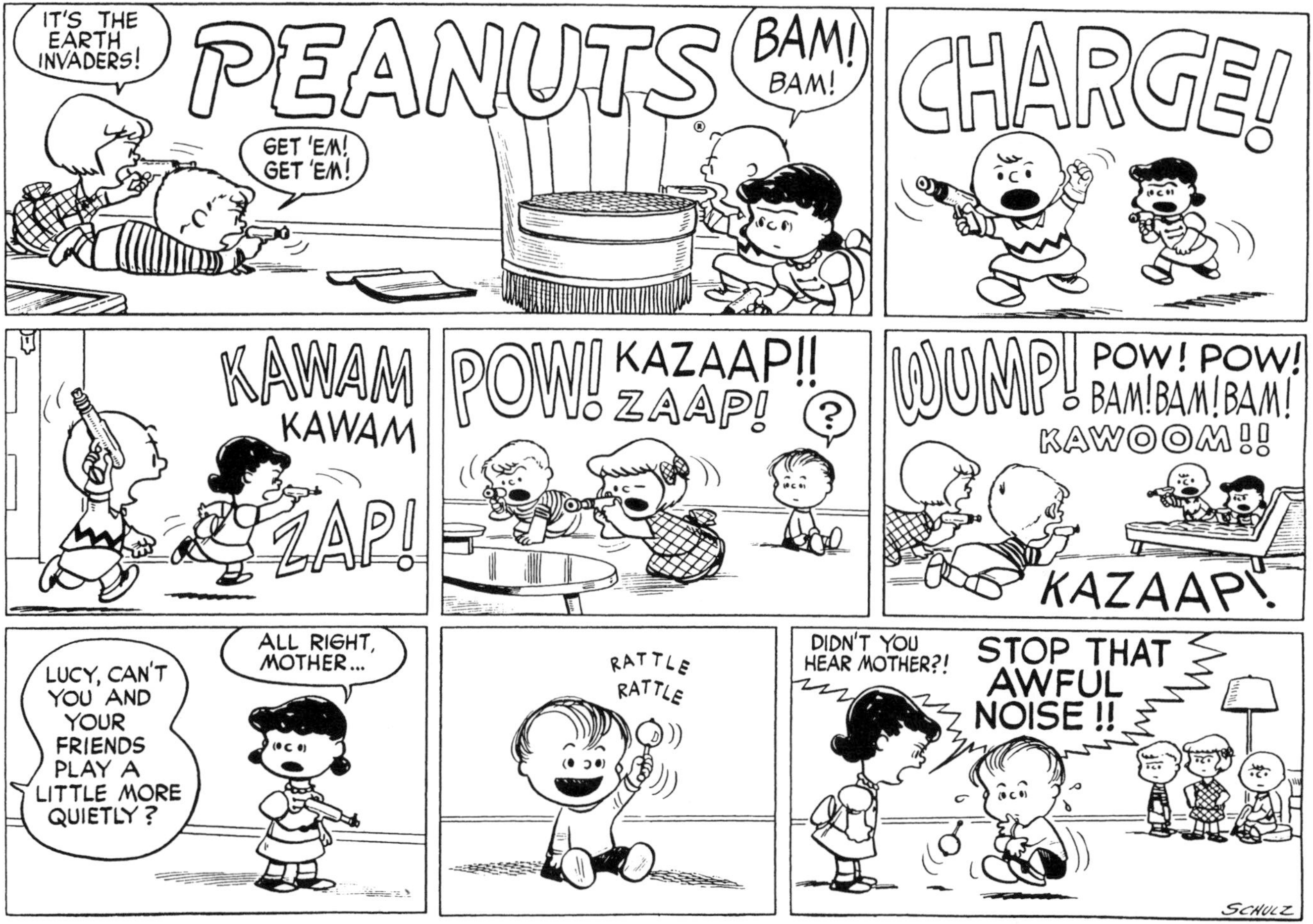
IT'S THE EARTH INVADERS!
PEANUTS
BAM! BAM!
GET 'EM! GET 'EM!
CHARGE!
KAWAM KAWAM
ZAP!
POW! KAZAAP!! ZAAP!
?
WUMP! POW! POW! BAM! BAM! BAM!
KAWOOM!!
KAZAAP!
LUCY, CAN'T YOU AND YOUR FRIENDS PLAY A LITTLE MORE QUIETLY?
ALL RIGHT, MOTHER...
RATTLE RATTLE
DIDN'T YOU HEAR MOTHER?!
STOP THAT AWFUL NOISE!!
SCHULZ

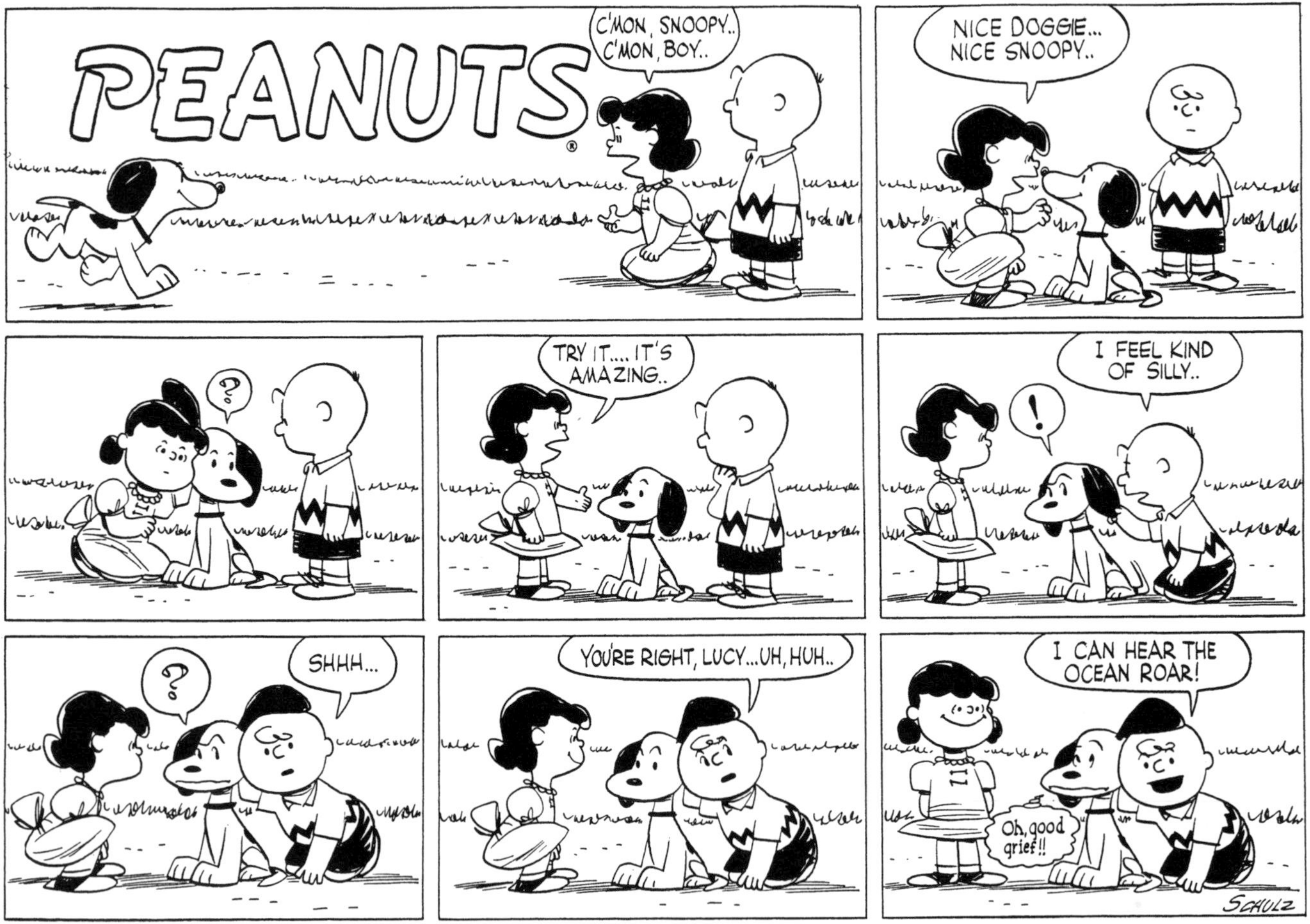
PEANUTS
C'MON, SNOOPY..
C'MON, BOY..
NICE DOGGIE...
NICE SNOOPY..
?
TRY IT.... IT'S
AMAZING..
!
I FEEL KIND
OF SILLY..
?
SHHH...
YOU'RE RIGHT, LUCY...UH, HUH..
I CAN HEAR THE
OCEAN ROAR!
Oh, good
grief!!
SCHULZ

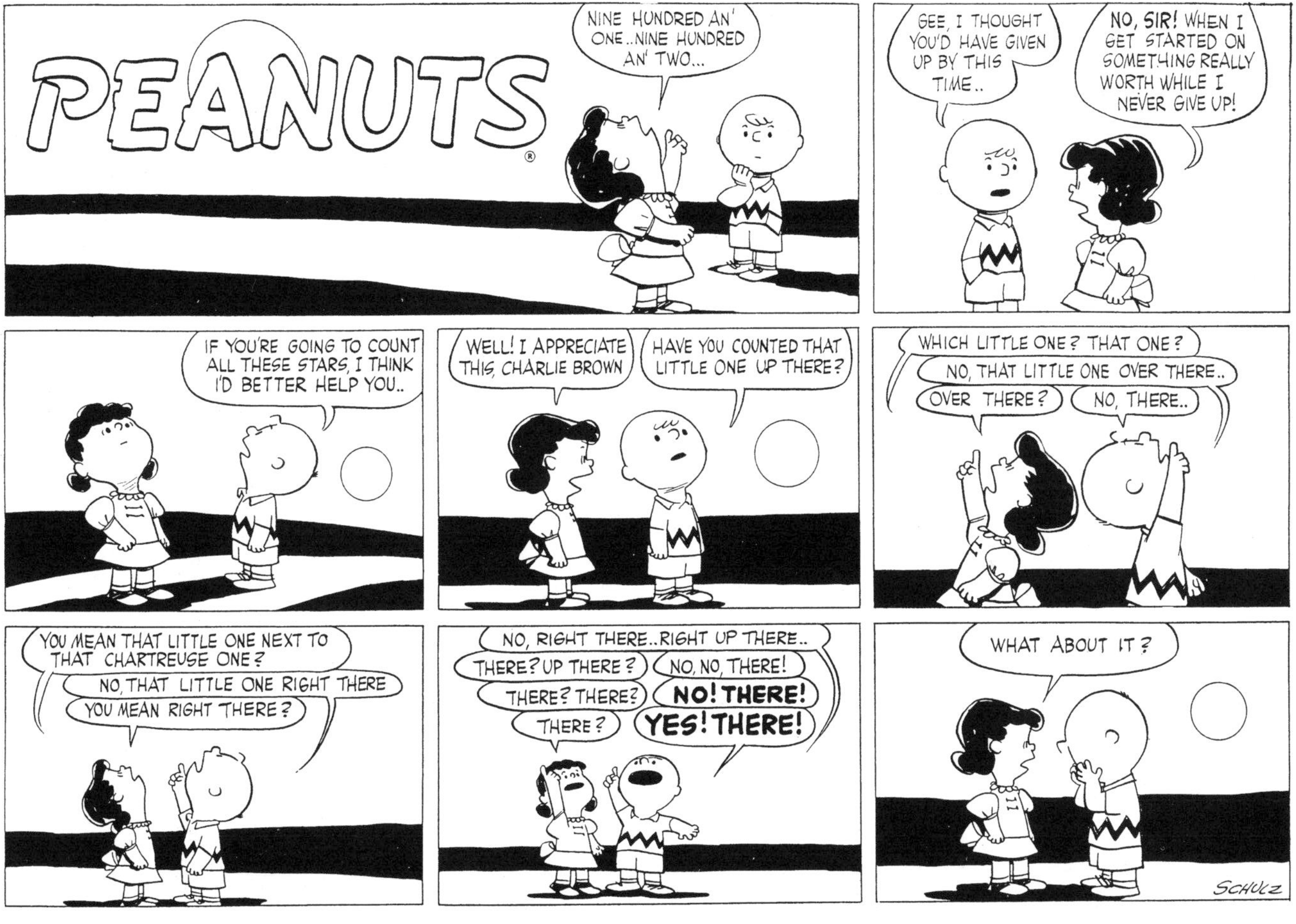
PEANUTS®
NINE HUNDRED AN' ONE..NINE HUNDRED AN' TWO...
GEE, I THOUGHT YOU'D HAVE GIVEN UP BY THIS TIME..
NO, SIR! WHEN I GET STARTED ON SOMETHING REALLY WORTH WHILE I NEVER GIVE UP!
IF YOU'RE GOING TO COUNT ALL THESE STARS, I THINK I'D BETTER HELP YOU..
WELL! I APPRECIATE THIS, CHARLIE BROWN
HAVE YOU COUNTED THAT LITTLE ONE UP THERE?
WHICH LITTLE ONE? THAT ONE?
NO, THAT LITTLE ONE OVER THERE..
OVER THERE?
NO, THERE..
YOU MEAN THAT LITTLE ONE NEXT TO THAT CHARTREUSE ONE?
NO, THAT LITTLE ONE RIGHT THERE
YOU MEAN RIGHT THERE?
NO, RIGHT THERE..RIGHT UP THERE..
THERE? UP THERE?
NO, NO, THERE!
THERE? THERE?
NO! THERE!
THERE?
YES! THERE!
WHAT ABOUT IT?
SCHULZ

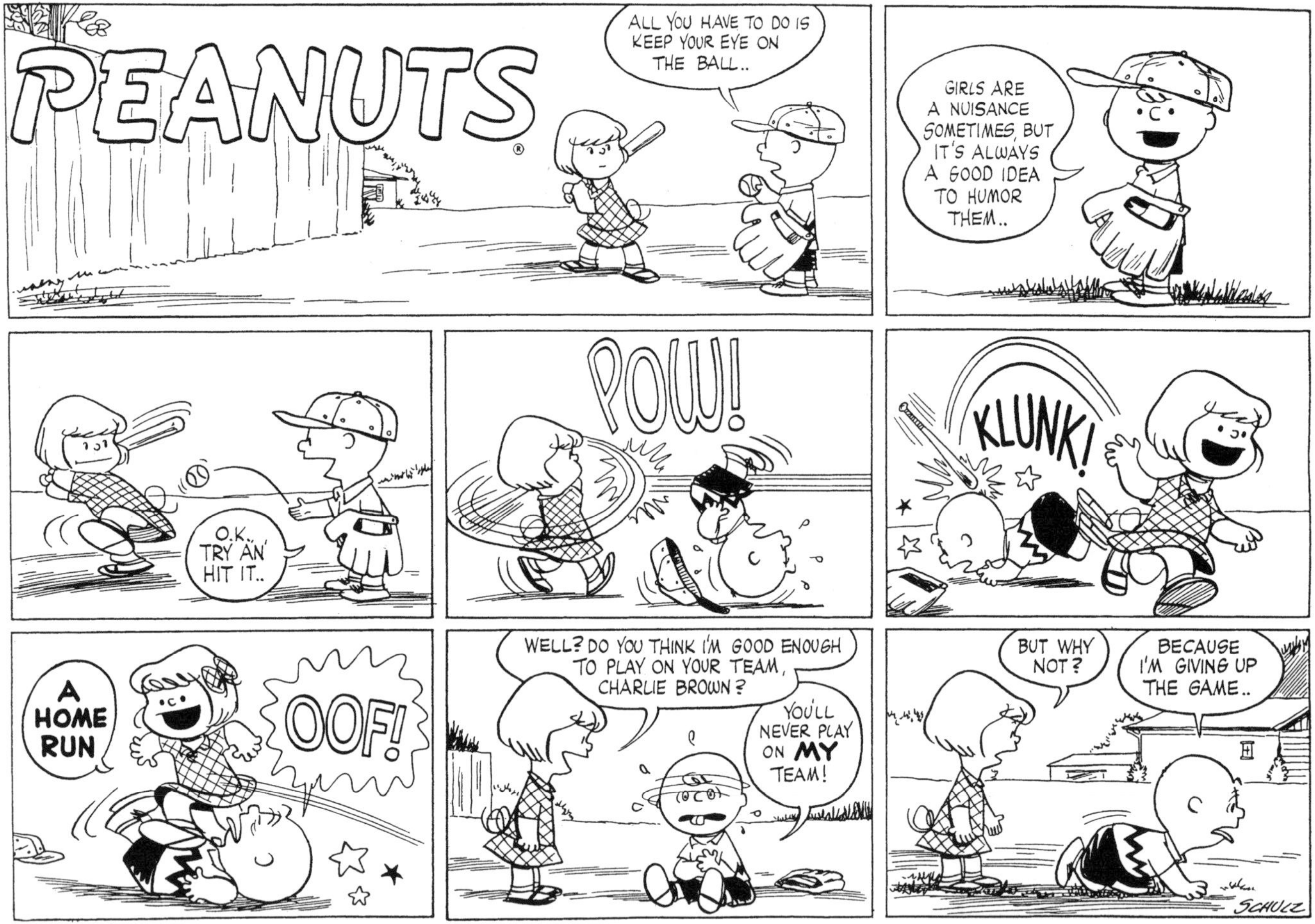
PEANUTS®
ALL YOU HAVE TO DO IS KEEP YOUR EYE ON THE BALL..
GIRLS ARE A NUISANCE SOMETIMES, BUT IT'S ALWAYS A GOOD IDEA TO HUMOR THEM..
O.K.. TRY AN' HIT IT..
POW!
KLUNK!
A HOME RUN
OOF!
WELL? DO YOU THINK I'M GOOD ENOUGH TO PLAY ON YOUR TEAM, CHARLIE BROWN?
YOU'LL NEVER PLAY ON MY TEAM!
BUT WHY NOT?
BECAUSE I'M GIVING UP THE GAME..
SCHULZ

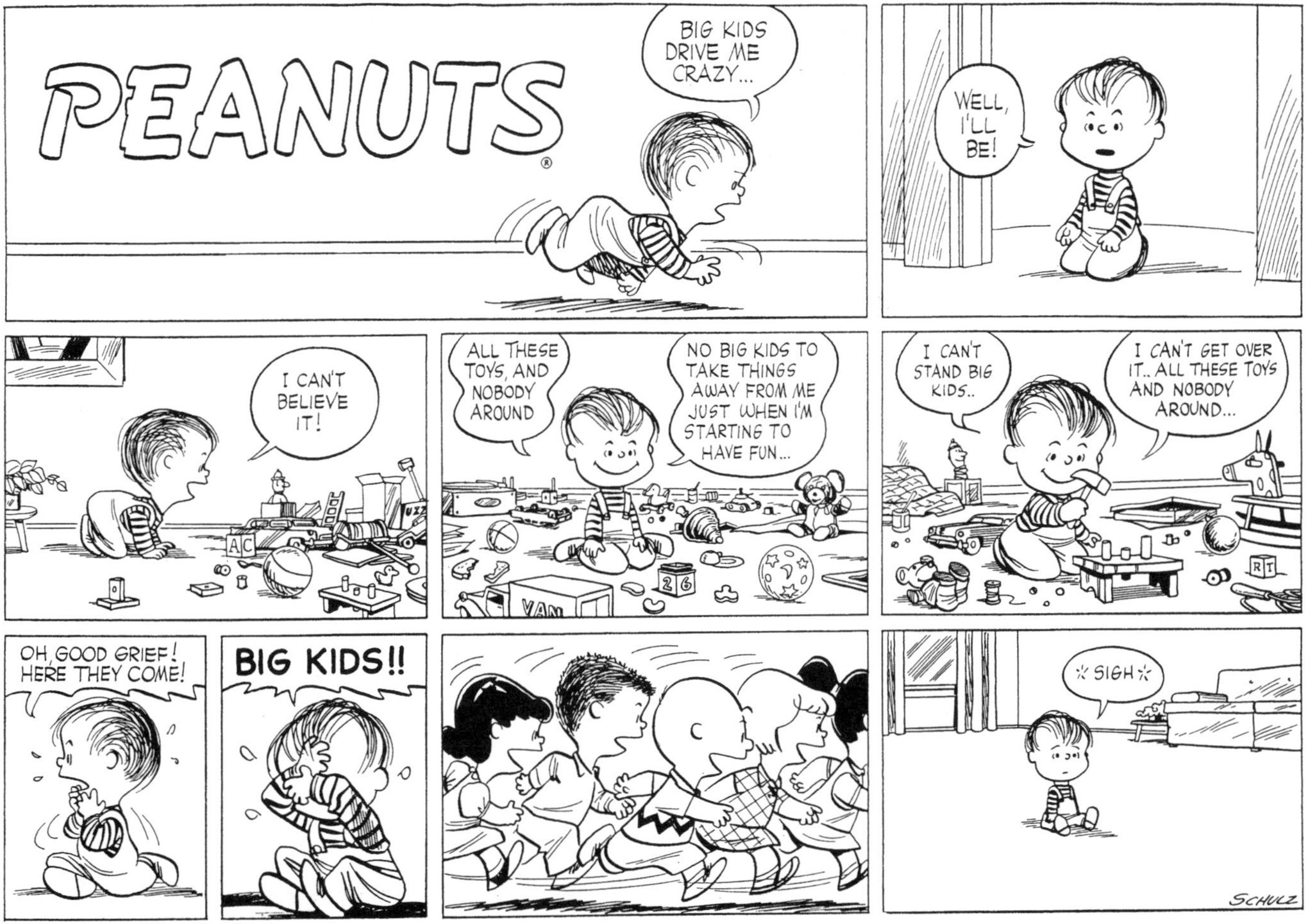
PEANUTS®
BIG KIDS DRIVE ME CRAZY...
WELL, I'LL BE!
I CAN'T BELIEVE IT!
ALL THESE TOYS, AND NOBODY AROUND
NO BIG KIDS TO TAKE THINGS AWAY FROM ME JUST WHEN I'M STARTING TO HAVE FUN...
I CAN'T STAND BIG KIDS..
I CAN'T GET OVER IT.. ALL THESE TOYS AND NOBODY AROUND...
OH, GOOD GRIEF! HERE THEY COME!
BIG KIDS!!
SIGH
SCHULZ

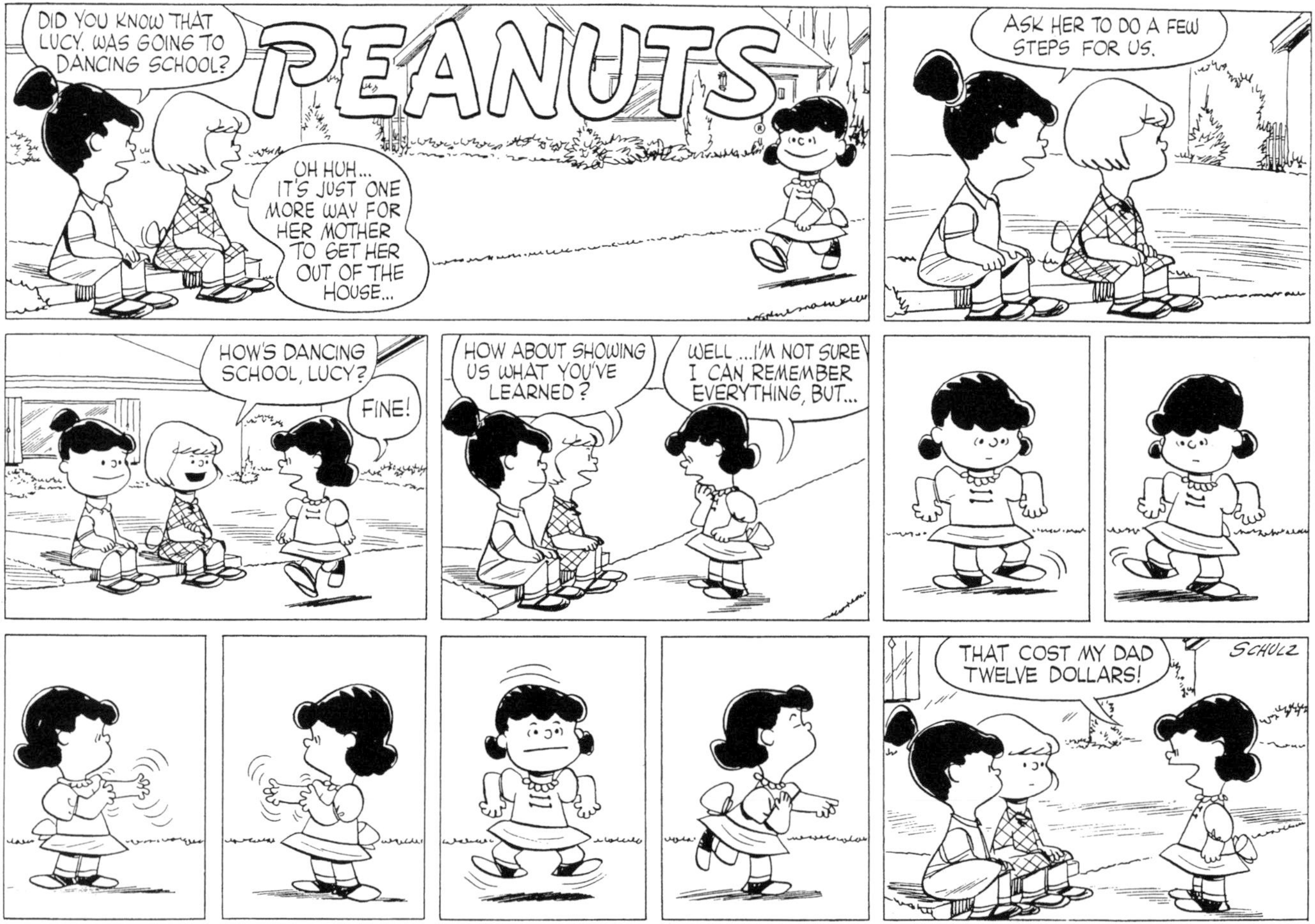
PEANUTS
DID YOU KNOW THAT LUCY WAS GOING TO DANCING SCHOOL?
OH HUH... IT'S JUST ONE MORE WAY FOR HER MOTHER TO GET HER OUT OF THE HOUSE...
ASK HER TO DO A FEW STEPS FOR US.
HOW'S DANCING SCHOOL, LUCY?
FINE!
HOW ABOUT SHOWING US WHAT YOU'VE LEARNED?
WELL ...I'M NOT SURE I CAN REMEMBER EVERYTHING, BUT...
SCHULZ
THAT COST MY DAD TWELVE DOLLARS!

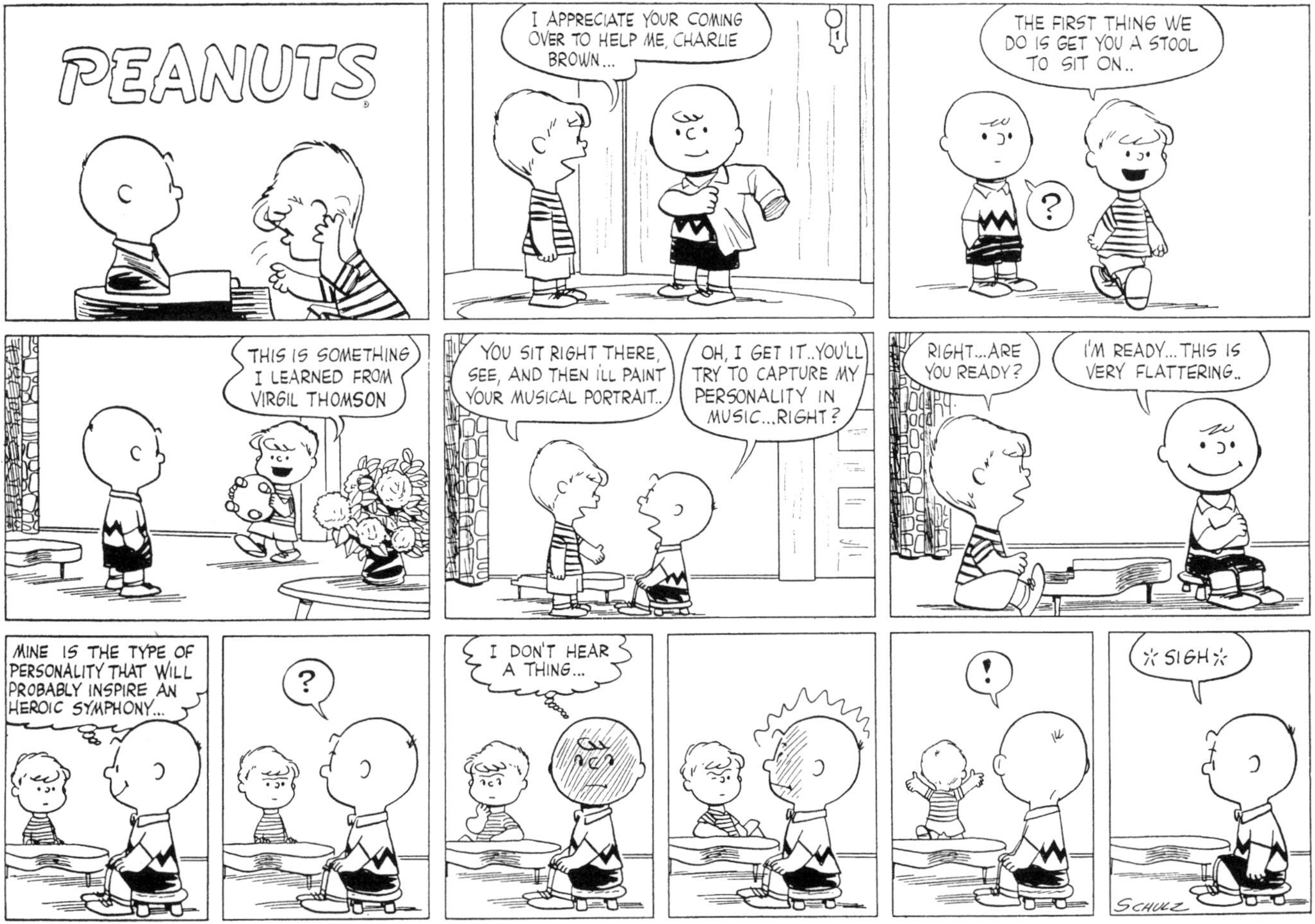
PEANUTS
I APPRECIATE YOUR COMING OVER TO HELP ME, CHARLIE BROWN...
THE FIRST THING WE DO IS GET YOU A STOOL TO SIT ON..
?
THIS IS SOMETHING I LEARNED FROM VIRGIL THOMSON
YOU SIT RIGHT THERE, SEE, AND THEN I'LL PAINT YOUR MUSICAL PORTRAIT..
OH, I GET IT..YOU'LL TRY TO CAPTURE MY PERSONALITY IN MUSIC...RIGHT?
RIGHT...ARE YOU READY?
I'M READY... THIS IS VERY FLATTERING..
MINE IS THE TYPE OF PERSONALITY THAT WILL PROBABLY INSPIRE AN HEROIC SYMPHONY...
?
I DON'T HEAR A THING...
!
SIGH
SCHULZ

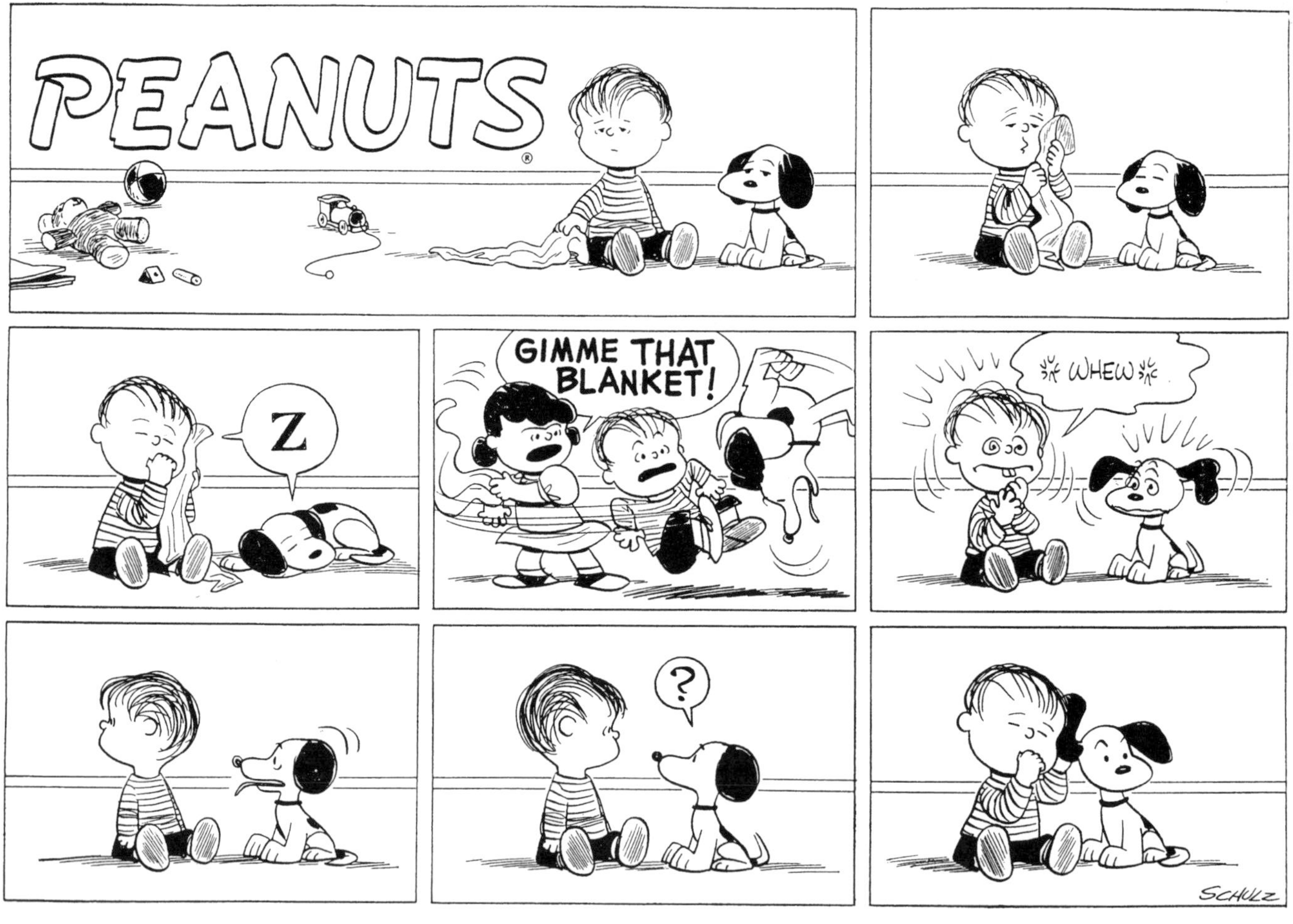
PEANUTS
Z
GIMME THAT BLANKET!
WHEW
?
SCHULZ

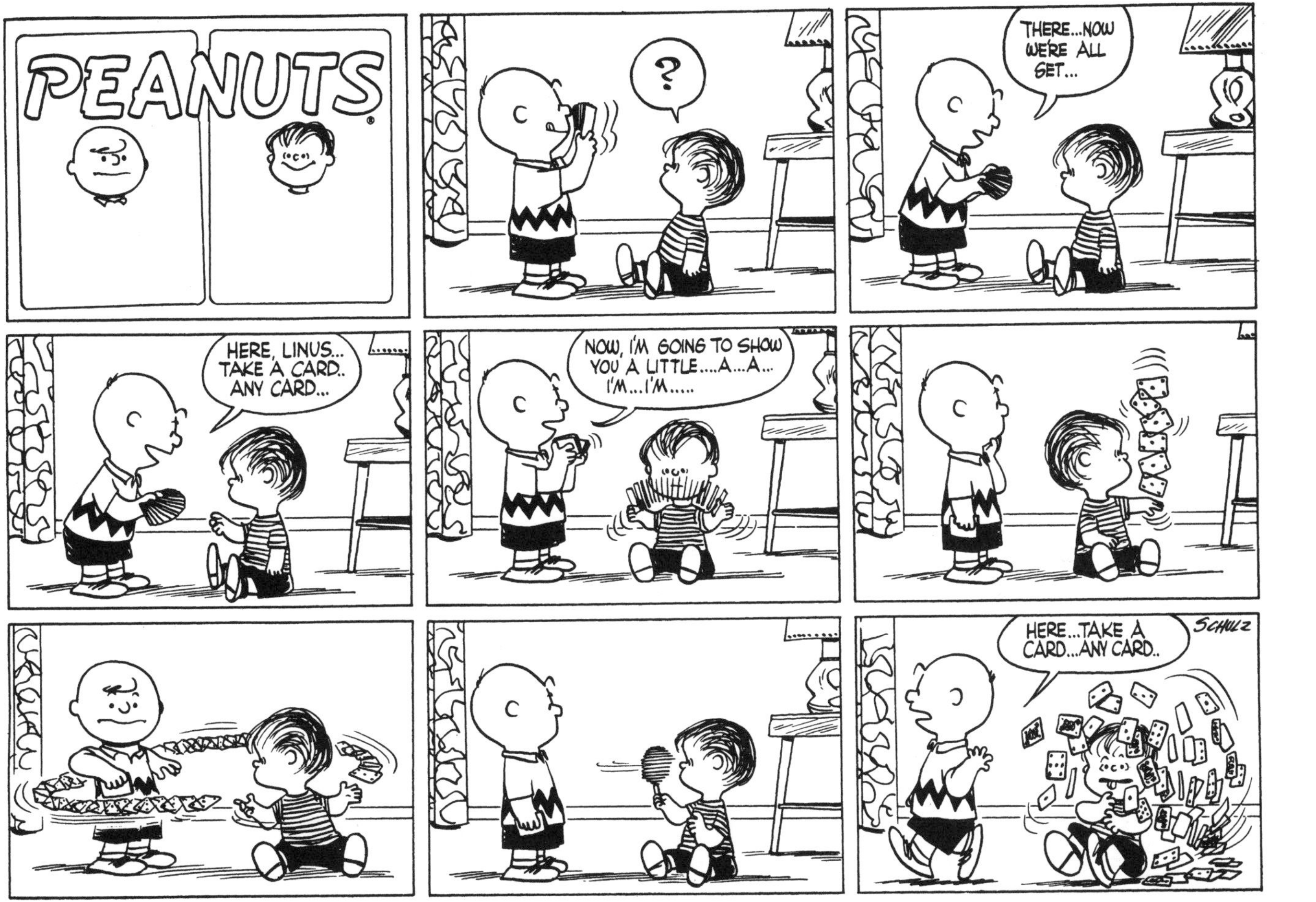
PEANUTS
?
THERE...NOW WE'RE ALL SET...
HERE, LINUS... TAKE A CARD.. ANY CARD...
NOW, I'M GOING TO SHOW YOU A LITTLE....A...A... I'M...I'M.....
HERE...TAKE A CARD...ANY CARD..
SCHULZ

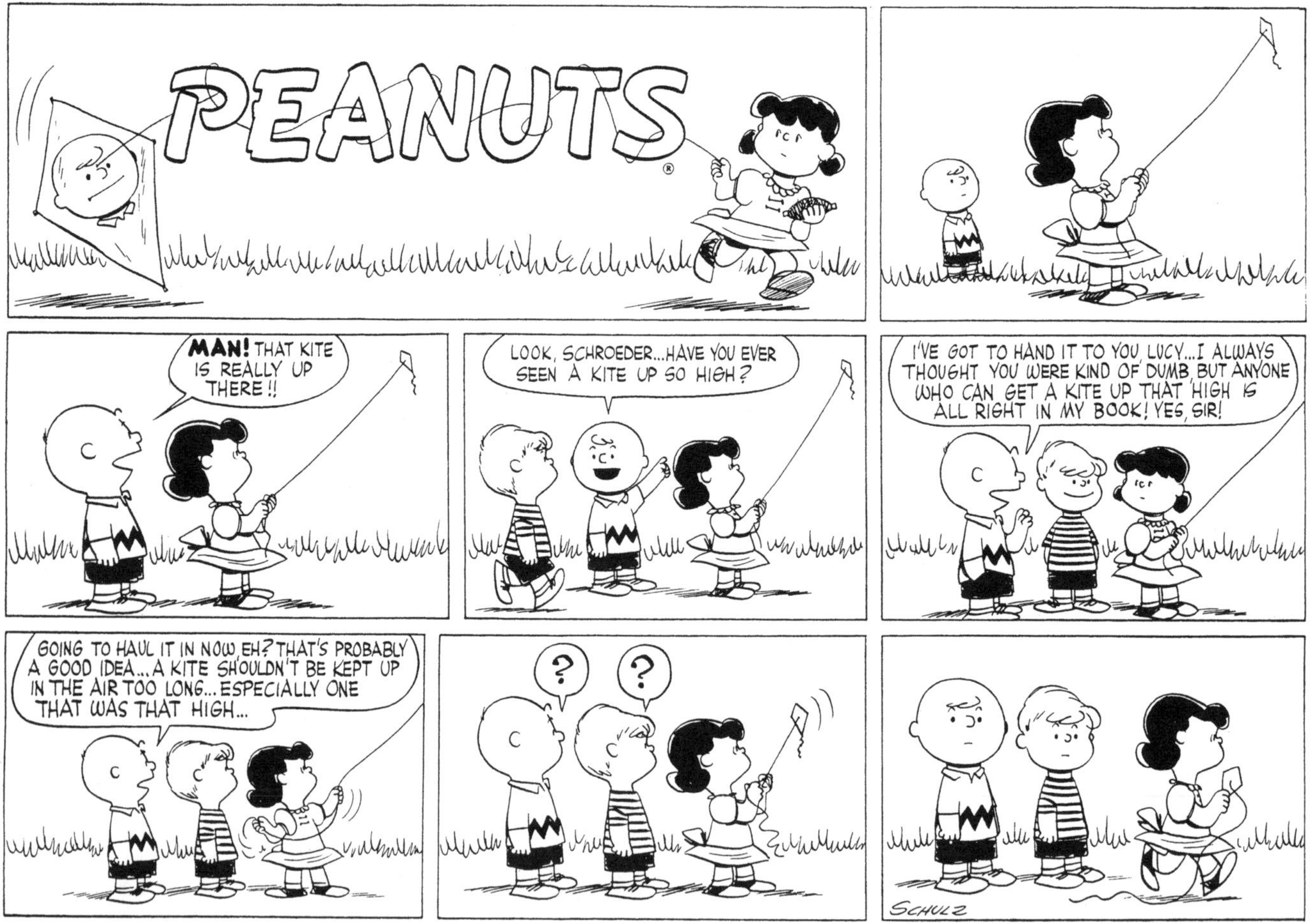
PEANUTS®
MAN! THAT KITE IS REALLY UP THERE!!
LOOK, SCHROEDER...HAVE YOU EVER SEEN A KITE UP SO HIGH?
I'VE GOT TO HAND IT TO YOU, LUCY...I ALWAYS THOUGHT YOU WERE KIND OF DUMB, BUT ANYONE WHO CAN GET A KITE UP THAT HIGH IS ALL RIGHT IN MY BOOK! YES, SIR!
GOING TO HAUL IT IN NOW, EH? THAT'S PROBABLY A GOOD IDEA...A KITE SHOULDN'T BE KEPT UP IN THE AIR TOO LONG...ESPECIALLY ONE THAT WAS THAT HIGH...
?
?
SCHULZ

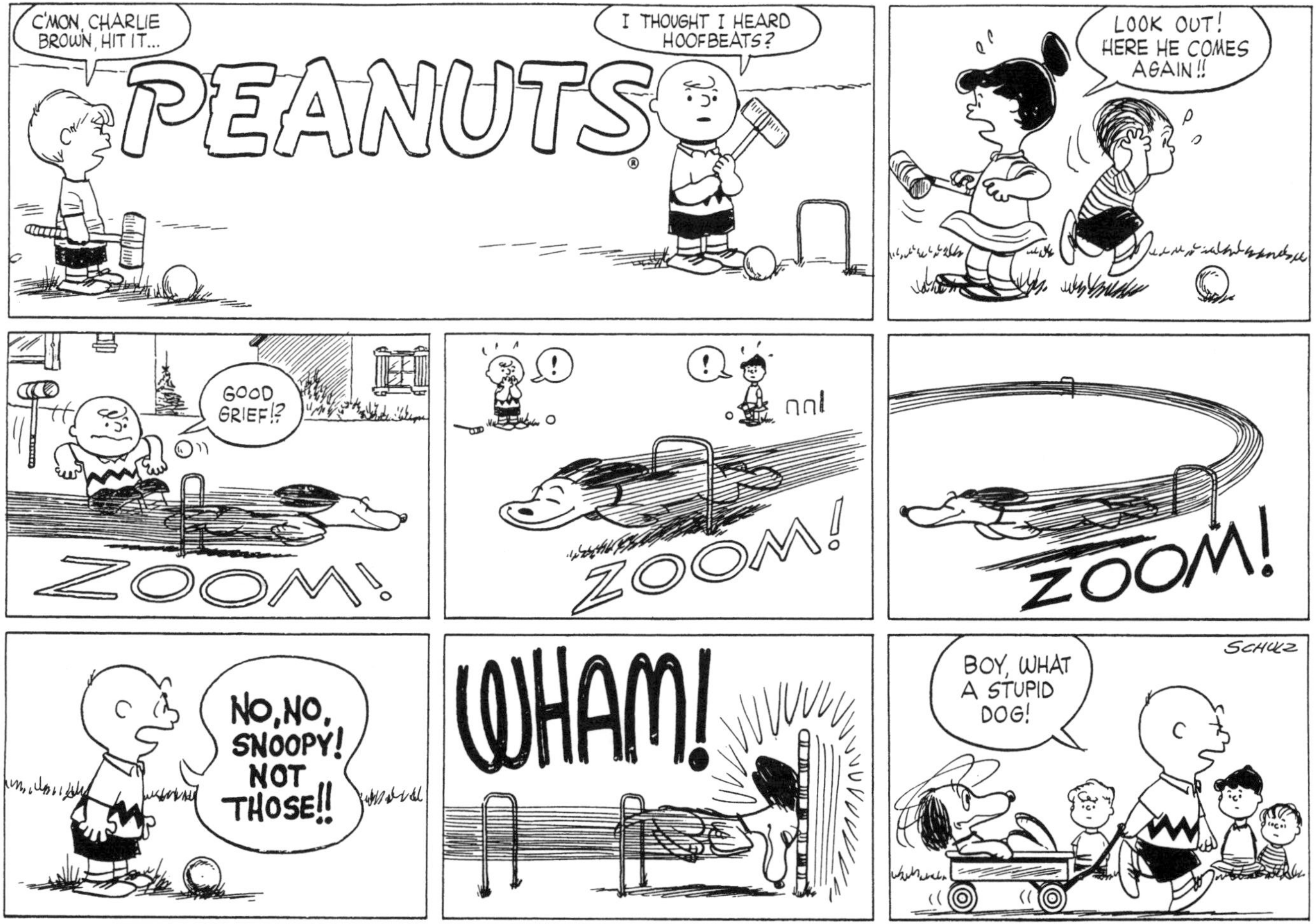

C'MON, CHARLIE BROWN, HIT IT...
PEANUTS®
I THOUGHT I HEARD HOOFBEATS?
LOOK OUT! HERE HE COMES AGAIN!!
GOOD GRIEF!?
ZOOM!
!
!
ZOOM!
ZOOM!
NO, NO, SNOOPY! NOT THOSE!!
WHAM!
SCHULZ
BOY, WHAT A STUPID DOG!

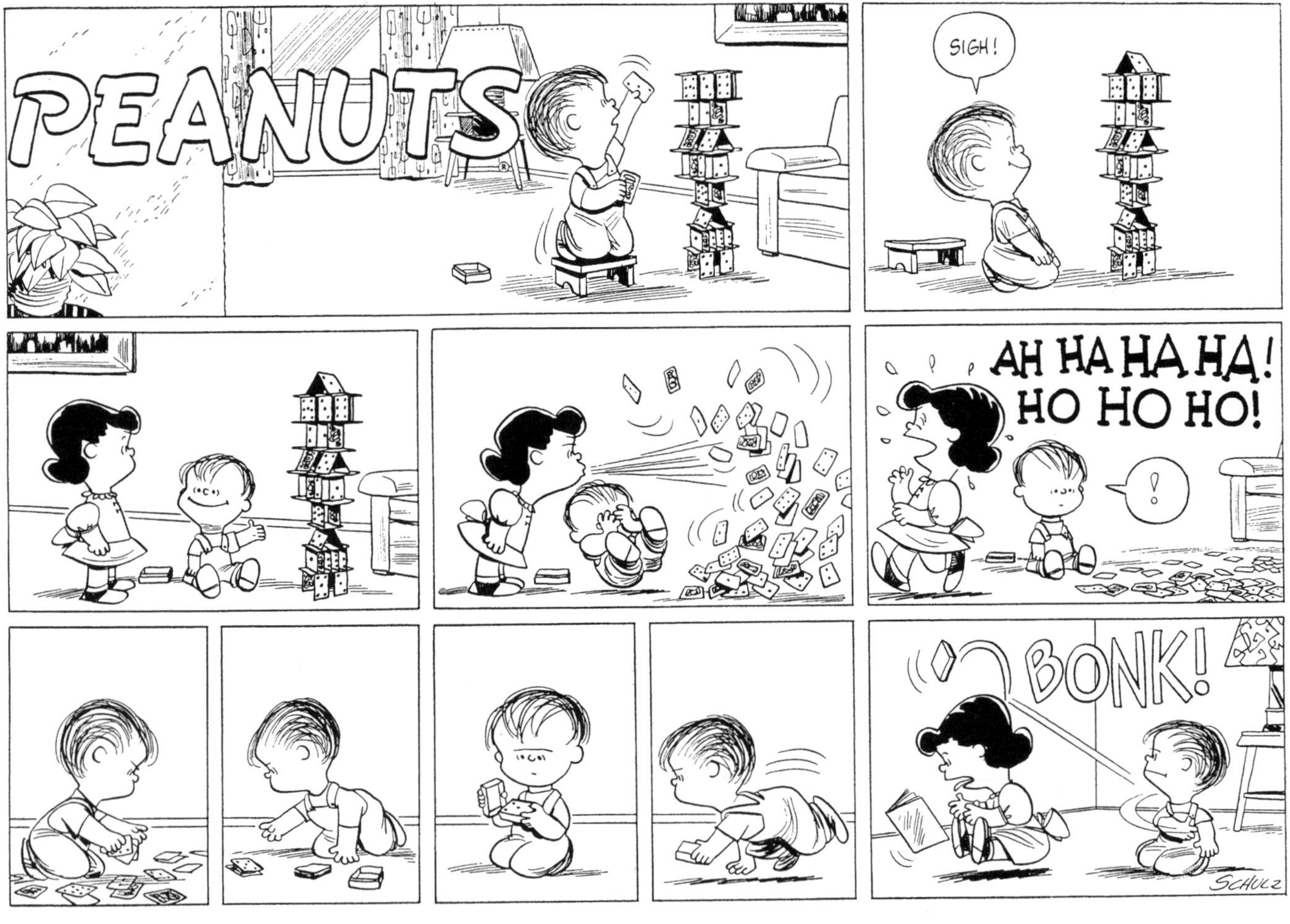
PEANUTS
SIGH!
AH HA HA HA!
HO HO HO!
!
BONK!
SCHULZ

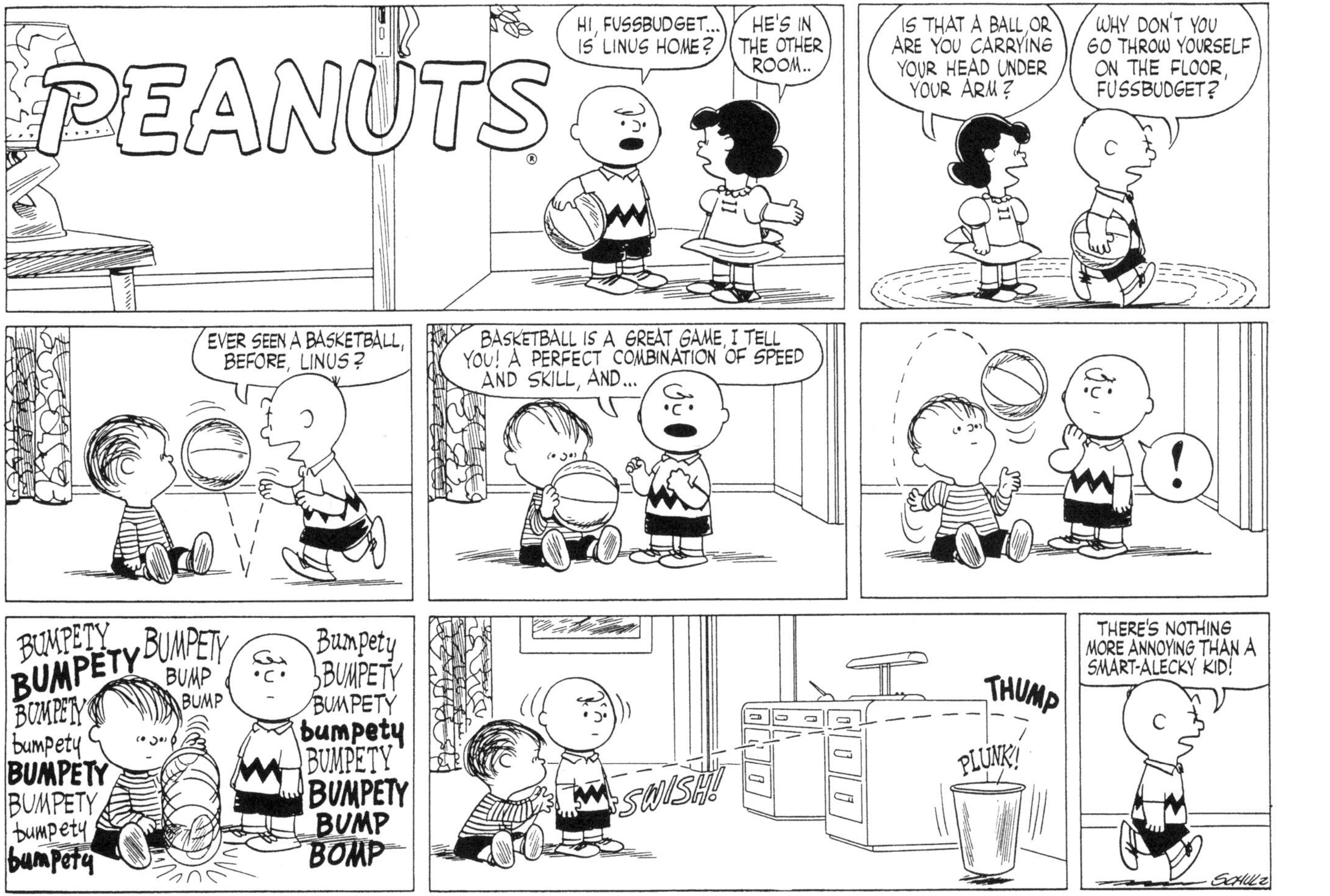
PEANUTS
HI, FUSSBUDGET... IS LINUS HOME?
HE'S IN THE OTHER ROOM..
IS THAT A BALL, OR ARE YOU CARRYING YOUR HEAD UNDER YOUR ARM?
WHY DON'T YOU GO THROW YOURSELF ON THE FLOOR, FUSSBUDGET?
EVER SEEN A BASKETBALL, BEFORE, LINUS?
BASKETBALL IS A GREAT GAME, I TELL YOU! A PERFECT COMBINATION OF SPEED AND SKILL, AND...
!
BUMPETY BUMPETY BUMPETY bumpety BUMPETY BUMPETY bumpety bumpety
BUMPETY BUMP BUMP
Bumpety BUMPETY BUMPETY bumpety BUMPETY BUMPETY BUMP BOMP
THUMP
SWISH!
PLUNK!
THERE'S NOTHING MORE ANNOYING THAN A SMART-ALECKY KID!
SCHULZ

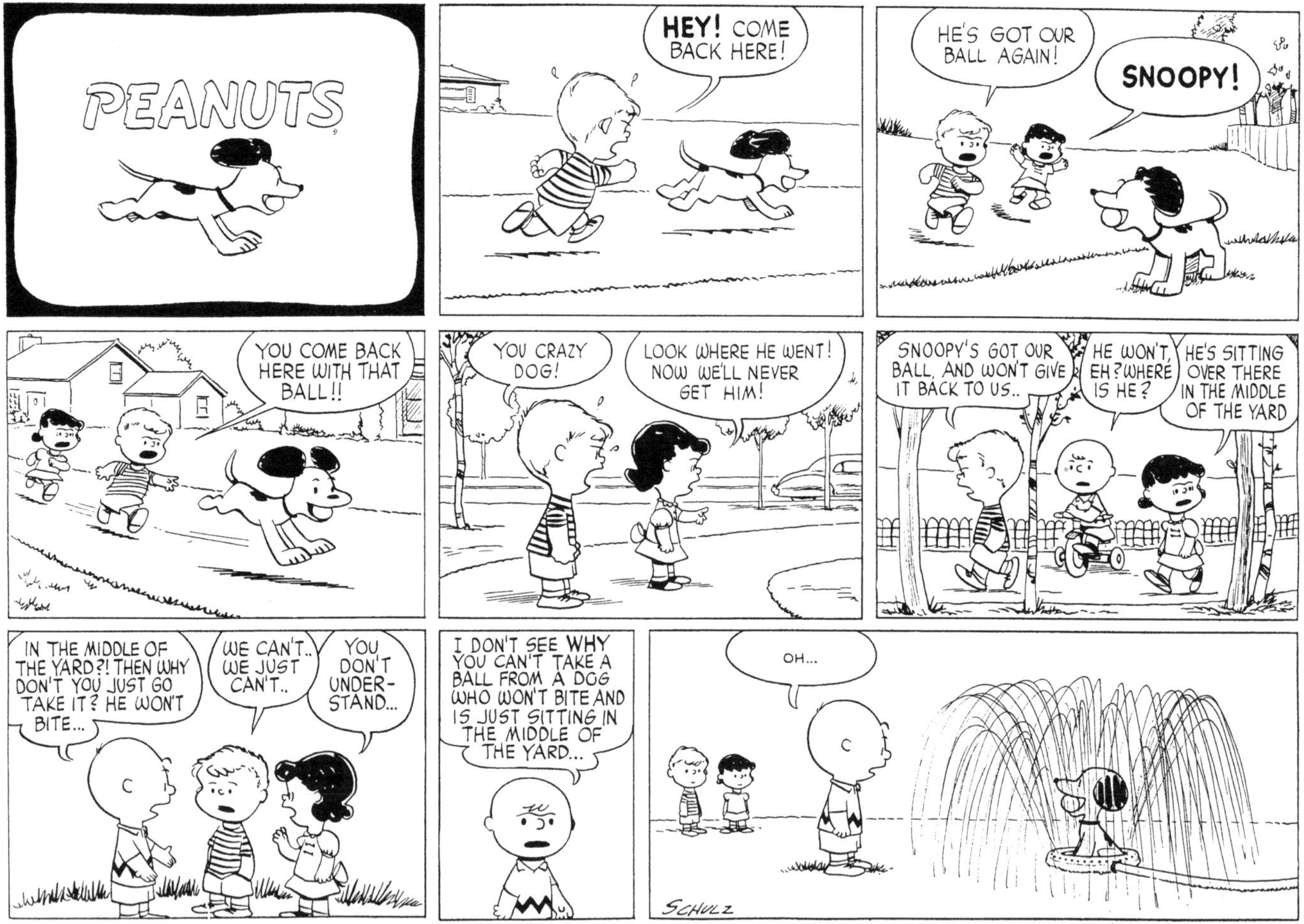
PEANUTS
HEY! COME BACK HERE!
HE'S GOT OUR BALL AGAIN!
SNOOPY!
YOU COME BACK HERE WITH THAT BALL!!
YOU CRAZY DOG!
LOOK WHERE HE WENT! NOW WE'LL NEVER GET HIM!
SNOOPY'S GOT OUR BALL, AND WON'T GIVE IT BACK TO US..
HE WON'T, EH? WHERE IS HE?
HE'S SITTING OVER THERE IN THE MIDDLE OF THE YARD
IN THE MIDDLE OF THE YARD?! THEN WHY DON'T YOU JUST GO TAKE IT? HE WON'T BITE...
WE CAN'T.. WE JUST CAN'T..
YOU DON'T UNDER-STAND...
I DON'T SEE WHY YOU CAN'T TAKE A BALL FROM A DOG WHO WON'T BITE AND IS JUST SITTING IN THE MIDDLE OF THE YARD...
OH...
SCHULZ

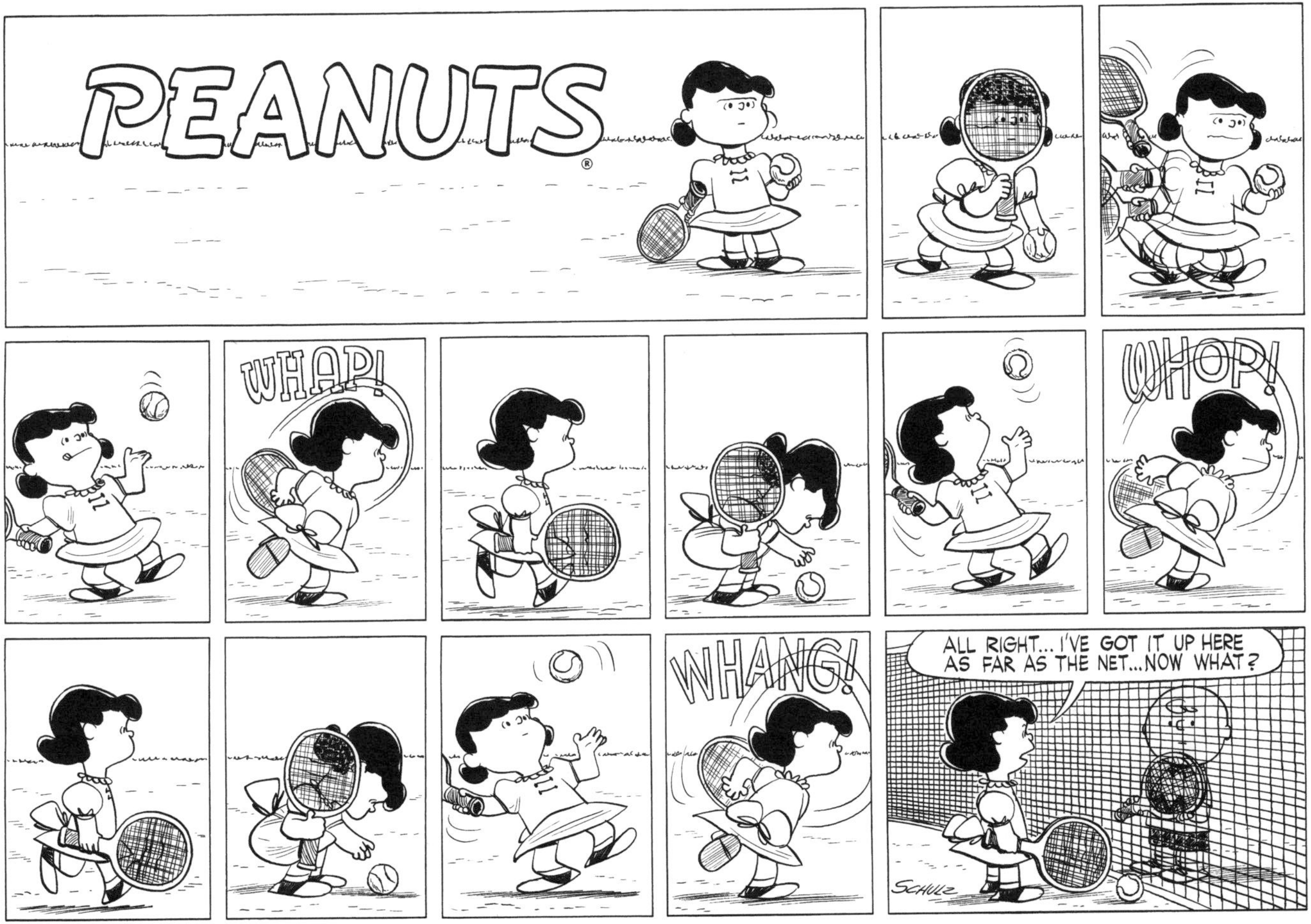
PEANUTS
WHAP!
WHOP!
WHANG!
ALL RIGHT... I'VE GOT IT UP HERE AS FAR AS THE NET...NOW WHAT?
SCHULZ

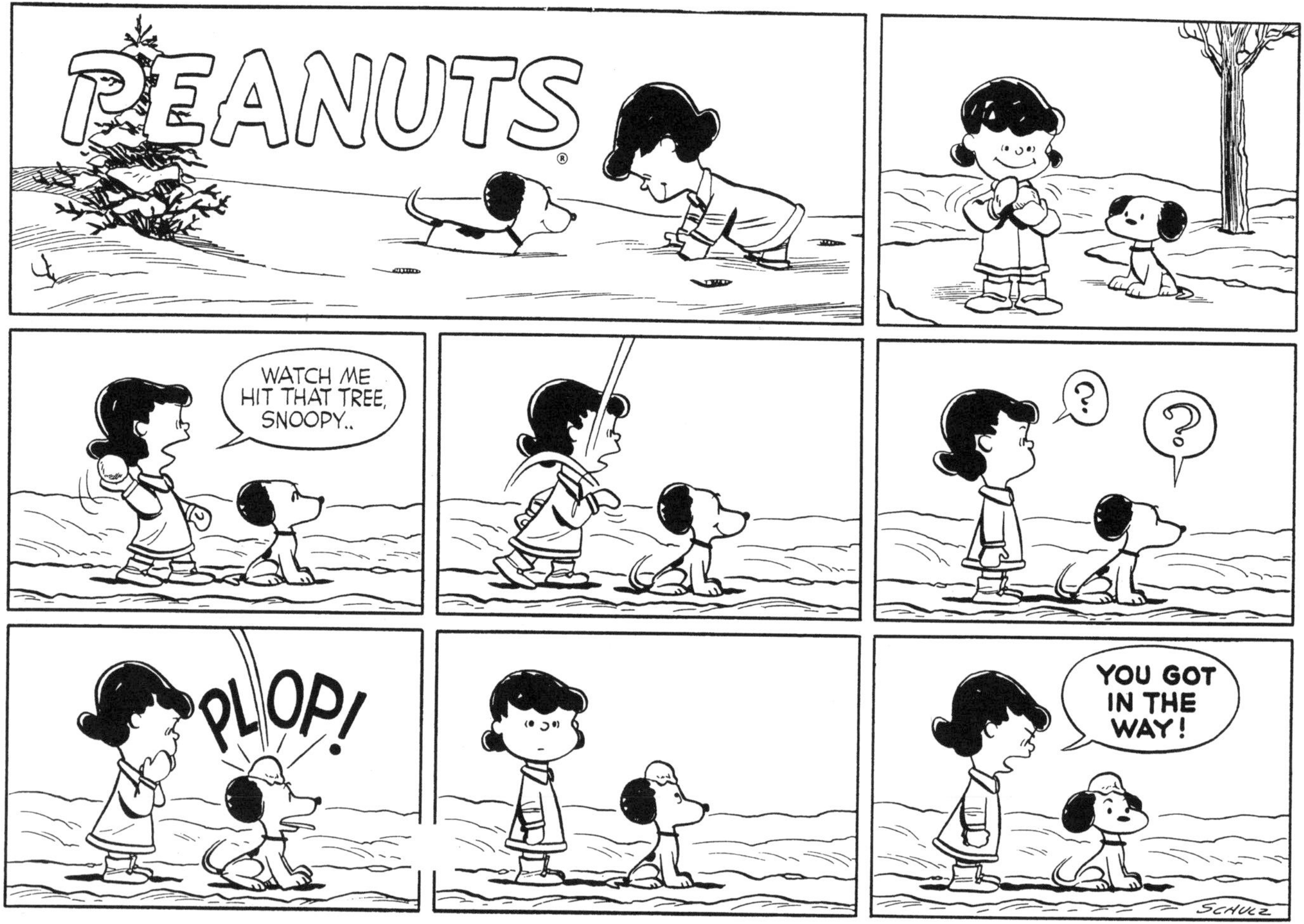
PEANUTS®
WATCH ME HIT THAT TREE, SNOOPY..
?
?
PLOP!
YOU GOT IN THE WAY!
SCHULZ

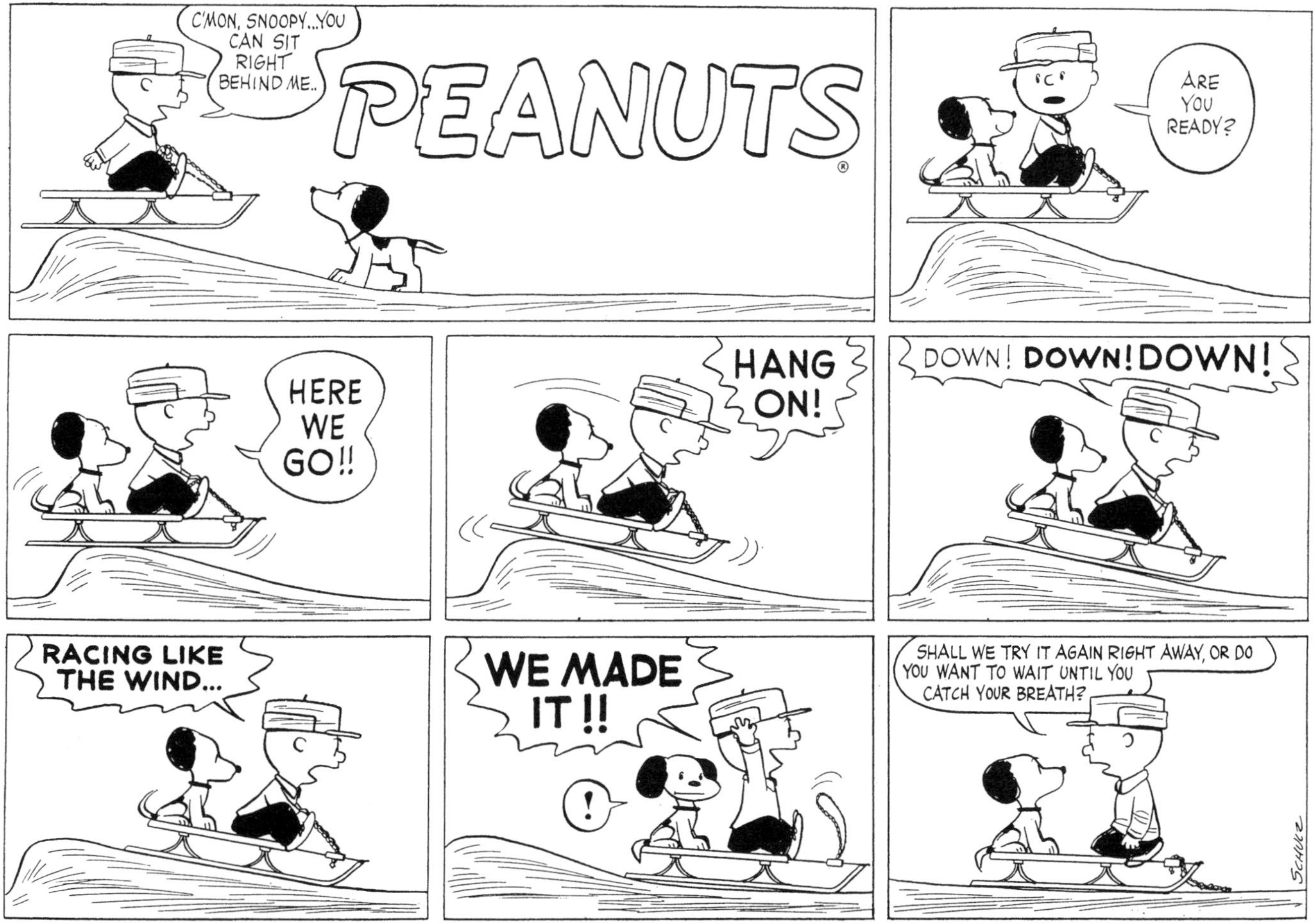
C'MON, SNOOPY...YOU CAN SIT RIGHT BEHIND ME..
PEANUTS
ARE YOU READY?
HERE WE GO!!
HANG ON!
DOWN! DOWN! DOWN!
RACING LIKE THE WIND...
WE MADE IT!!
!
SHALL WE TRY IT AGAIN RIGHT AWAY, OR DO YOU WANT TO WAIT UNTIL YOU CATCH YOUR BREATH?
SCHULZ

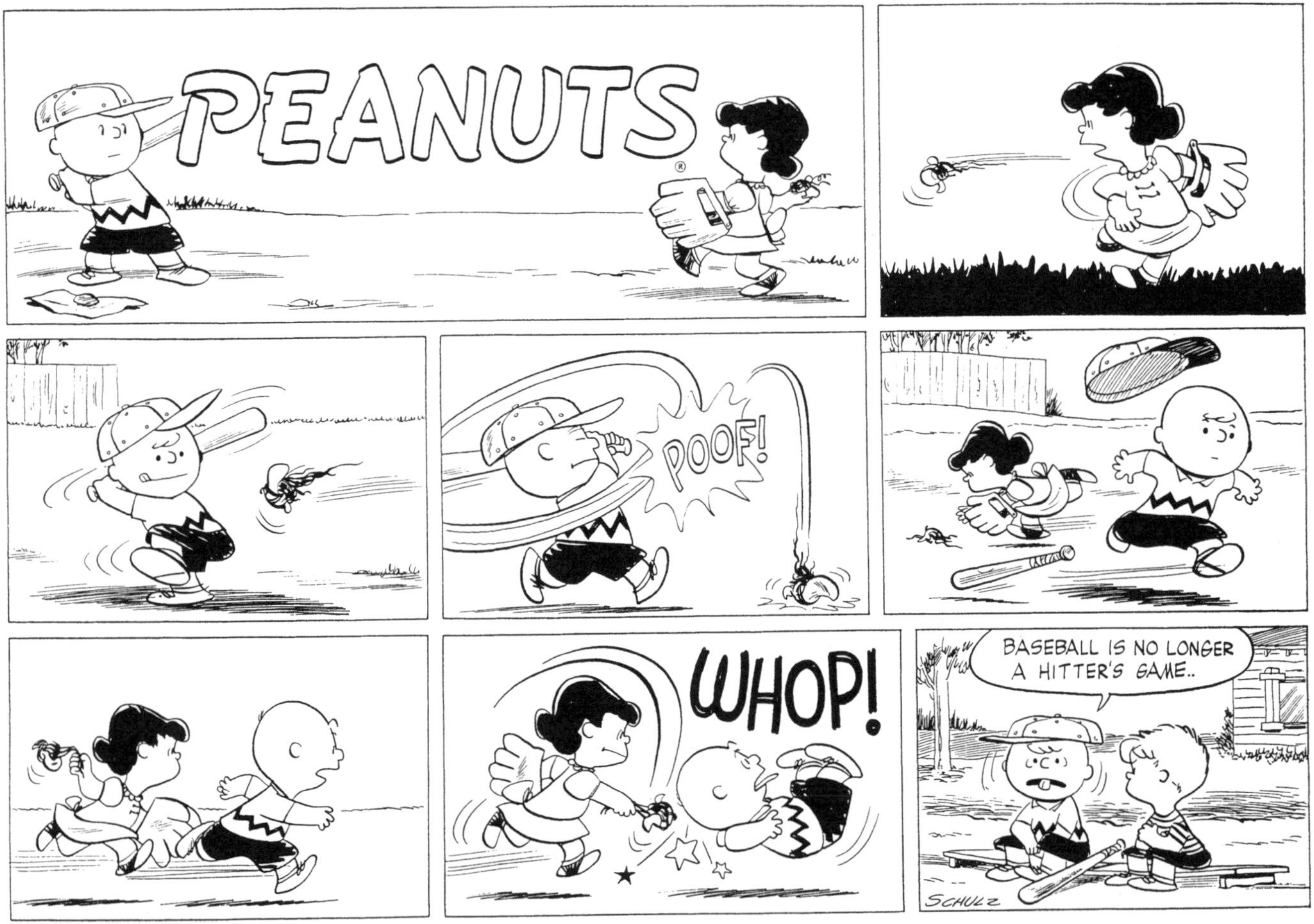
PEANUTS
POOF!
WHOP!
BASEBALL IS NO LONGER A HITTER'S GAME..
SCHULZ

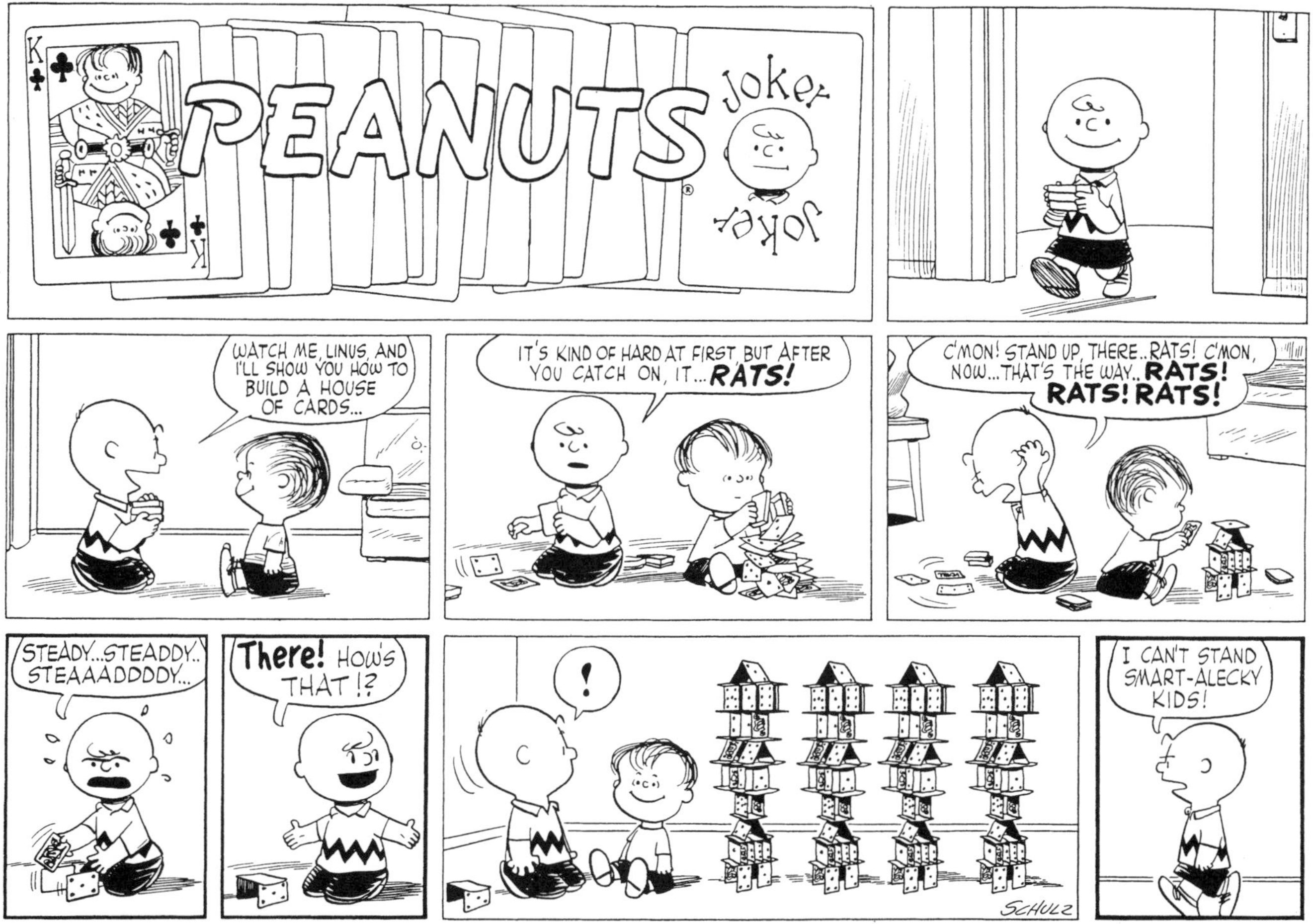
PEANUTS
Joker
Joker
WATCH ME, LINUS, AND I'LL SHOW YOU HOW TO BUILD A HOUSE OF CARDS...
IT'S KIND OF HARD AT FIRST BUT AFTER YOU CATCH ON, IT... RATS!
C'MON! STAND UP, THERE.. RATS! C'MON, NOW... THAT'S THE WAY.. RATS! RATS! RATS!
STEADY...STEADDY.. STEAAADDDDY...
There! HOW'S THAT !?
!
SCHULZ
I CAN'T STAND SMART-ALECKY KIDS!

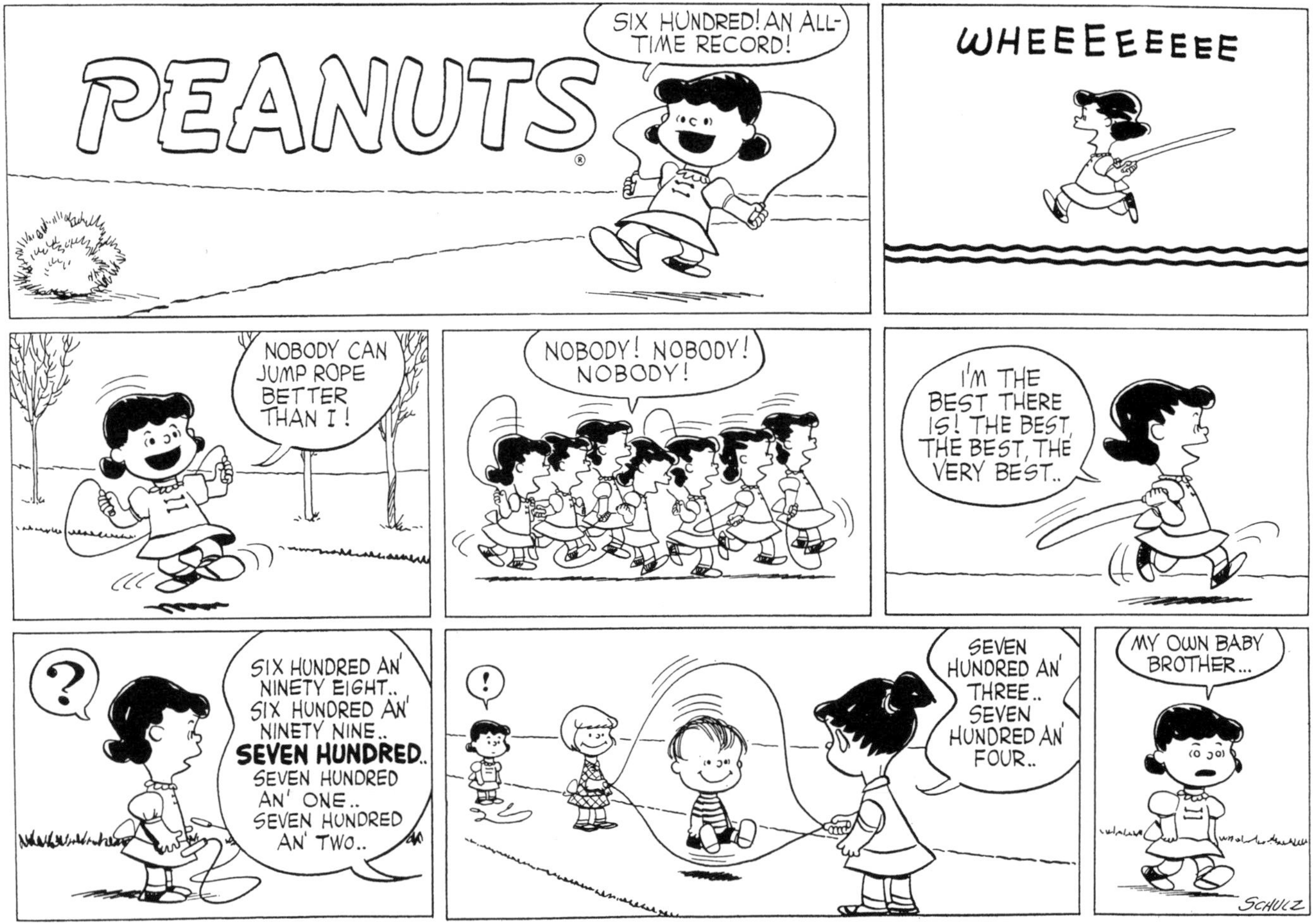
PEANUTS
SIX HUNDRED! AN ALL-TIME RECORD!
WHEEEEEEEE
NOBODY CAN JUMP ROPE BETTER THAN I!
NOBODY! NOBODY! NOBODY!
I'M THE BEST THERE IS! THE BEST, THE BEST, THE VERY BEST..
?
SIX HUNDRED AN' NINETY EIGHT.. SIX HUNDRED AN' NINETY NINE.. **SEVEN HUNDRED**.. SEVEN HUNDRED AN' ONE.. SEVEN HUNDRED AN' TWO..
!
SEVEN HUNDRED AN' THREE.. SEVEN HUNDRED AN' FOUR..
MY OWN BABY BROTHER...
SCHULZ

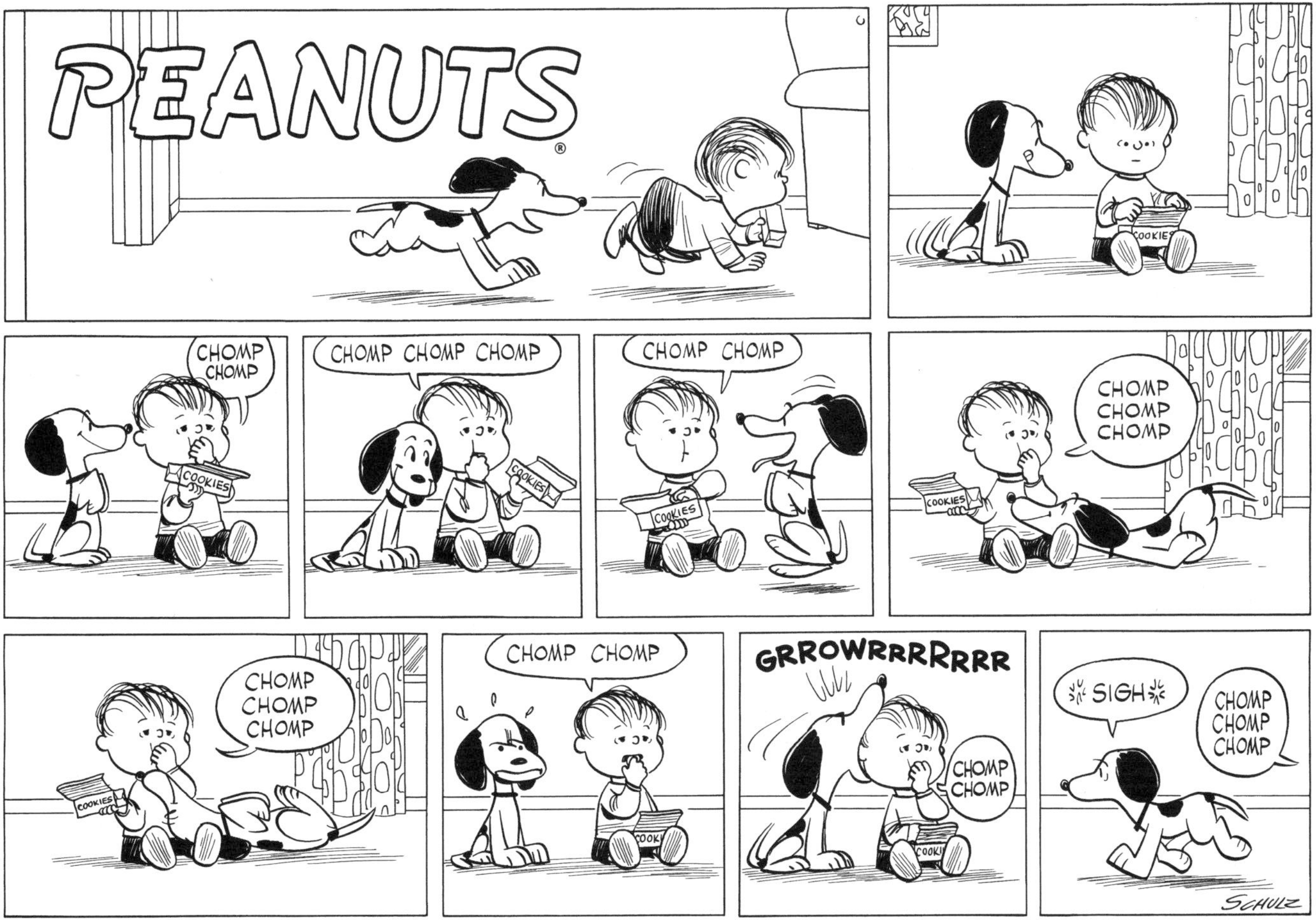
PEANUTS
COOKIES
CHOMP CHOMP
COOKIES
CHOMP CHOMP CHOMP
COOKIES
CHOMP CHOMP
COOKIES
CHOMP CHOMP CHOMP
COOKIES
CHOMP CHOMP CHOMP
COOKIES
CHOMP CHOMP
GRROWRRRRRrrr
CHOMP CHOMP
SIGH
CHOMP CHOMP CHOMP
SCHULZ

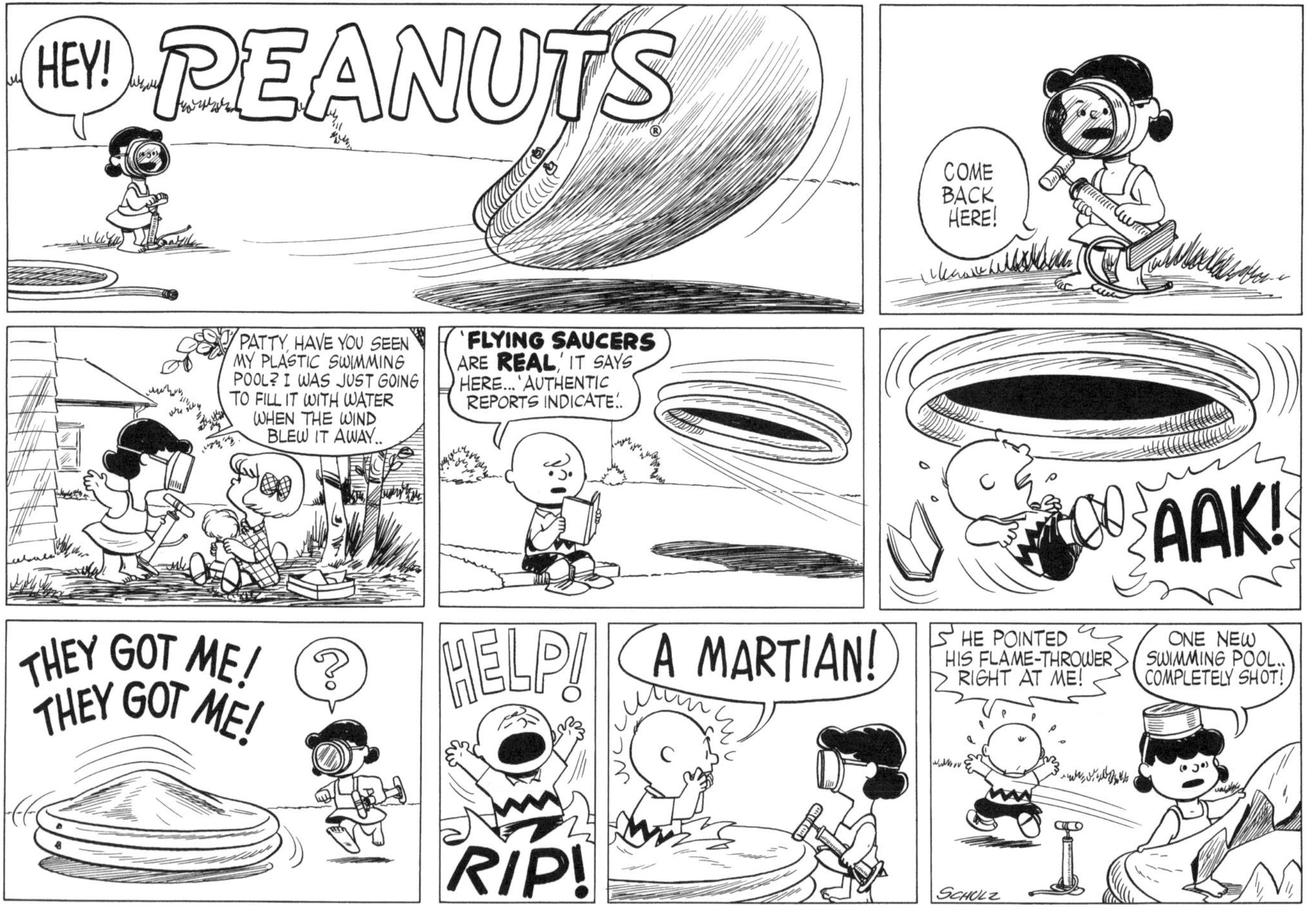
HEY!
PEANUTS
COME BACK HERE!
PATTY, HAVE YOU SEEN MY PLASTIC SWIMMING POOL? I WAS JUST GOING TO FILL IT WITH WATER WHEN THE WIND BLEW IT AWAY..
'FLYING SAUCERS ARE REAL,' IT SAYS HERE...'AUTHENTIC REPORTS INDICATE'..
AAK!
THEY GOT ME! THEY GOT ME!
?
HELP!
RIP!
A MARTIAN!
HE POINTED HIS FLAME-THROWER RIGHT AT ME!
ONE NEW SWIMMING POOL.. COMPLETELY SHOT!
SCHULZ

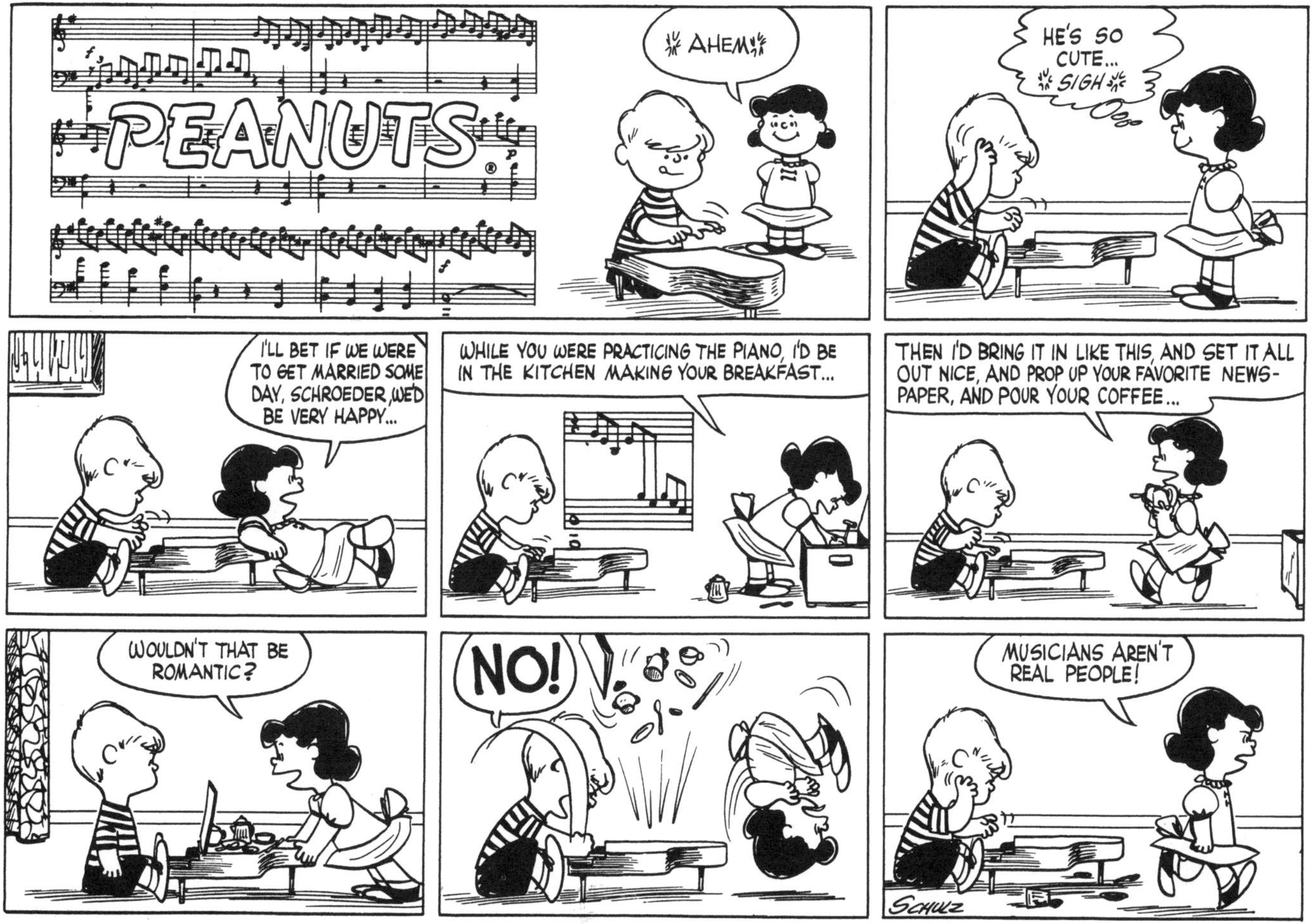
PEANUTS®
AHEM
HE'S SO CUTE... SIGH
I'LL BET IF WE WERE TO GET MARRIED SOME DAY, SCHROEDER, WE'D BE VERY HAPPY...
WHILE YOU WERE PRACTICING THE PIANO, I'D BE IN THE KITCHEN MAKING YOUR BREAKFAST...
THEN I'D BRING IT IN LIKE THIS, AND SET IT ALL OUT NICE, AND PROP UP YOUR FAVORITE NEWS-PAPER, AND POUR YOUR COFFEE...
WOULDN'T THAT BE ROMANTIC?
NO!
MUSICIANS AREN'T REAL PEOPLE!
SCHULZ

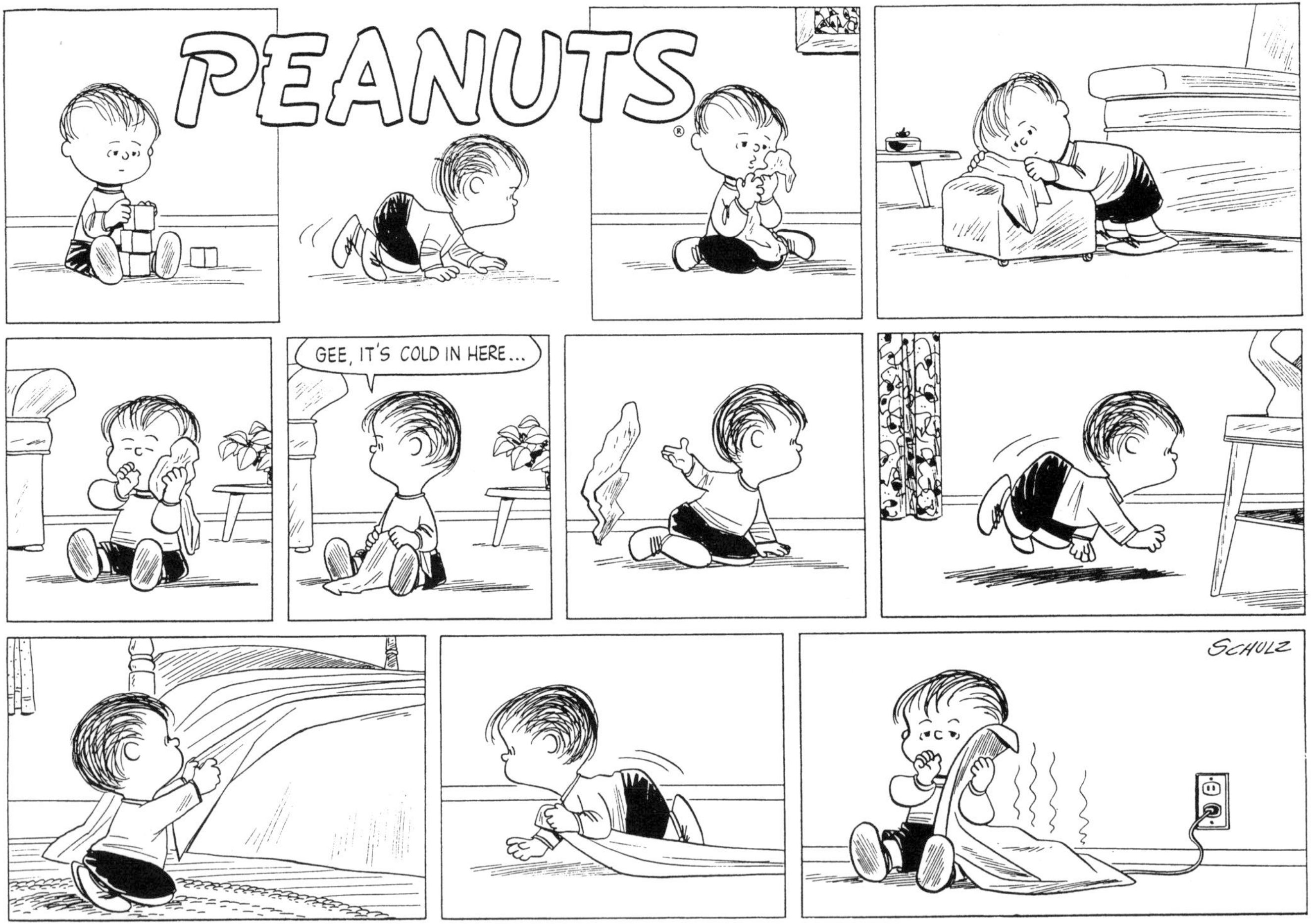
PEANUTS
GEE, IT'S COLD IN HERE...
SCHULZ

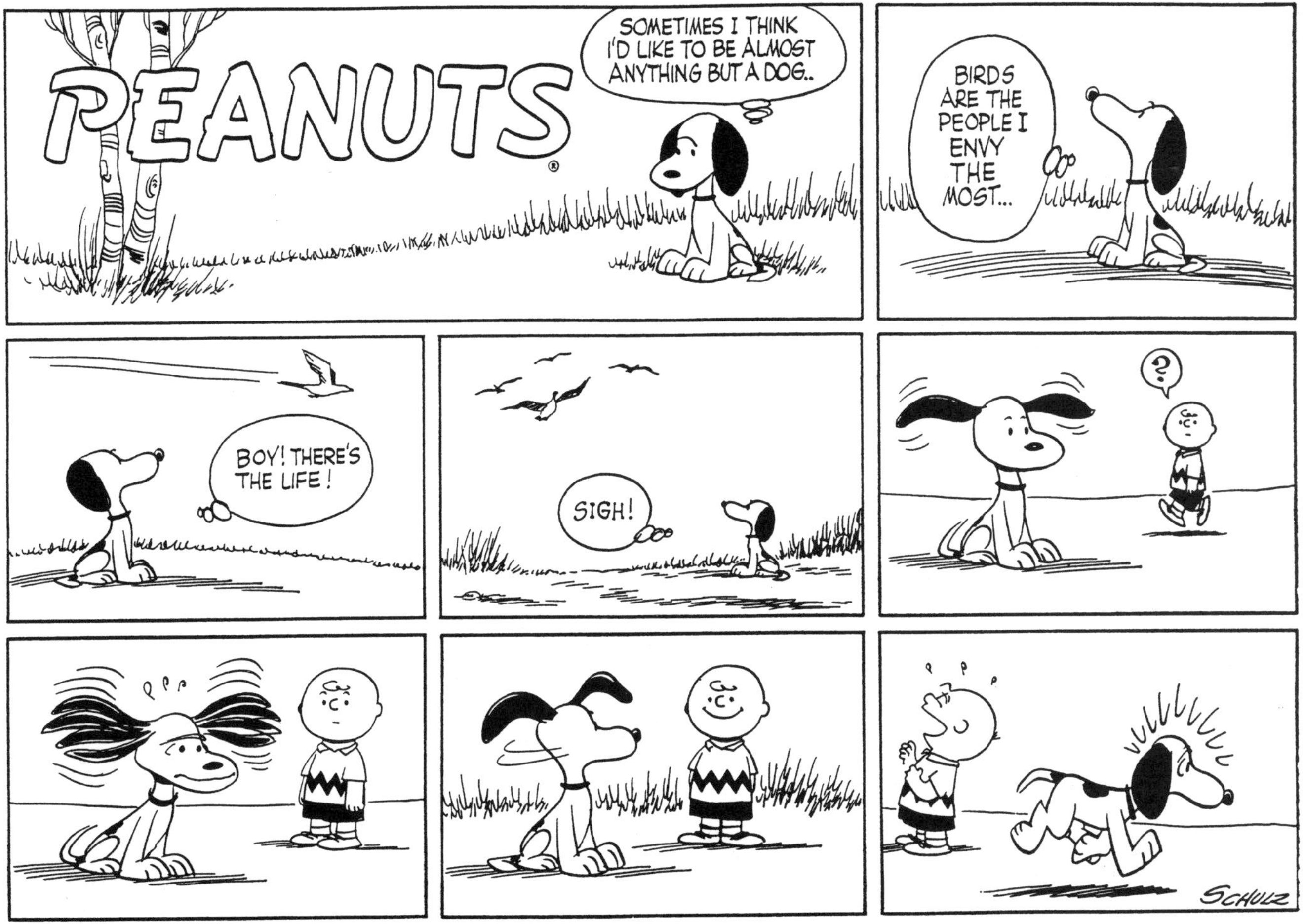
PEANUTS®
SOMETIMES I THINK I'D LIKE TO BE ALMOST ANYTHING BUT A DOG..
BIRDS ARE THE PEOPLE I ENVY THE MOST...
BOY! THERE'S THE LIFE!
SIGH!
?
SCHULZ

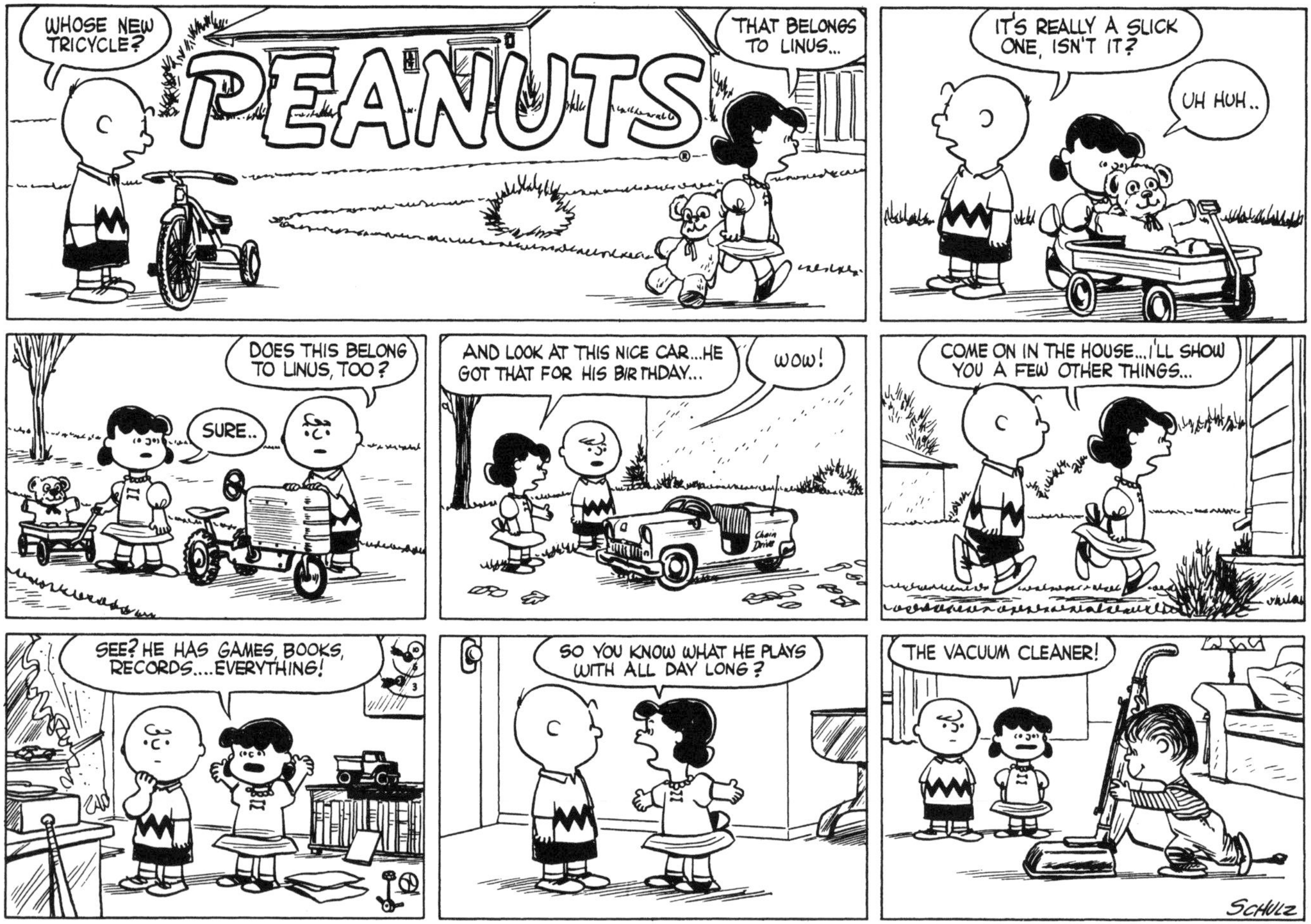
WHOSE NEW TRICYCLE?
PEANUTS
THAT BELONGS TO LINUS...
IT'S REALLY A SLICK ONE, ISN'T IT?
UH HUH..
DOES THIS BELONG TO LINUS, TOO?
SURE..
AND LOOK AT THIS NICE CAR...HE GOT THAT FOR HIS BIRTHDAY...
WOW!
Chain Drive
COME ON IN THE HOUSE...I'LL SHOW YOU A FEW OTHER THINGS...
SEE? HE HAS GAMES, BOOKS, RECORDS....EVERYTHING!
SO YOU KNOW WHAT HE PLAYS WITH ALL DAY LONG?
THE VACUUM CLEANER!
SCHULZ

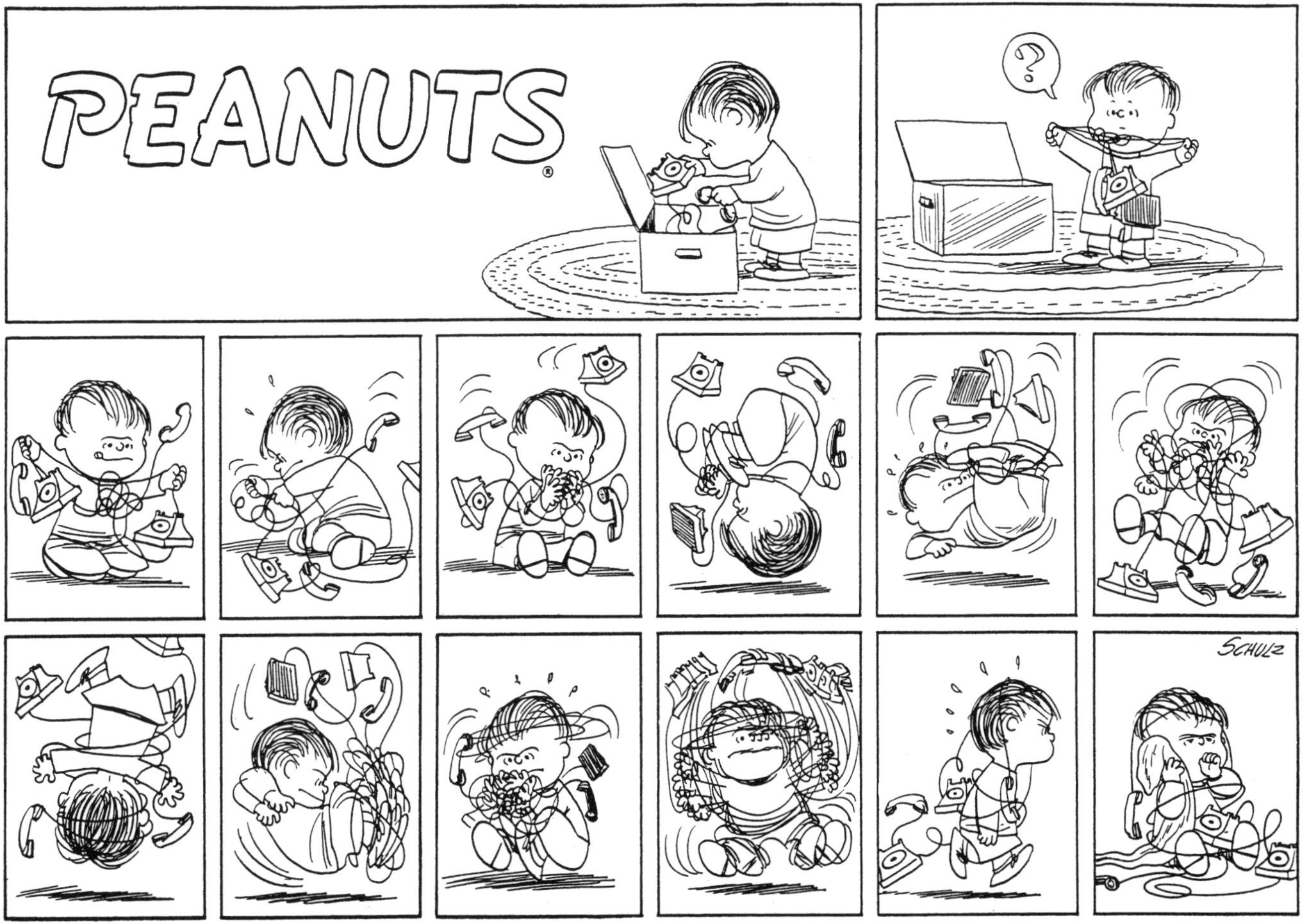
PEANUTS
?
SCHULZ

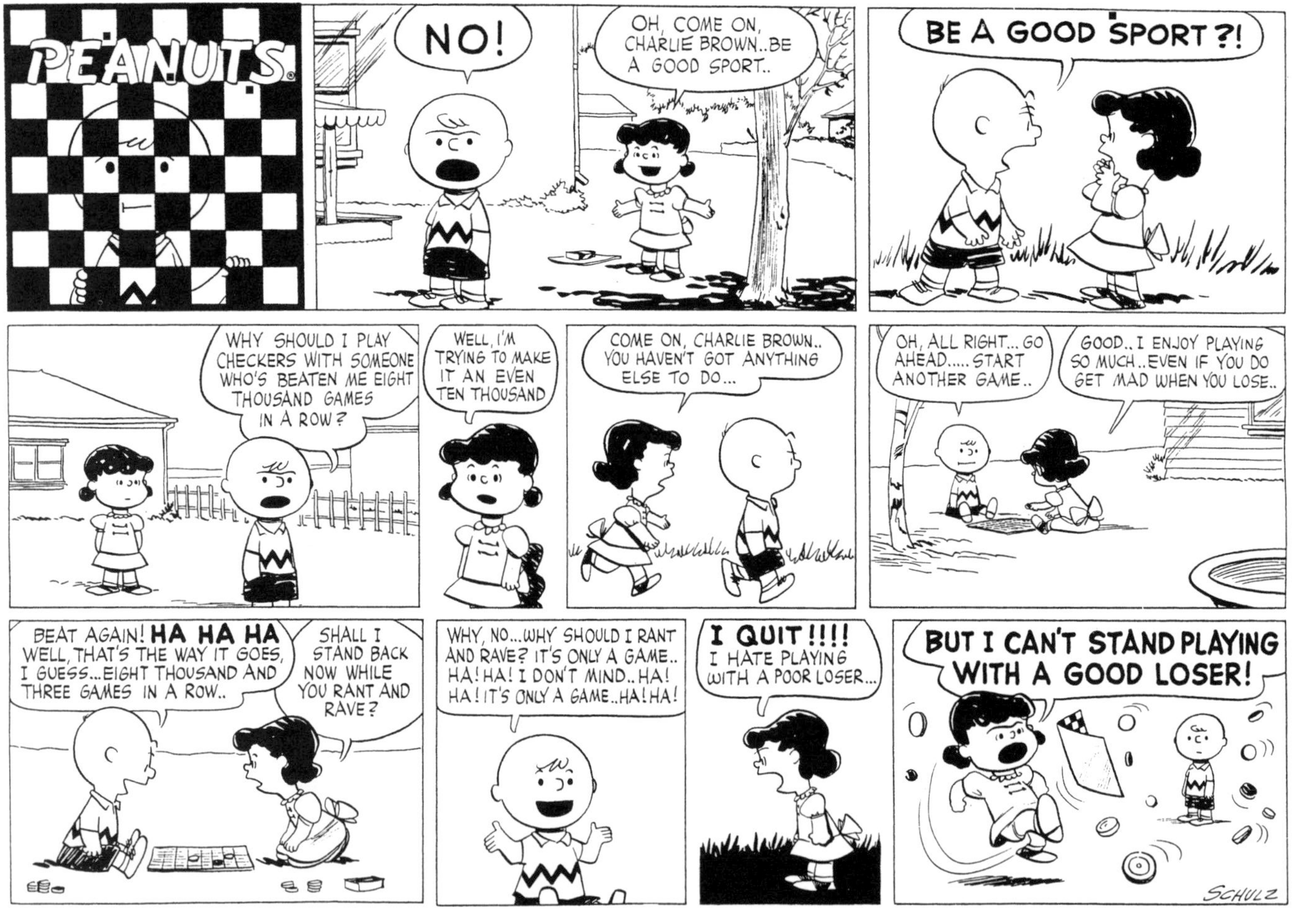
PEANUTS
NO!
OH, COME ON, CHARLIE BROWN..BE A GOOD SPORT..
BE A GOOD SPORT?!
WHY SHOULD I PLAY CHECKERS WITH SOMEONE WHO'S BEATEN ME EIGHT THOUSAND GAMES IN A ROW?
WELL, I'M TRYING TO MAKE IT AN EVEN TEN THOUSAND
COME ON, CHARLIE BROWN.. YOU HAVEN'T GOT ANYTHING ELSE TO DO...
OH, ALL RIGHT... GO AHEAD..... START ANOTHER GAME..
GOOD.. I ENJOY PLAYING SO MUCH..EVEN IF YOU DO GET MAD WHEN YOU LOSE..
BEAT AGAIN! HA HA HA WELL, THAT'S THE WAY IT GOES, I GUESS...EIGHT THOUSAND AND THREE GAMES IN A ROW..
SHALL I STAND BACK NOW WHILE YOU RANT AND RAVE?
WHY, NO...WHY SHOULD I RANT AND RAVE? IT'S ONLY A GAME.. HA! HA! I DON'T MIND.. HA! HA! IT'S ONLY A GAME..HA! HA!
I QUIT!!!! I HATE PLAYING WITH A POOR LOSER...
BUT I CAN'T STAND PLAYING WITH A GOOD LOSER!
SCHULZ

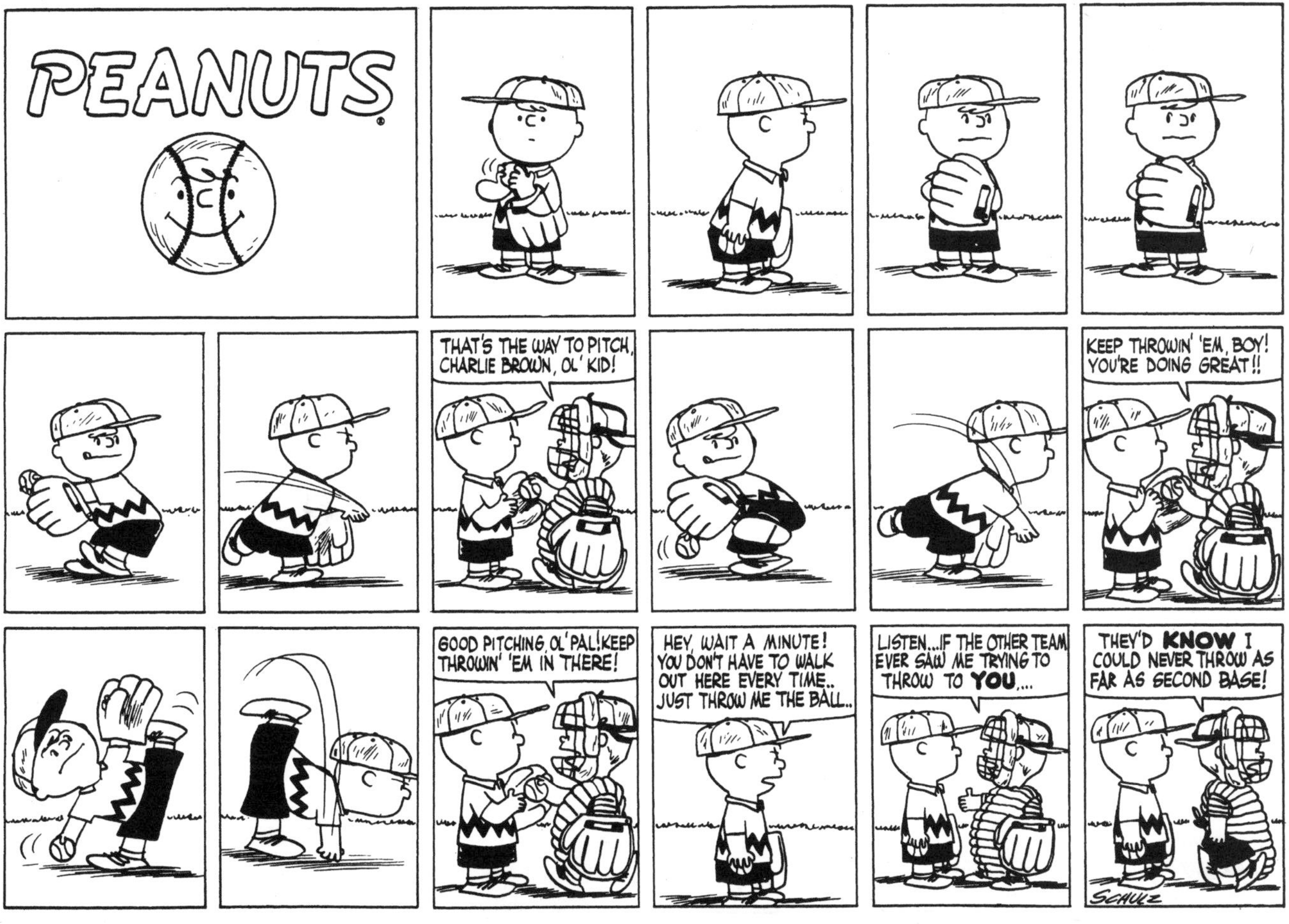
PEANUTS
THAT'S THE WAY TO PITCH, CHARLIE BROWN, OL' KID!
KEEP THROWIN' 'EM, BOY! YOU'RE DOING GREAT!!
GOOD PITCHING, OL' PAL! KEEP THROWIN' 'EM IN THERE!
HEY, WAIT A MINUTE! YOU DON'T HAVE TO WALK OUT HERE EVERY TIME.. JUST THROW ME THE BALL..
LISTEN...IF THE OTHER TEAM EVER SAW ME TRYING TO THROW TO YOU....
THEY'D KNOW I COULD NEVER THROW AS FAR AS SECOND BASE!
SCHULZ

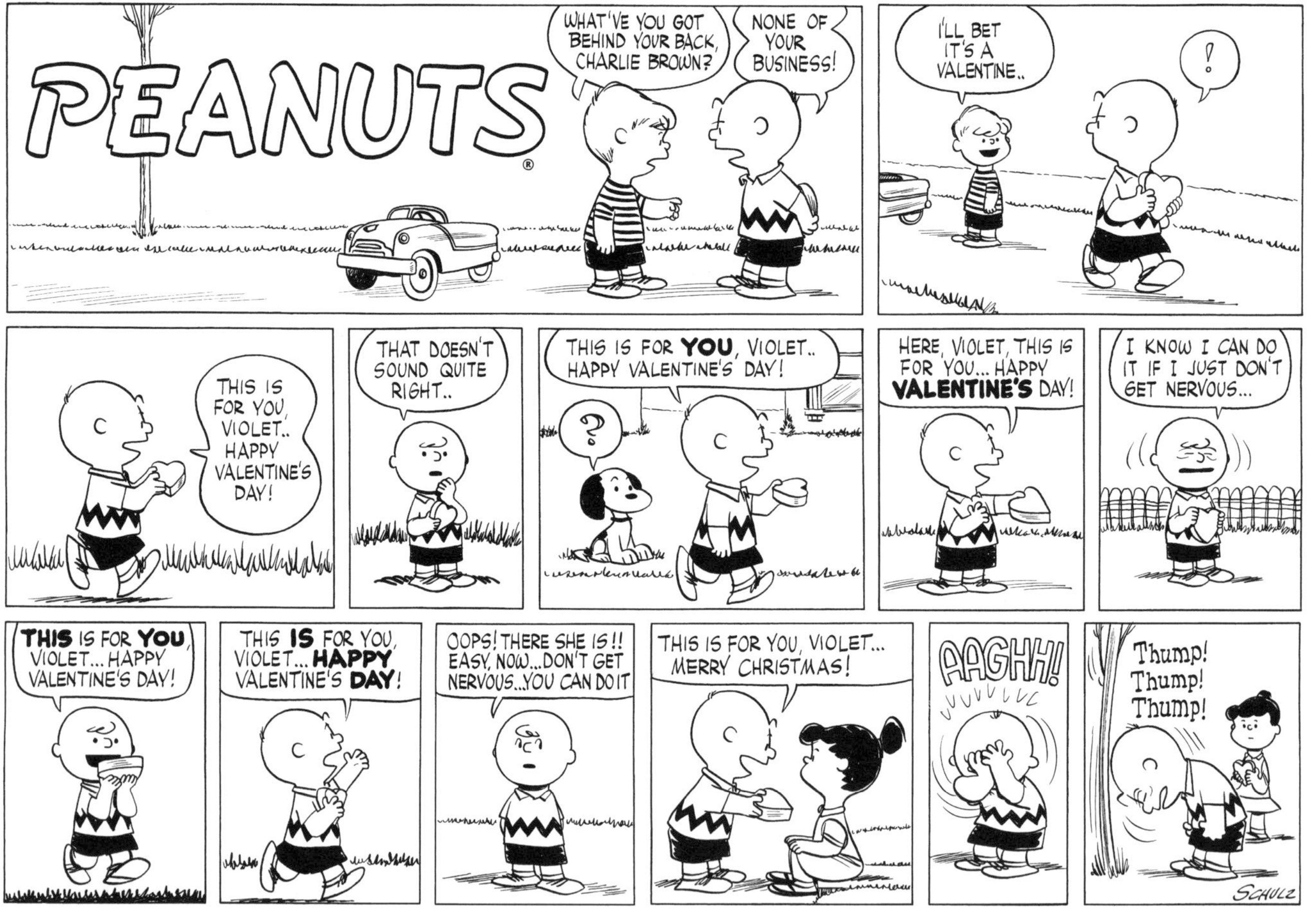
PEANUTS®
WHAT'VE YOU GOT BEHIND YOUR BACK, CHARLIE BROWN?
NONE OF YOUR BUSINESS!
I'LL BET IT'S A VALENTINE..
!
THIS IS FOR YOU, VIOLET.. HAPPY VALENTINE'S DAY!
THAT DOESN'T SOUND QUITE RIGHT..
THIS IS FOR YOU, VIOLET.. HAPPY VALENTINE'S DAY!
?
HERE, VIOLET, THIS IS FOR YOU... HAPPY VALENTINE'S DAY!
I KNOW I CAN DO IT IF I JUST DON'T GET NERVOUS...
THIS IS FOR YOU, VIOLET... HAPPY VALENTINE'S DAY!
THIS IS FOR YOU, VIOLET... HAPPY VALENTINE'S DAY!
OOPS! THERE SHE IS!! EASY, NOW... DON'T GET NERVOUS... YOU CAN DO IT
THIS IS FOR YOU, VIOLET... MERRY CHRISTMAS!
AAGHH!
Thump! Thump! Thump!
SCHULZ

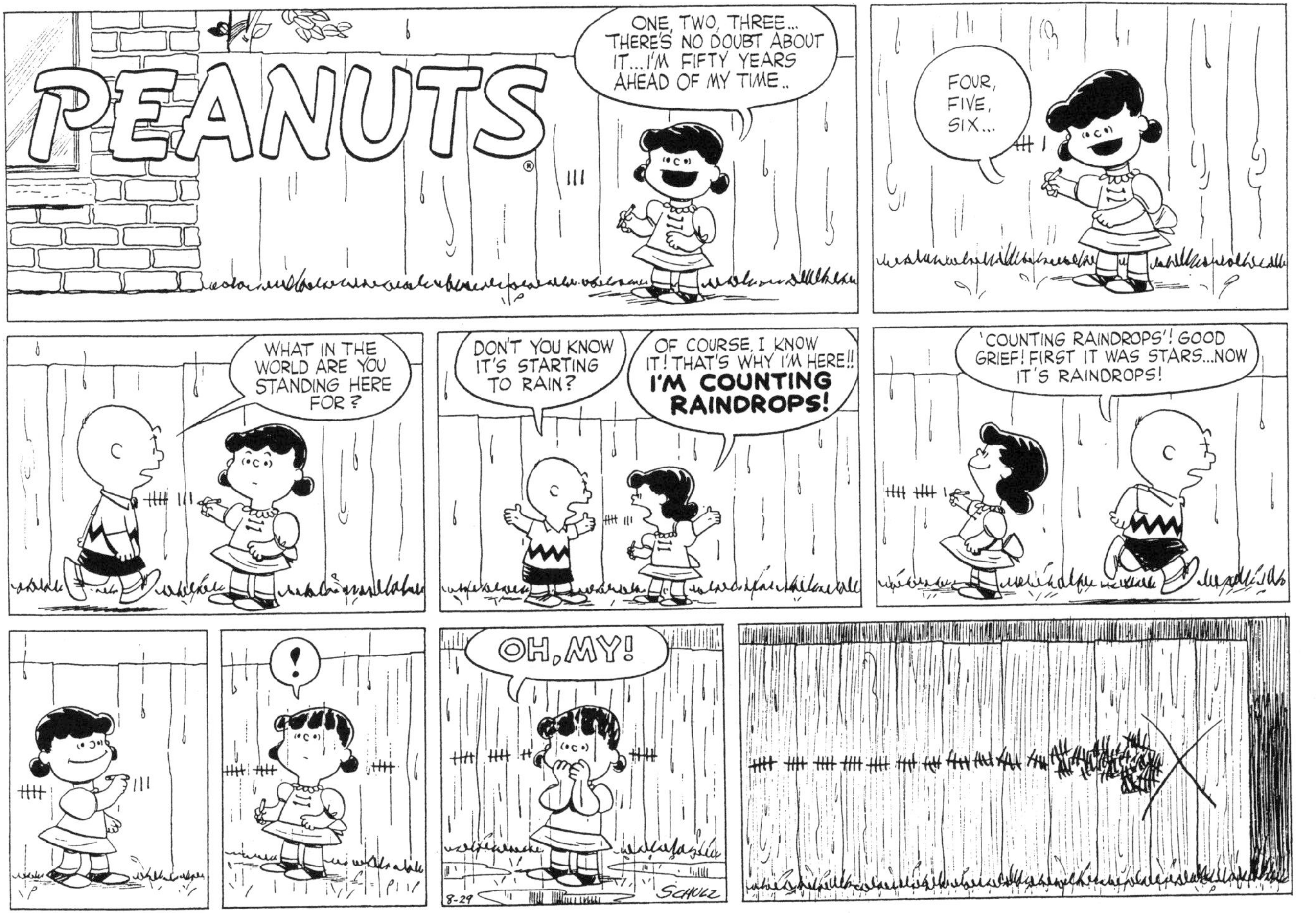
PEANUTS
ONE, TWO, THREE... THERE'S NO DOUBT ABOUT IT...I'M FIFTY YEARS AHEAD OF MY TIME..
FOUR, FIVE, SIX...
WHAT IN THE WORLD ARE YOU STANDING HERE FOR?
DON'T YOU KNOW IT'S STARTING TO RAIN?
OF COURSE, I KNOW IT! THAT'S WHY I'M HERE!! I'M COUNTING RAINDROPS!
'COUNTING RAINDROPS'! GOOD GRIEF! FIRST IT WAS STARS...NOW IT'S RAINDROPS!
!
OH, MY!
8-29
SCHULZ

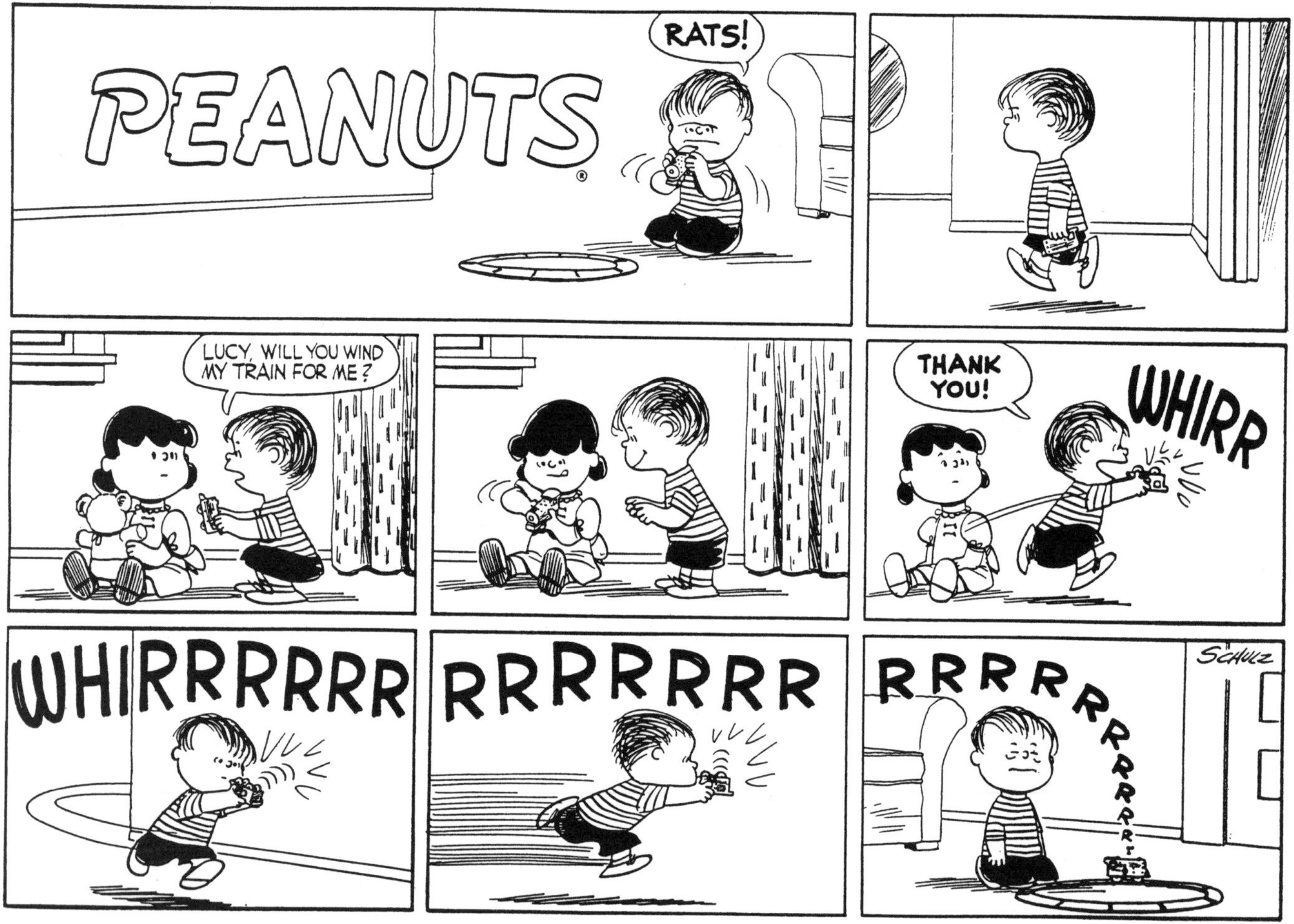
PEANUTS
RATS!
LUCY, WILL YOU WIND MY TRAIN FOR ME?
THANK YOU!
WHIRR
WHIRRRRRRR
RRRRRRRR
RRRRRRRRRRR
SCHULZ

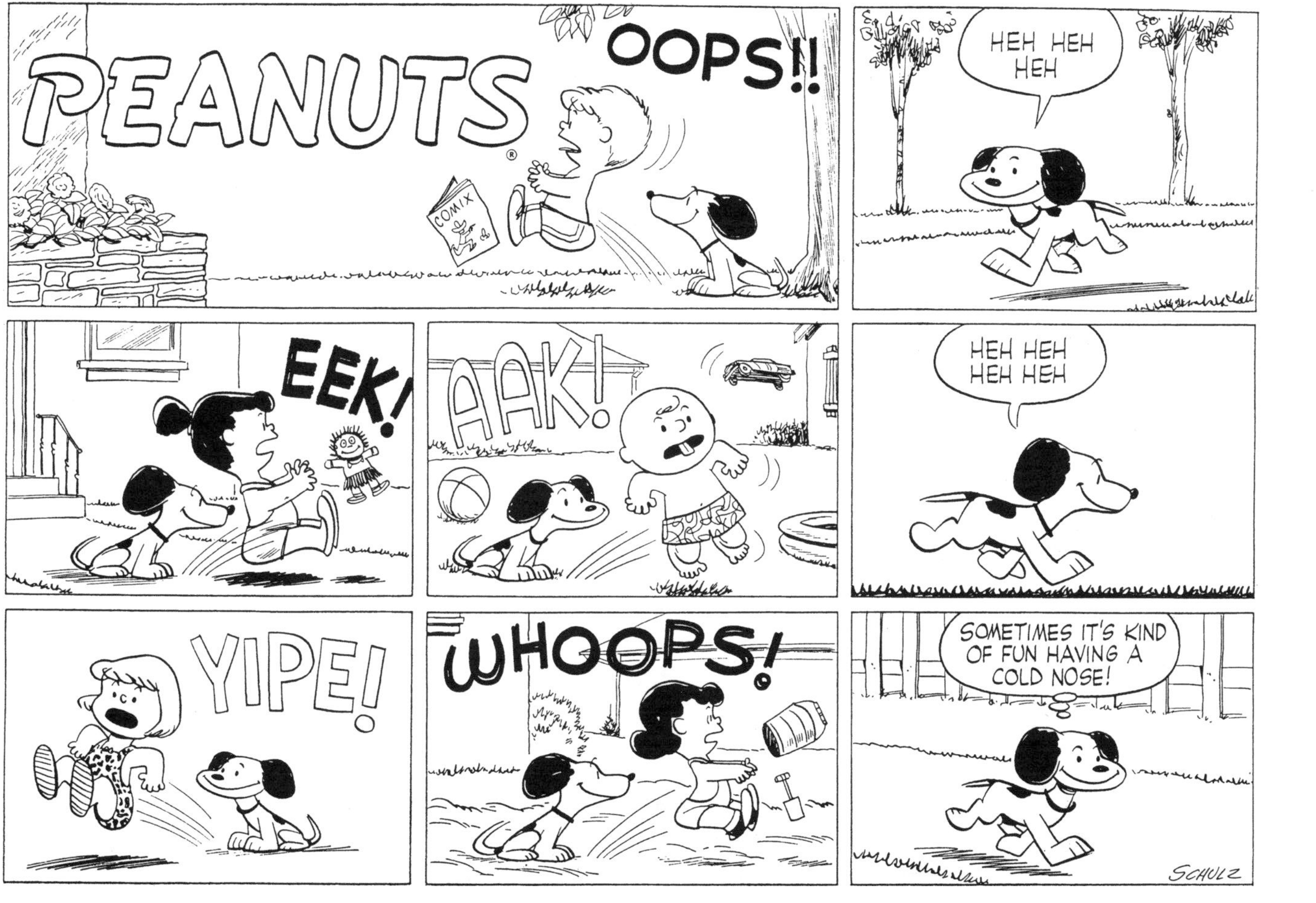
PEANUTS®
OOPS!!
COMIX
HEH HEH HEH
EEK!
AAK!
HEH HEH HEH HEH
YIPE!
WHOOPS!
SOMETIMES IT'S KIND OF FUN HAVING A COLD NOSE!
SCHULZ

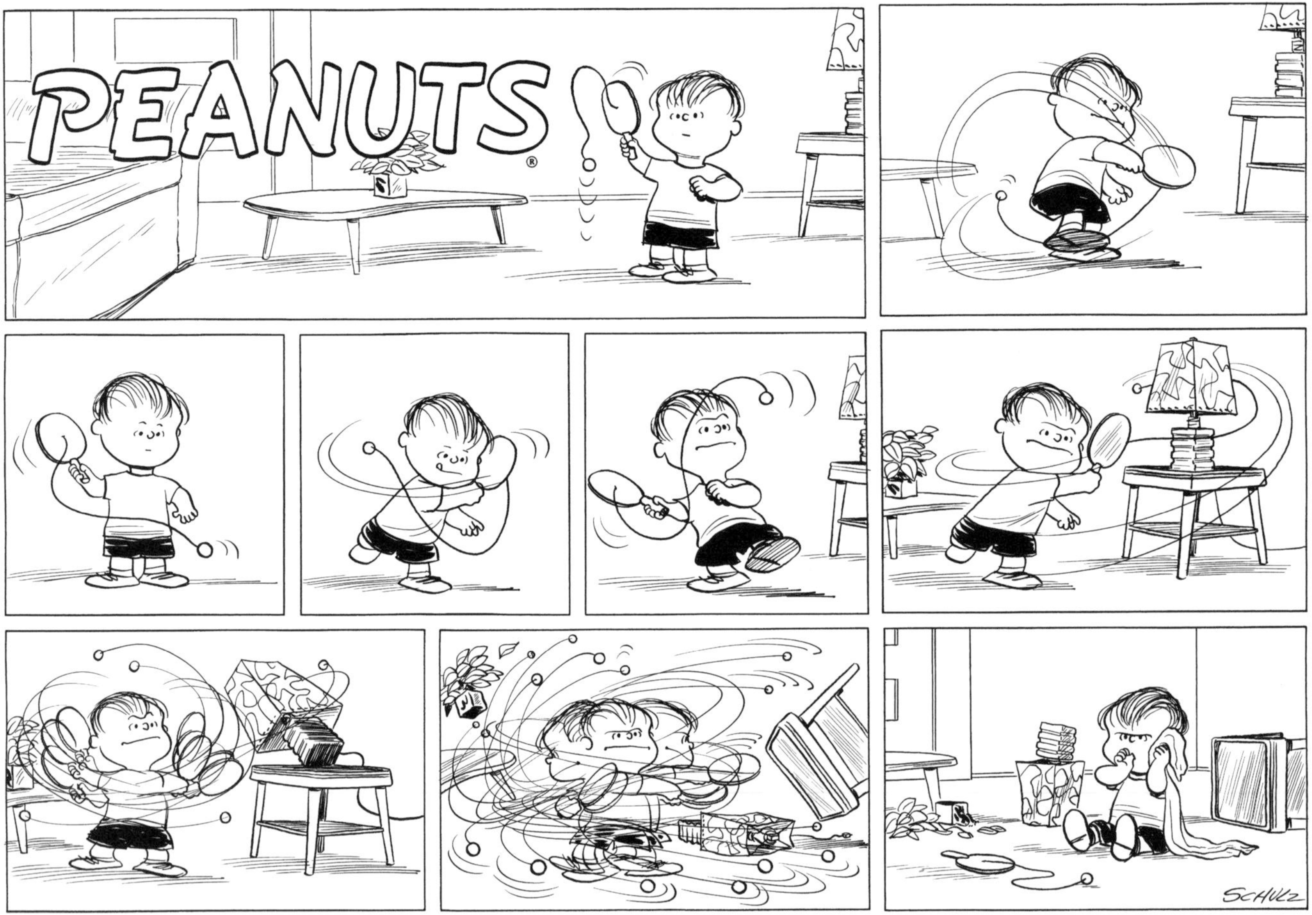
PEANUTS
SCHULZ

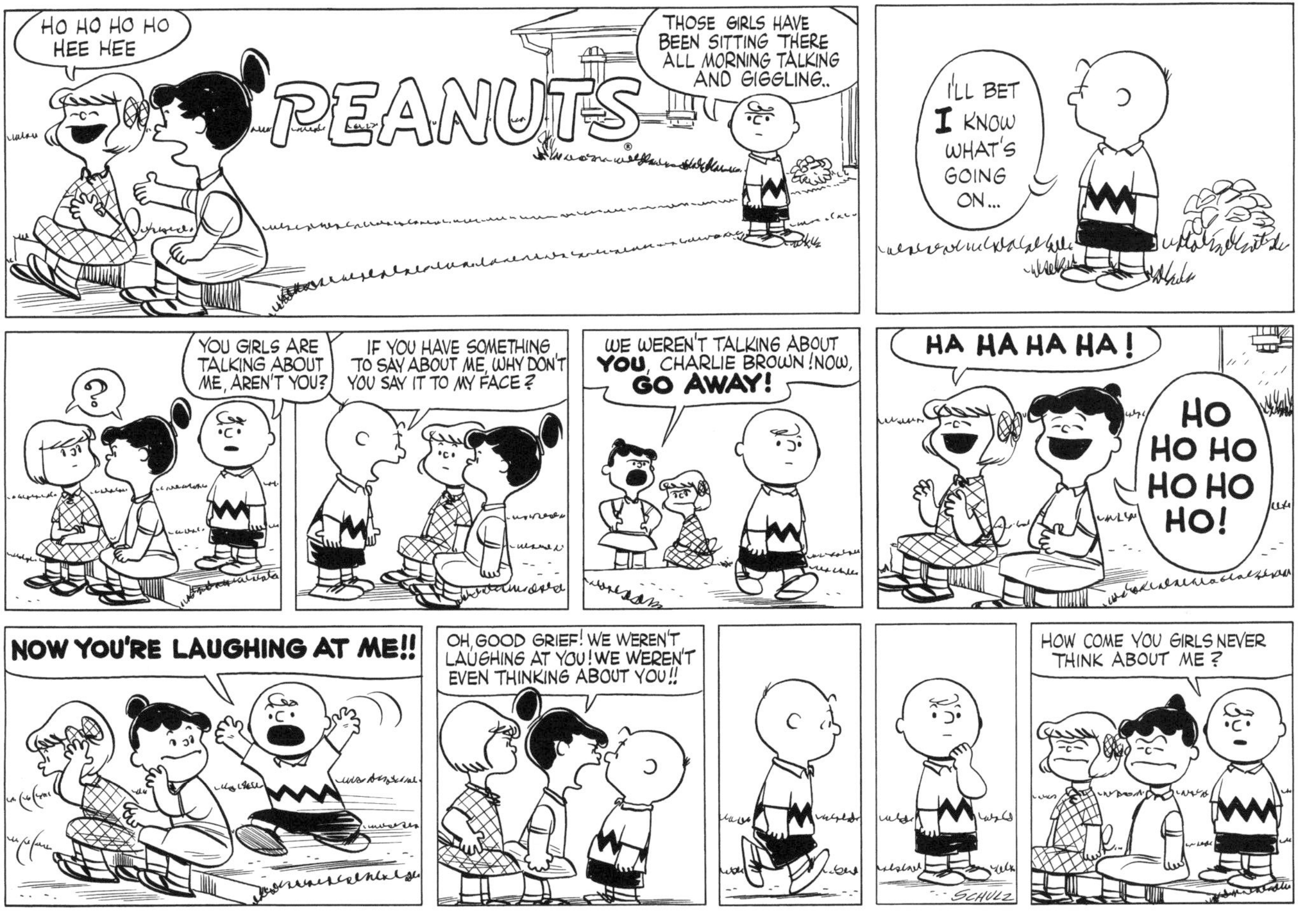
HO HO HO HO HEE HEE
PEANUTS®
THOSE GIRLS HAVE BEEN SITTING THERE ALL MORNING TALKING AND GIGGLING..
I'LL BET I KNOW WHAT'S GOING ON...
?
YOU GIRLS ARE TALKING ABOUT ME, AREN'T YOU?
IF YOU HAVE SOMETHING TO SAY ABOUT ME, WHY DON'T YOU SAY IT TO MY FACE?
WE WEREN'T TALKING ABOUT YOU, CHARLIE BROWN! NOW, GO AWAY!
HA HA HA HA!
HO HO HO HO HO HO!
NOW YOU'RE LAUGHING AT ME!!
OH, GOOD GRIEF! WE WEREN'T LAUGHING AT YOU! WE WEREN'T EVEN THINKING ABOUT YOU!!
SCHULZ
HOW COME YOU GIRLS NEVER THINK ABOUT ME?

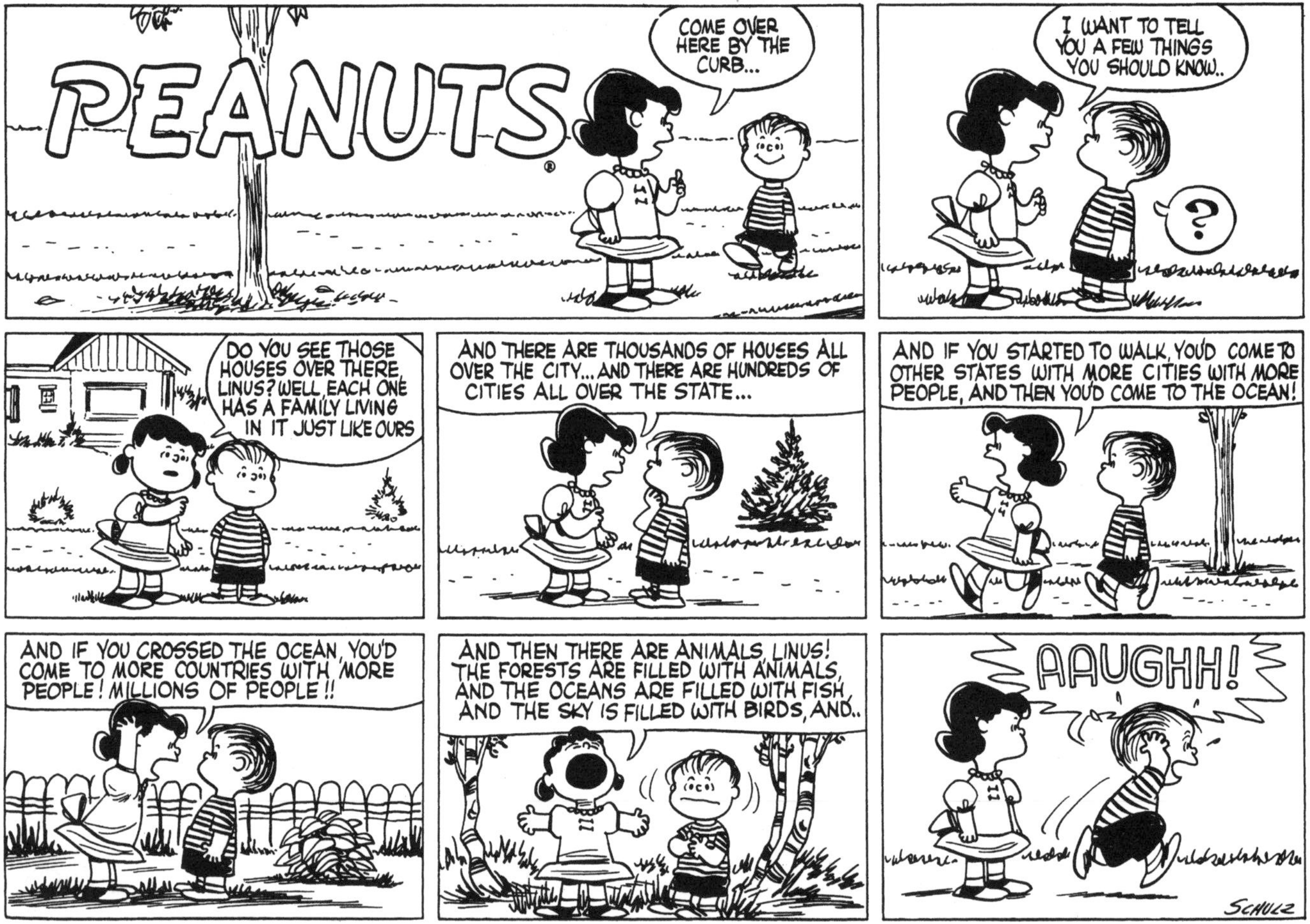
PEANUTS®
COME OVER HERE BY THE CURB...
I WANT TO TELL YOU A FEW THINGS YOU SHOULD KNOW..
?
DO YOU SEE THOSE HOUSES OVER THERE, LINUS? WELL, EACH ONE HAS A FAMILY LIVING IN IT JUST LIKE OURS
AND THERE ARE THOUSANDS OF HOUSES ALL OVER THE CITY... AND THERE ARE HUNDREDS OF CITIES ALL OVER THE STATE...
AND IF YOU STARTED TO WALK, YOU'D COME TO OTHER STATES WITH MORE CITIES WITH MORE PEOPLE, AND THEN YOU'D COME TO THE OCEAN!
AND IF YOU CROSSED THE OCEAN, YOU'D COME TO MORE COUNTRIES WITH MORE PEOPLE! MILLIONS OF PEOPLE!!
AND THEN THERE ARE ANIMALS, LINUS! THE FORESTS ARE FILLED WITH ANIMALS, AND THE OCEANS ARE FILLED WITH FISH, AND THE SKY IS FILLED WITH BIRDS, AND..
AAUGHH!
SCHULZ

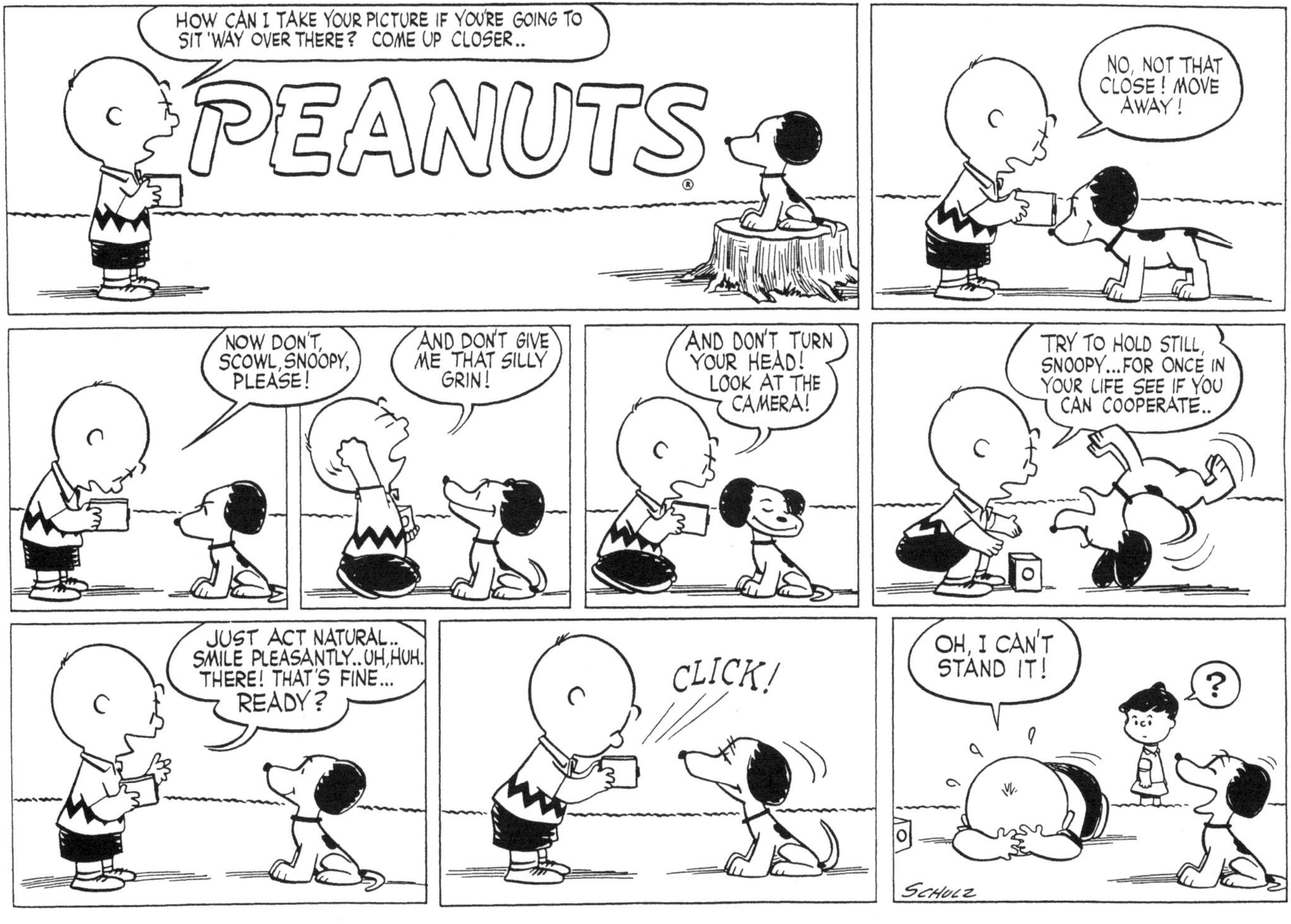
HOW CAN I TAKE YOUR PICTURE IF YOU'RE GOING TO SIT 'WAY OVER THERE? COME UP CLOSER..
PEANUTS®
NO, NOT THAT CLOSE! MOVE AWAY!
NOW DON'T SCOWL, SNOOPY, PLEASE!
AND DON'T GIVE ME THAT SILLY GRIN!
AND DON'T TURN YOUR HEAD! LOOK AT THE CAMERA!
TRY TO HOLD STILL, SNOOPY...FOR ONCE IN YOUR LIFE SEE IF YOU CAN COOPERATE..
JUST ACT NATURAL.. SMILE PLEASANTLY..UH,HUH. THERE! THAT'S FINE... READY?
CLICK!
OH, I CAN'T STAND IT!
?
SCHULZ

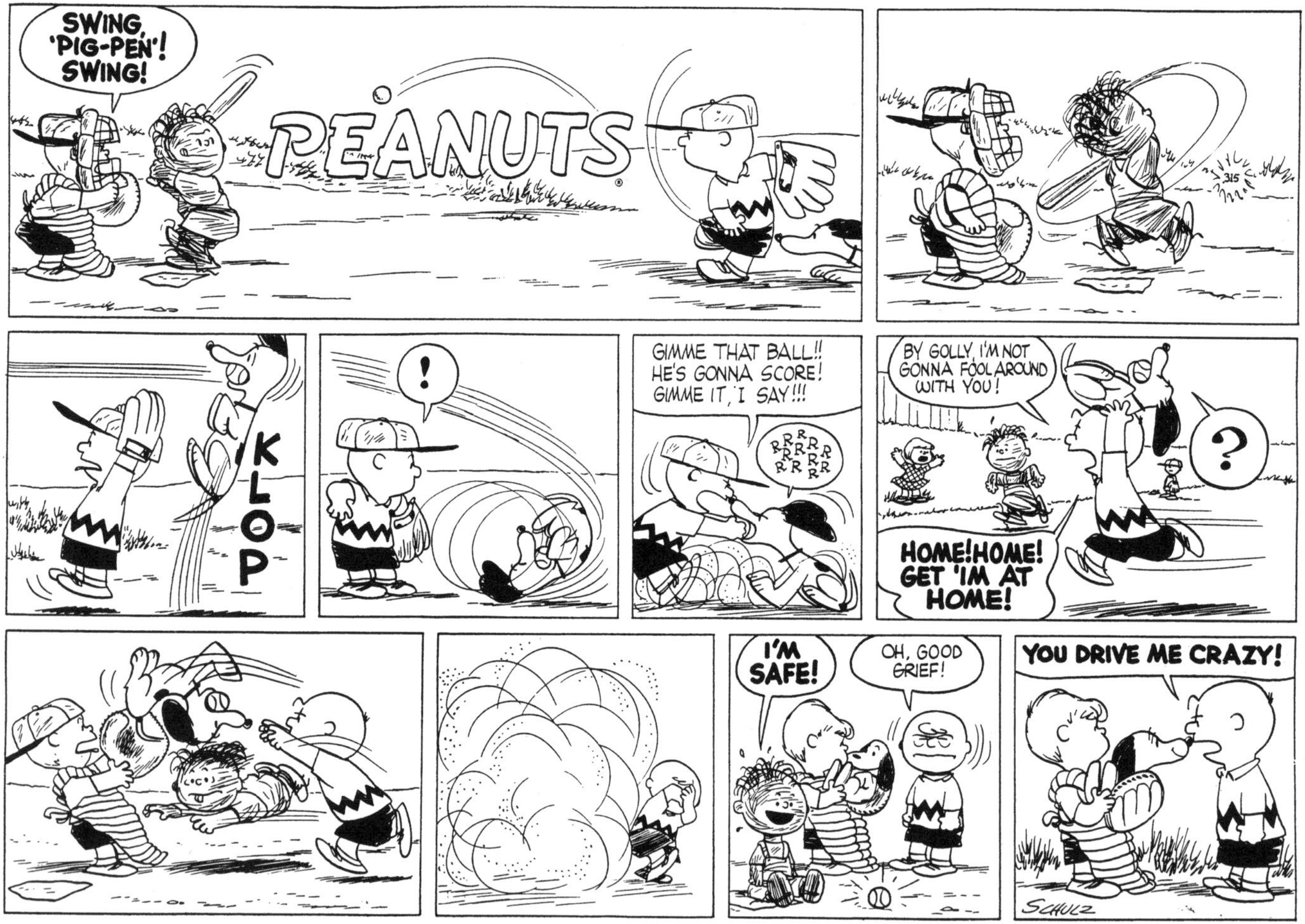

SWING, 'PIG-PEN'! SWING!
PEANUTS
KLOP
!
GIMME THAT BALL!! HE'S GONNA SCORE! GIMME IT, I SAY!!!
RRRRRRRRRRRR
BY GOLLY, I'M NOT GONNA FOOL AROUND WITH YOU!
HOME! HOME! GET 'IM AT HOME!
?
I'M SAFE!
OH, GOOD GRIEF!
YOU DRIVE ME CRAZY!
SCHULZ

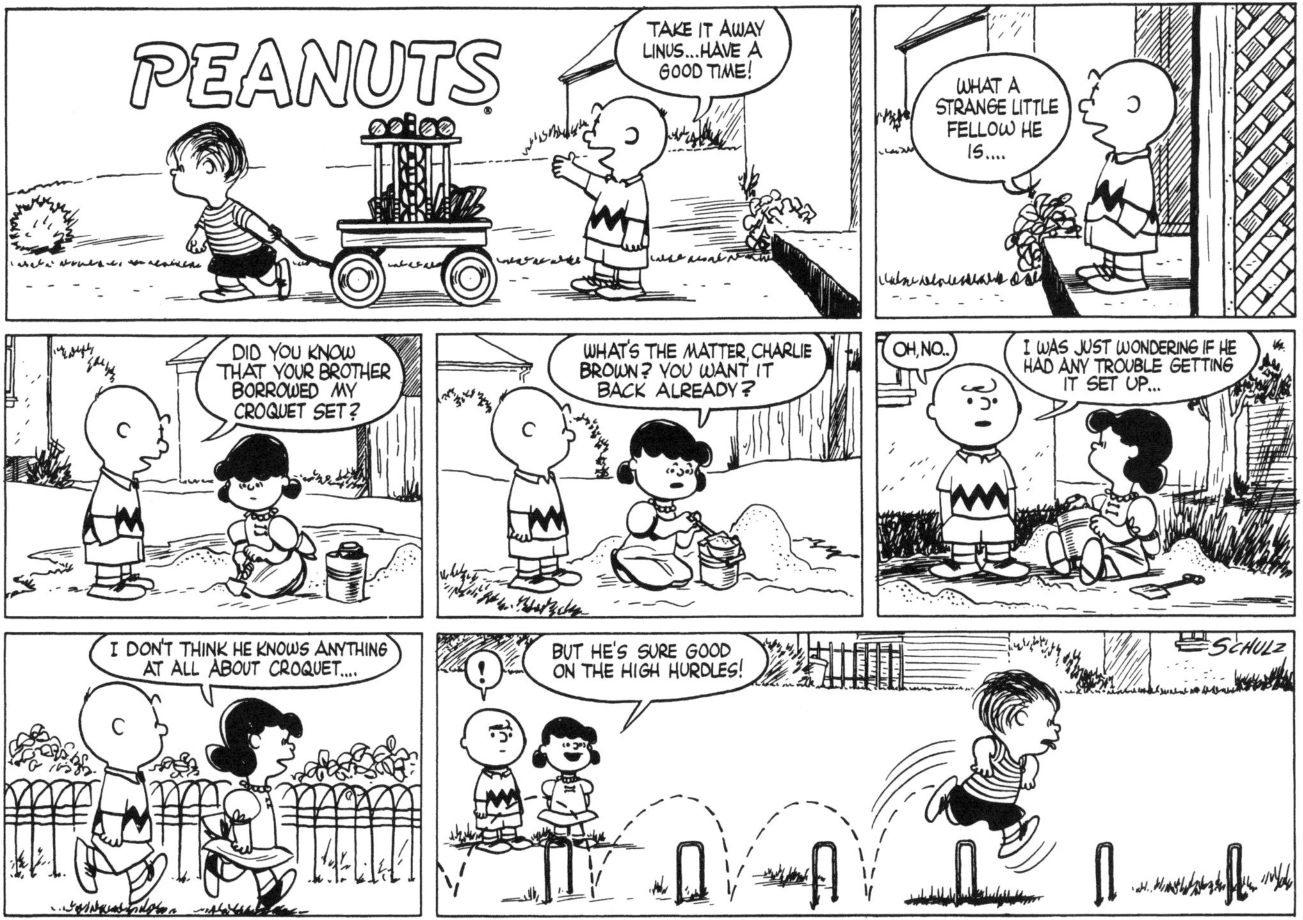
PEANUTS
TAKE IT AWAY LINUS...HAVE A GOOD TIME!
WHAT A STRANGE LITTLE FELLOW HE IS....
DID YOU KNOW THAT YOUR BROTHER BORROWED MY CROQUET SET?
WHAT'S THE MATTER, CHARLIE BROWN? YOU WANT IT BACK ALREADY?
OH, NO..
I WAS JUST WONDERING IF HE HAD ANY TROUBLE GETTING IT SET UP...
I DON'T THINK HE KNOWS ANYTHING AT ALL ABOUT CROQUET....
!
BUT HE'S SURE GOOD ON THE HIGH HURDLES!
SCHULZ

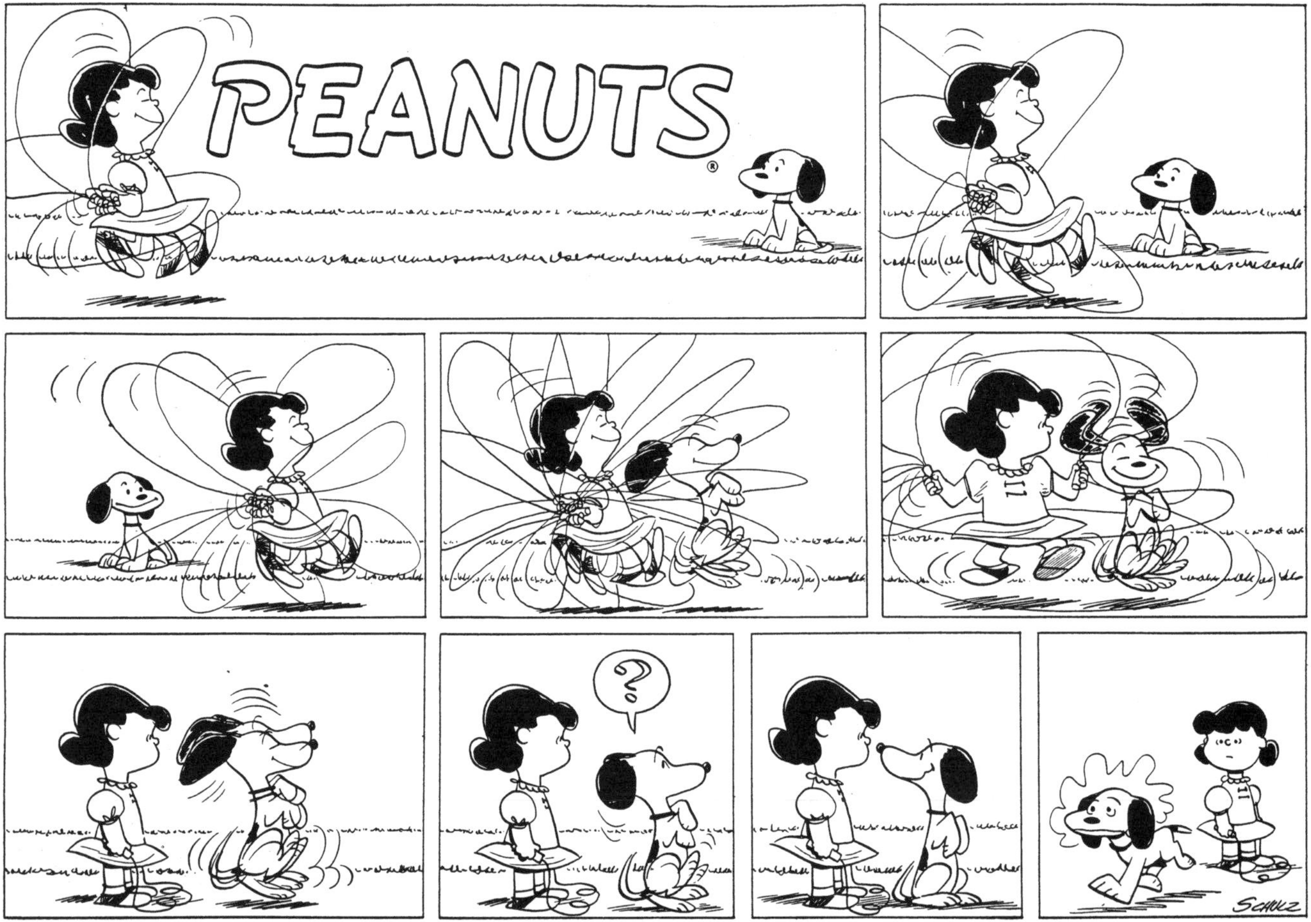
PEANUTS
?
SCHULZ

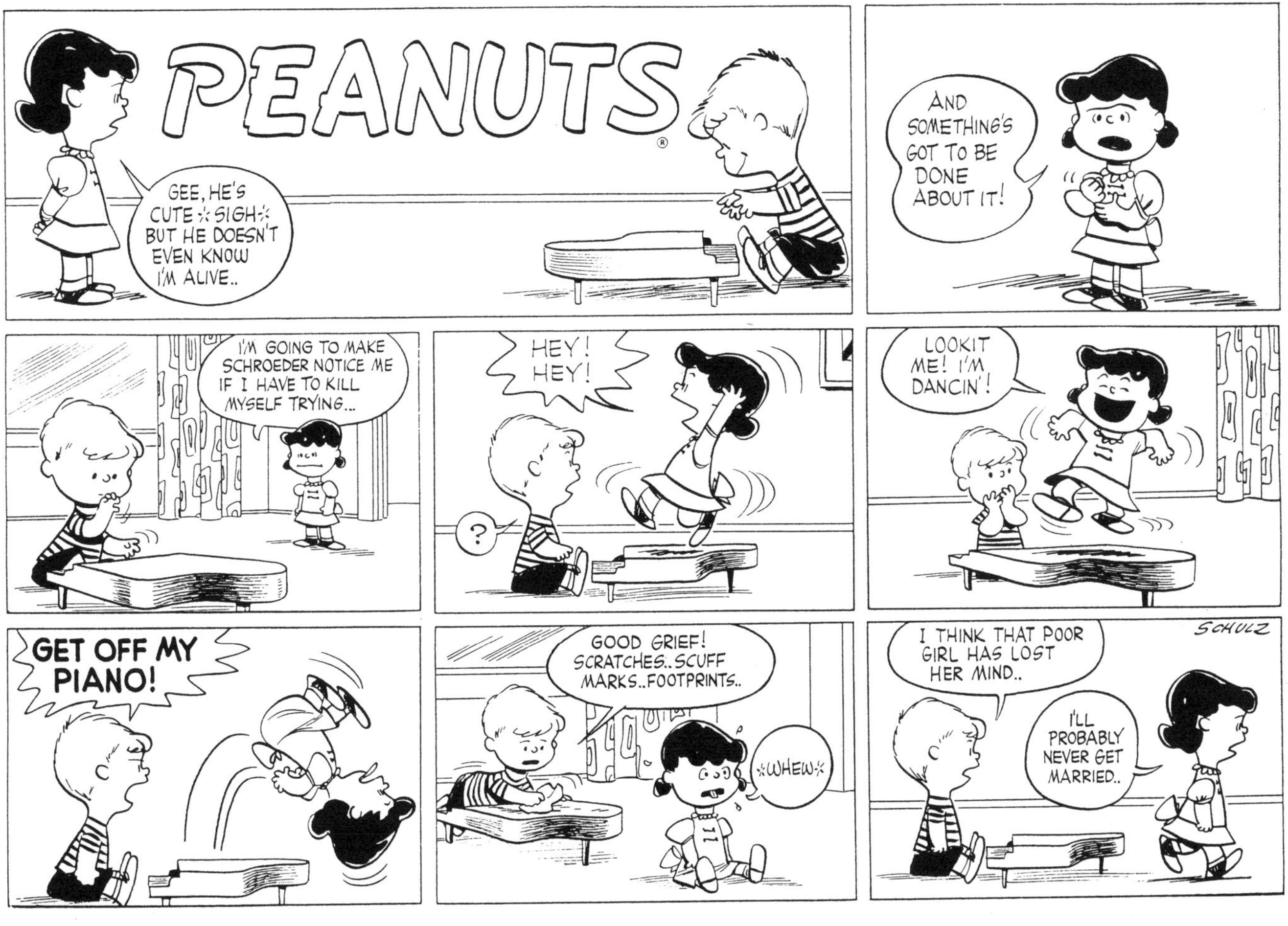
PEANUTS
GEE, HE'S CUTE ⁘SIGH⁘ BUT HE DOESN'T EVEN KNOW I'M ALIVE..
AND SOMETHING'S GOT TO BE DONE ABOUT IT!
I'M GOING TO MAKE SCHROEDER NOTICE ME IF I HAVE TO KILL MYSELF TRYING...
HEY! HEY!
?
LOOKIT ME! I'M DANCIN'!
GET OFF MY PIANO!
GOOD GRIEF! SCRATCHES..SCUFF MARKS..FOOTPRINTS..
⁘WHEW⁘
SCHULZ
I THINK THAT POOR GIRL HAS LOST HER MIND..
I'LL PROBABLY NEVER GET MARRIED..

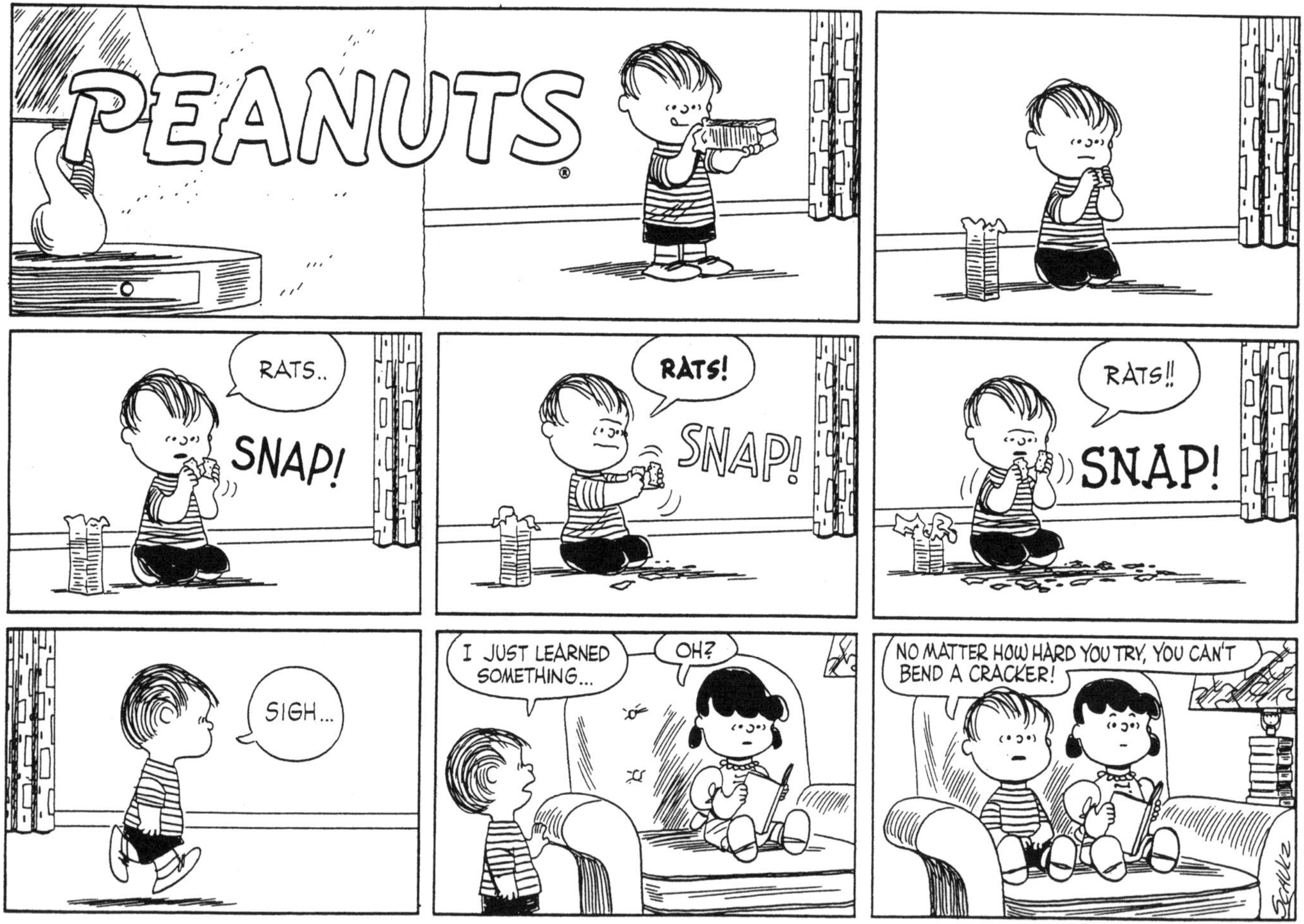
PEANUTS
RATS..
SNAP!
RATS!
SNAP!
RATS!!
SNAP!
SIGH...
I JUST LEARNED SOMETHING...
OH?
NO MATTER HOW HARD YOU TRY, YOU CAN'T BEND A CRACKER!
SCHULZ

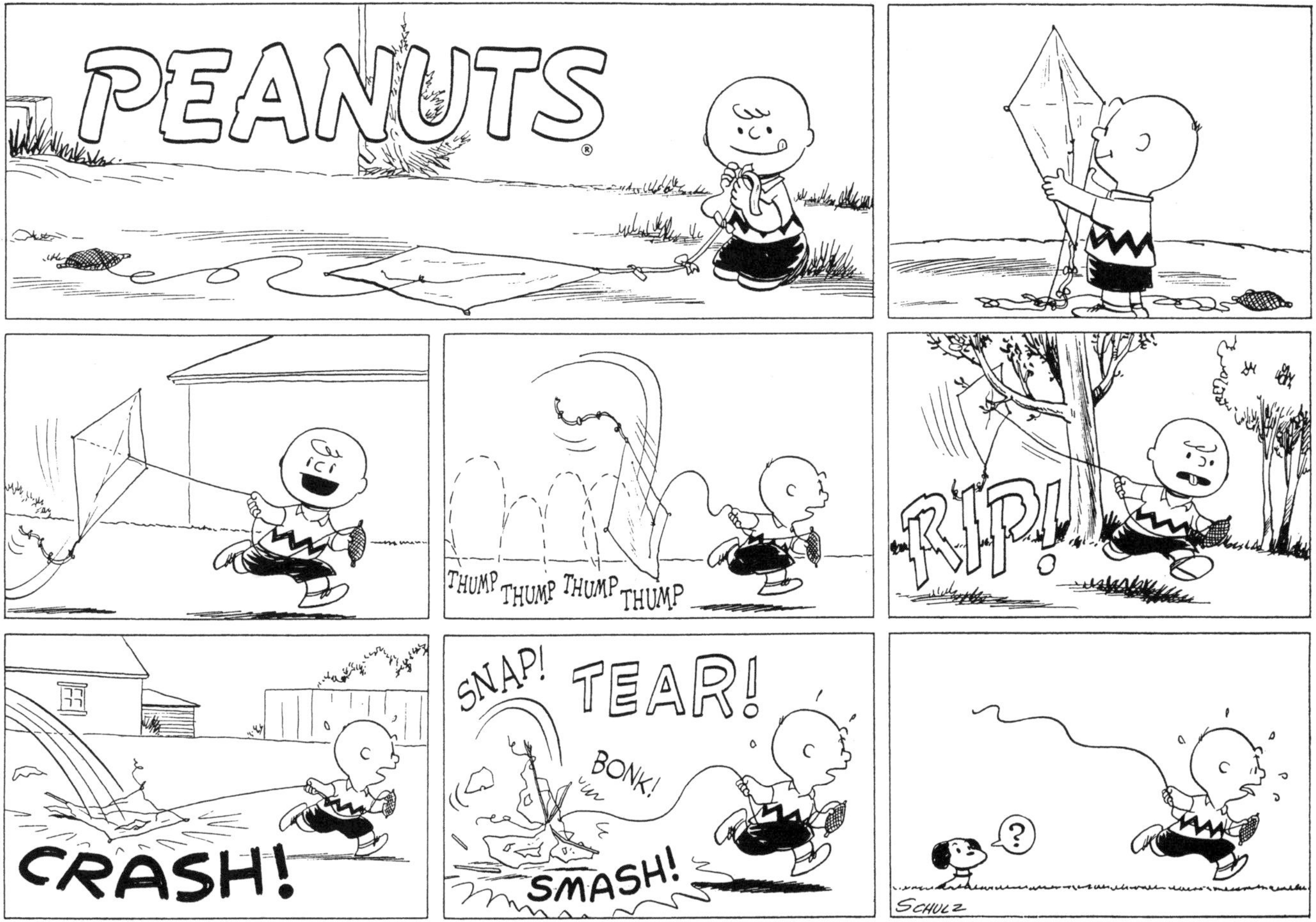
PEANUTS
THUMP THUMP THUMP THUMP
RIP!
CRASH!
SNAP!
TEAR!
BONK!
SMASH!
?
SCHULZ

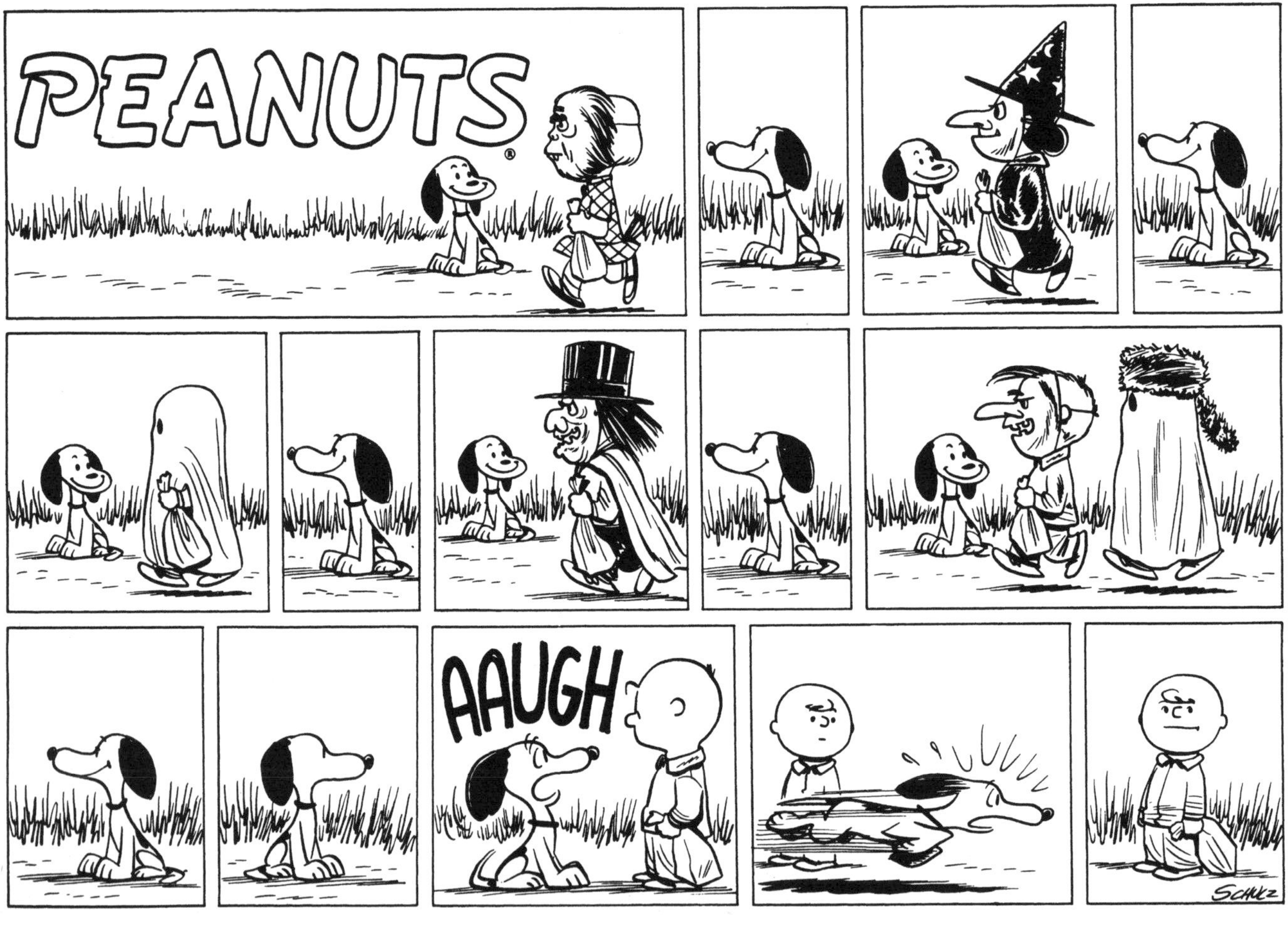
PEANUTS
AAUGH
SCHULZ

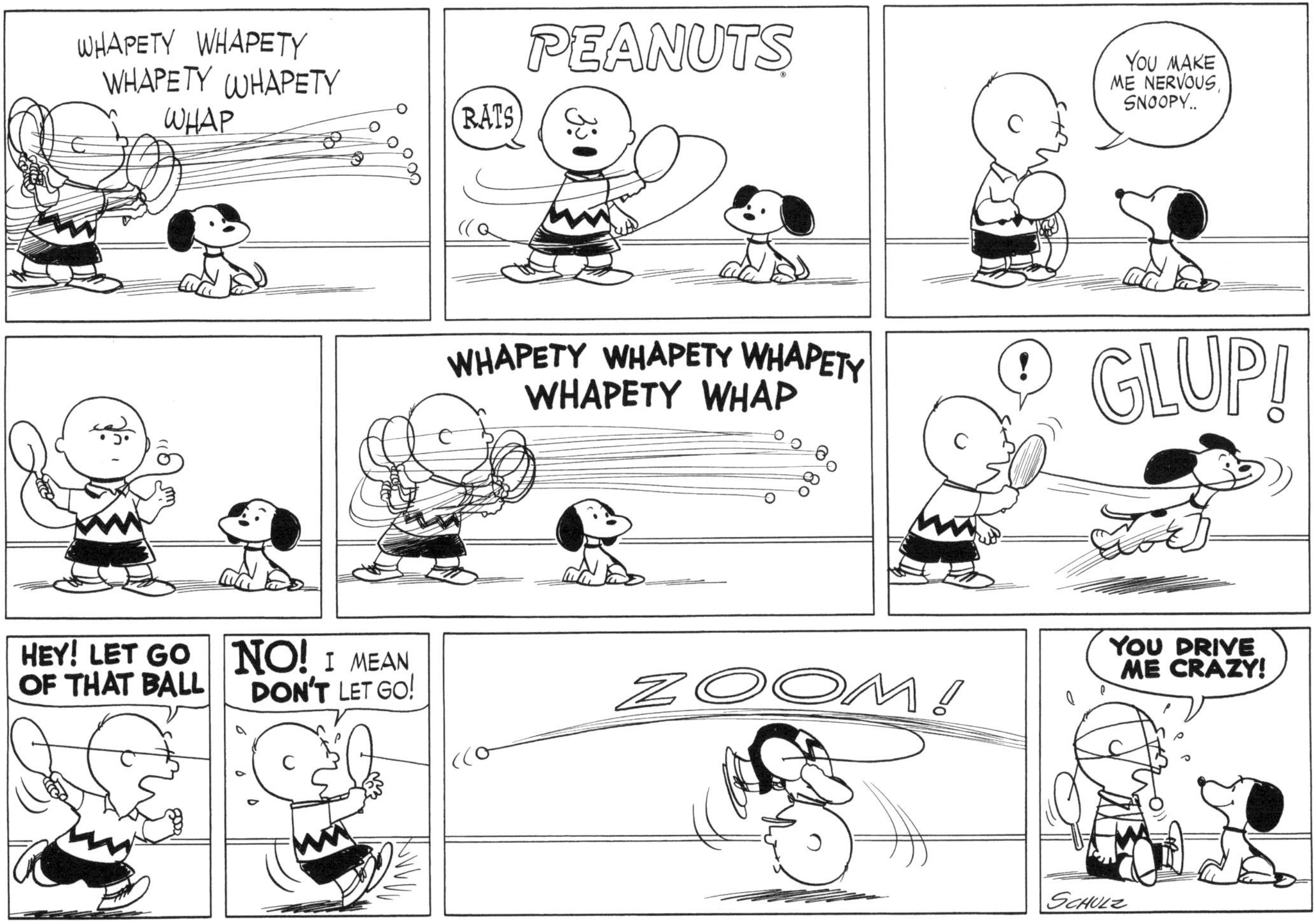
WHAPETY WHAPETY WHAPETY WHAPETY WHAP
PEANUTS
RATS
YOU MAKE ME NERVOUS, SNOOPY..
WHAPETY WHAPETY WHAPETY WHAPETY WHAPETY WHAP
!
GLUP!
HEY! LET GO OF THAT BALL
NO! I MEAN DON'T LET GO!
ZOOM!
YOU DRIVE ME CRAZY!
SCHULZ

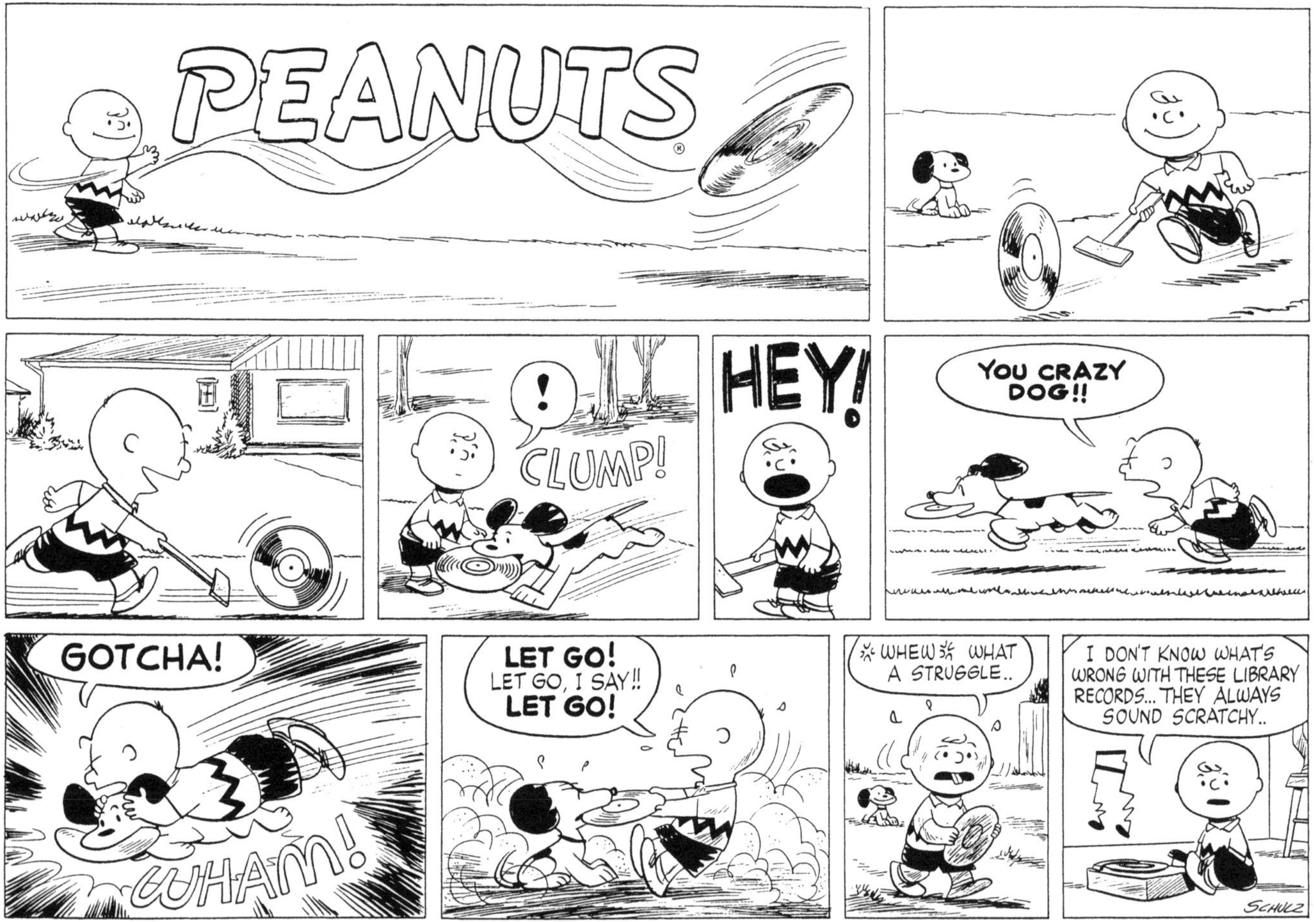
PEANUTS
!
CLUMP!
HEY!
YOU CRAZY DOG!!
GOTCHA!
WHAM!
LET GO! LET GO, I SAY!! LET GO!
WHEW WHAT A STRUGGLE..
I DON'T KNOW WHAT'S WRONG WITH THESE LIBRARY RECORDS... THEY ALWAYS SOUND SCRATCHY..
SCHULZ

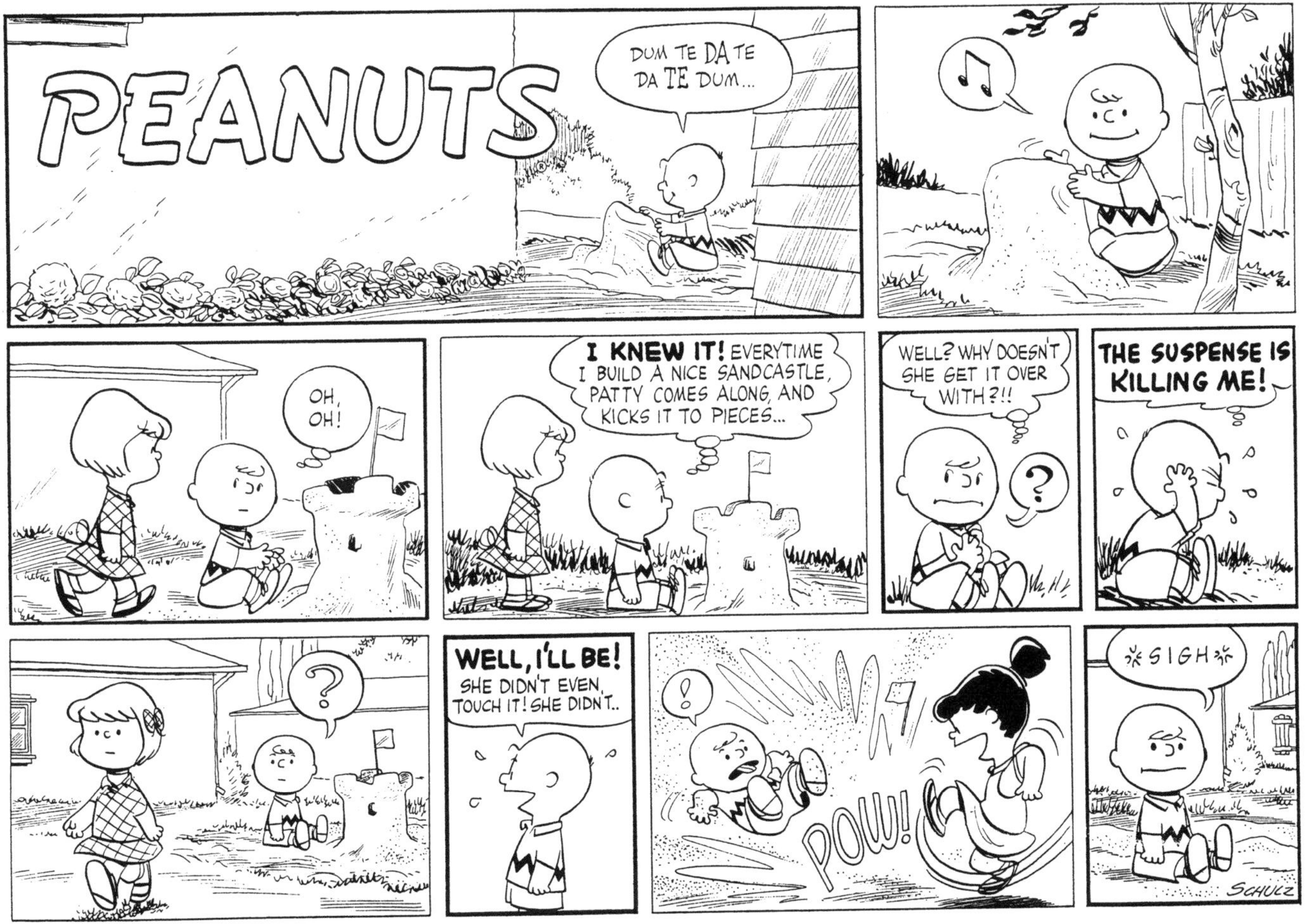
PEANUTS
DUM TE DA TE DA TE DUM...
OH, OH!
I KNEW IT! EVERYTIME I BUILD A NICE SANDCASTLE, PATTY COMES ALONG, AND KICKS IT TO PIECES...
WELL? WHY DOESN'T SHE GET IT OVER WITH?!!
THE SUSPENSE IS KILLING ME!
WELL, I'LL BE! SHE DIDN'T EVEN TOUCH IT! SHE DIDN'T..
!
POW!
SIGH
SCHULZ

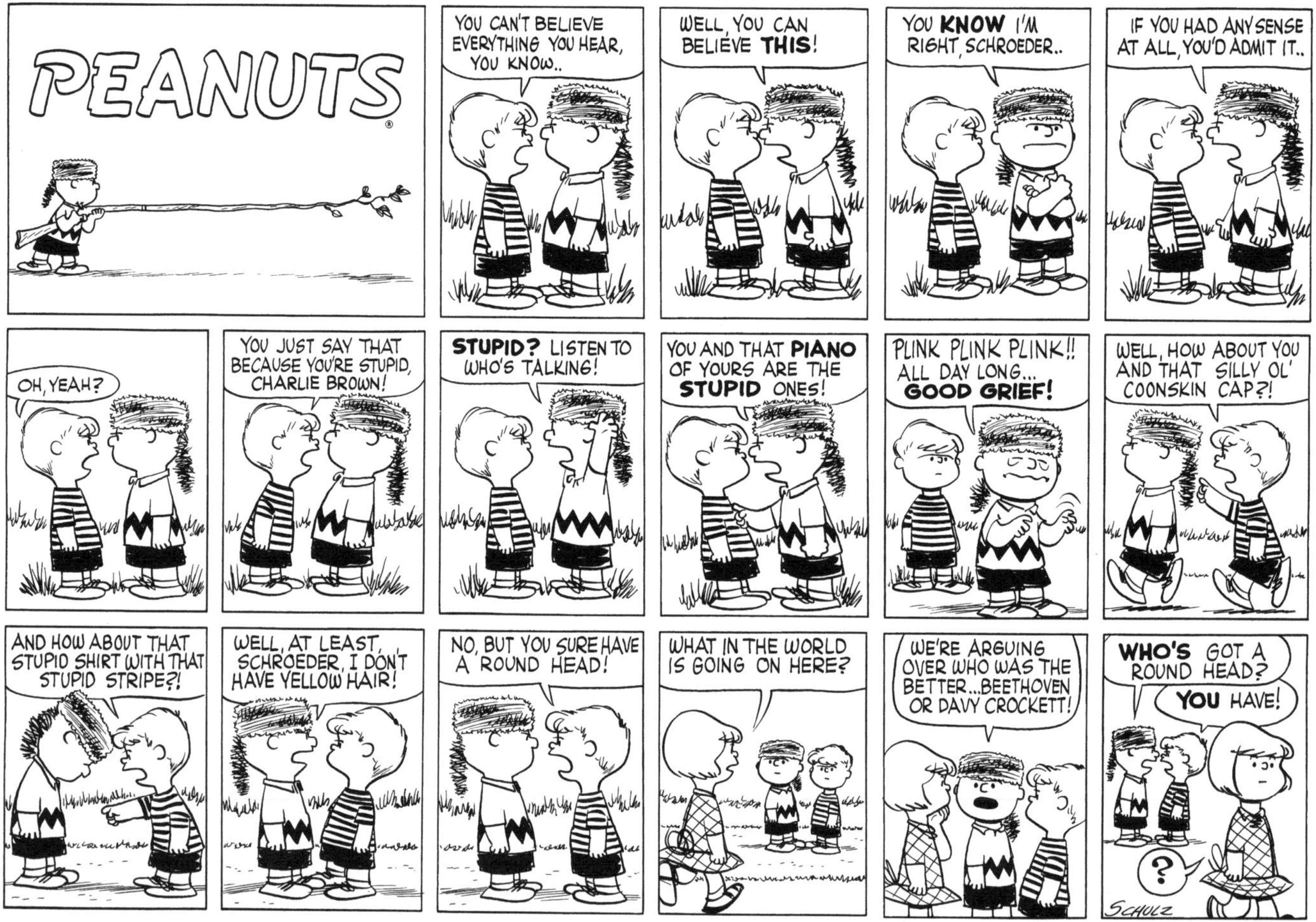
PEANUTS
YOU CAN'T BELIEVE EVERYTHING YOU HEAR, YOU KNOW..
WELL, YOU CAN BELIEVE THIS!
YOU KNOW I'M RIGHT, SCHROEDER..
IF YOU HAD ANY SENSE AT ALL, YOU'D ADMIT IT..
OH, YEAH?
YOU JUST SAY THAT BECAUSE YOU'RE STUPID, CHARLIE BROWN!
STUPID? LISTEN TO WHO'S TALKING!
YOU AND THAT PIANO OF YOURS ARE THE STUPID ONES!
PLINK PLINK PLINK!! ALL DAY LONG... GOOD GRIEF!
WELL, HOW ABOUT YOU AND THAT SILLY OL' COONSKIN CAP?!
AND HOW ABOUT THAT STUPID SHIRT WITH THAT STUPID STRIPE?!
WELL, AT LEAST, SCHROEDER, I DON'T HAVE YELLOW HAIR!
NO, BUT YOU SURE HAVE A ROUND HEAD!
WHAT IN THE WORLD IS GOING ON HERE?
WE'RE ARGUING OVER WHO WAS THE BETTER...BEETHOVEN OR DAVY CROCKETT!
WHO'S GOT A ROUND HEAD?
YOU HAVE!
?
SCHULZ

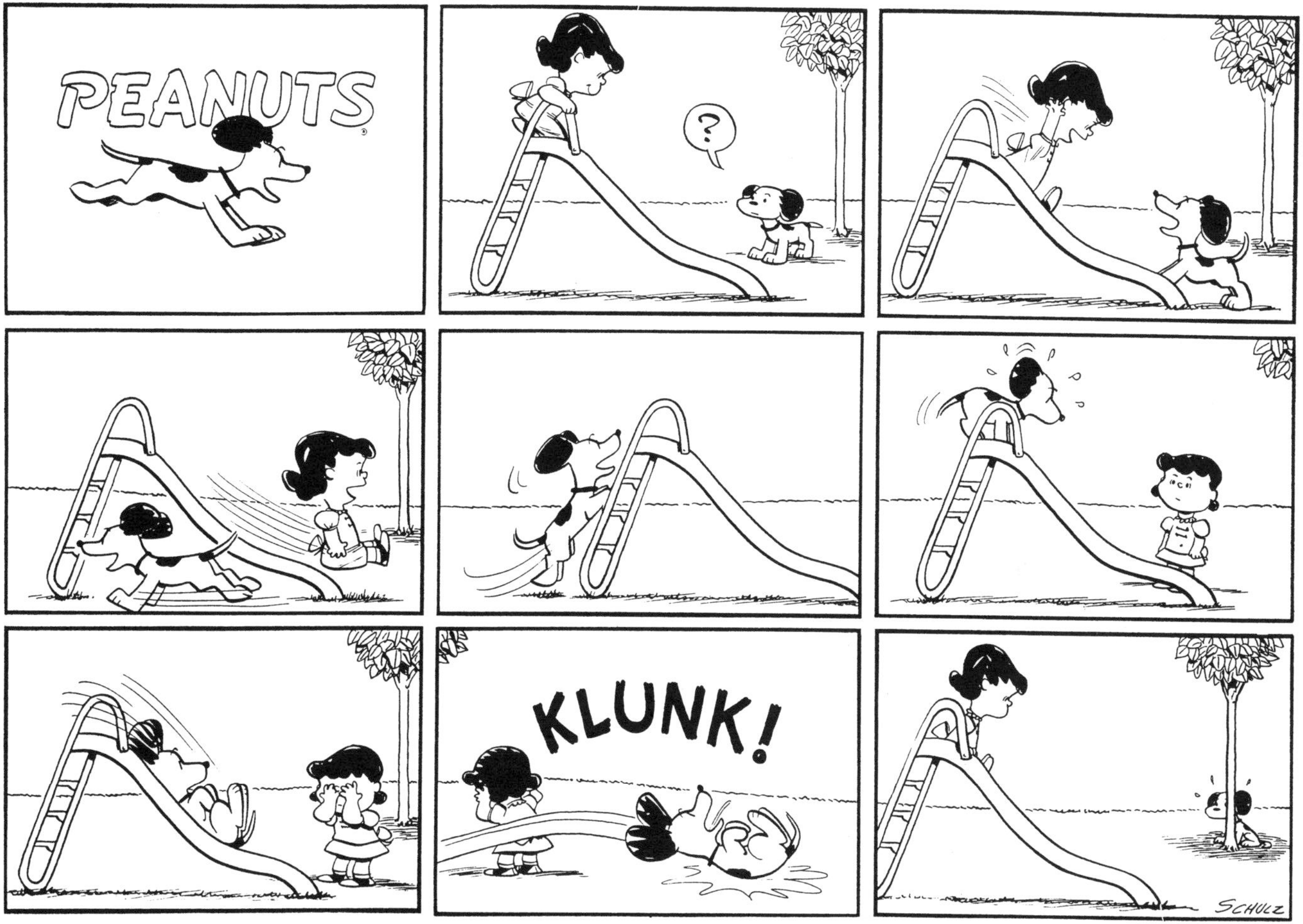
PEANUTS
?
KLUNK!
SCHULZ

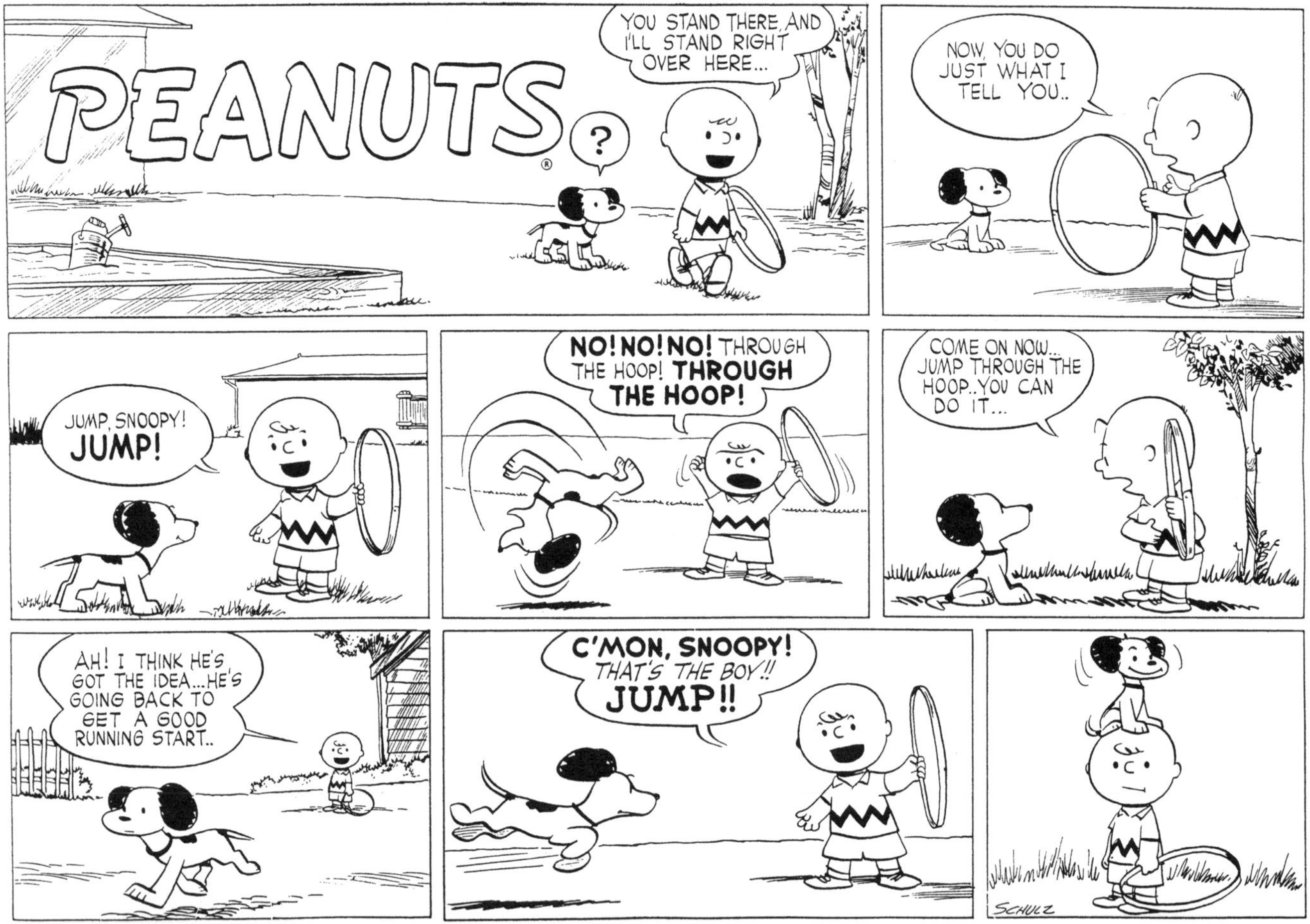
PEANUTS®
YOU STAND THERE, AND I'LL STAND RIGHT OVER HERE...
?
NOW, YOU DO JUST WHAT I TELL YOU..
JUMP, SNOOPY! JUMP!
NO! NO! NO! THROUGH THE HOOP! THROUGH THE HOOP!
COME ON NOW... JUMP THROUGH THE HOOP.. YOU CAN DO IT...
AH! I THINK HE'S GOT THE IDEA...HE'S GOING BACK TO GET A GOOD RUNNING START..
C'MON, SNOOPY! THAT'S THE BOY!! JUMP!!
SCHULZ

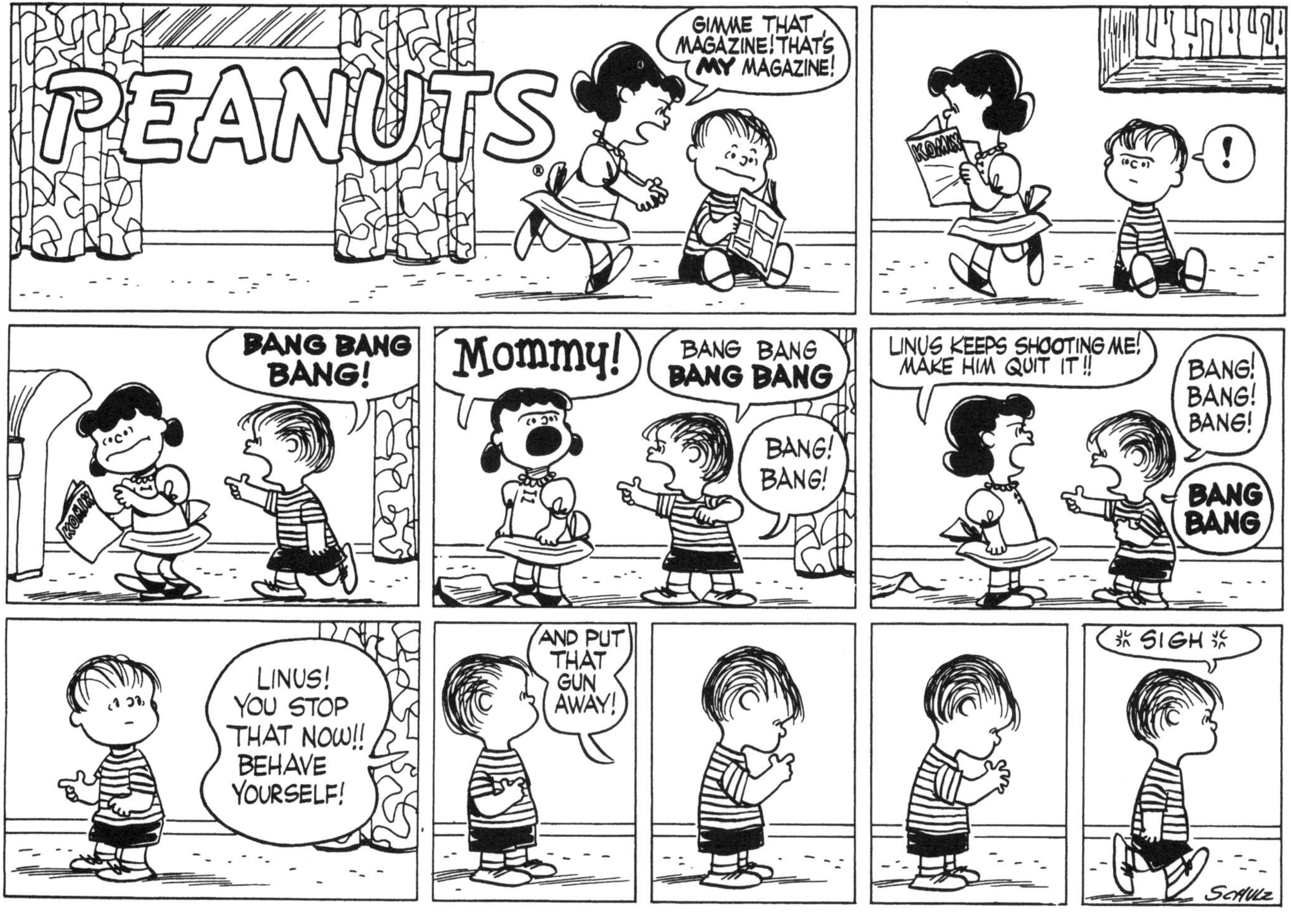
PEANUTS
GIMME THAT MAGAZINE! THAT'S MY MAGAZINE!
KOMIX
!
BANG BANG BANG!
KOMIX
Mommy!
BANG BANG BANG BANG
BANG! BANG!
LINUS KEEPS SHOOTING ME! MAKE HIM QUIT IT!!
BANG! BANG! BANG!
BANG BANG
LINUS! YOU STOP THAT NOW!! BEHAVE YOURSELF!
AND PUT THAT GUN AWAY!
SIGH
SCHULZ

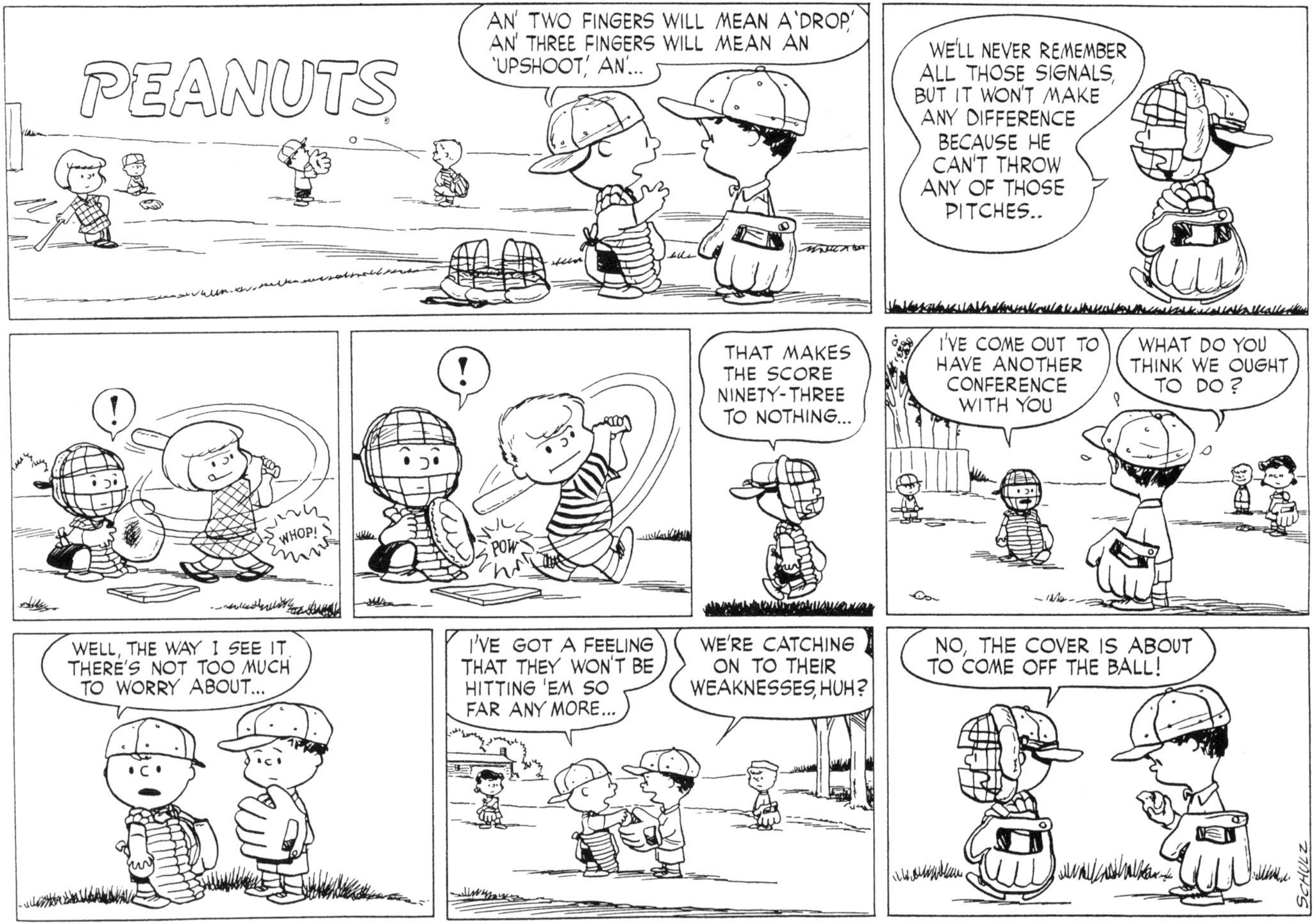
PEANUTS
AN' TWO FINGERS WILL MEAN A 'DROP,' AN' THREE FINGERS WILL MEAN AN 'UPSHOOT,' AN'...
WE'LL NEVER REMEMBER ALL THOSE SIGNALS, BUT IT WON'T MAKE ANY DIFFERENCE BECAUSE HE CAN'T THROW ANY OF THOSE PITCHES..
!
WHOP!
!
POW
THAT MAKES THE SCORE NINETY-THREE TO NOTHING...
I'VE COME OUT TO HAVE ANOTHER CONFERENCE WITH YOU
WHAT DO YOU THINK WE OUGHT TO DO?
WELL, THE WAY I SEE IT THERE'S NOT TOO MUCH TO WORRY ABOUT...
I'VE GOT A FEELING THAT THEY WON'T BE HITTING 'EM SO FAR ANY MORE...
WE'RE CATCHING ON TO THEIR WEAKNESSES, HUH?
NO, THE COVER IS ABOUT TO COME OFF THE BALL!
SCHULZ

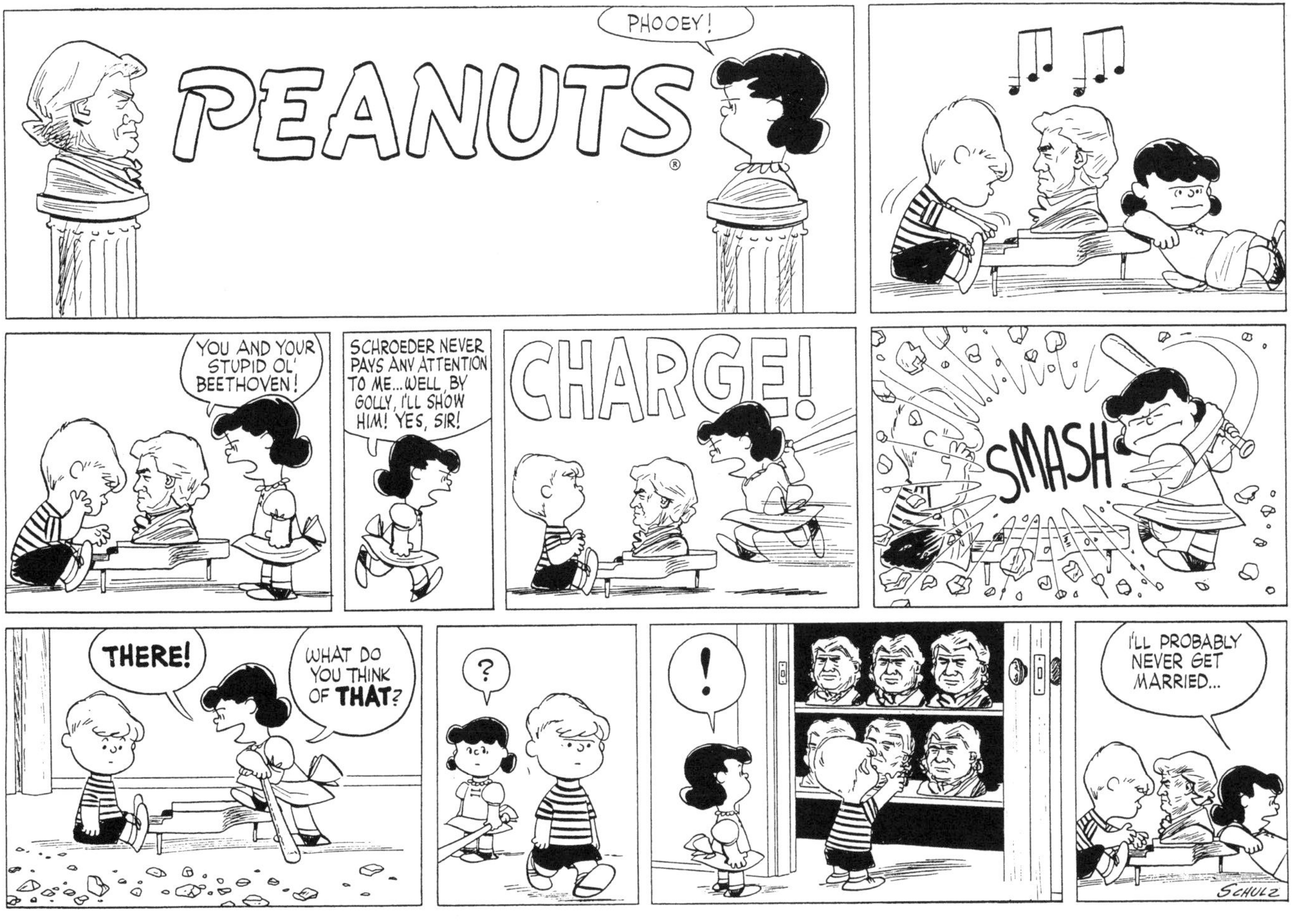
PEANUTS®
PHOOEY!
YOU AND YOUR STUPID OL' BEETHOVEN!
SCHROEDER NEVER PAYS ANY ATTENTION TO ME...WELL, BY GOLLY, I'LL SHOW HIM! YES, SIR!
CHARGE!
SMASH
THERE!
WHAT DO YOU THINK OF THAT?
?
!
I'LL PROBABLY NEVER GET MARRIED...
SCHULZ

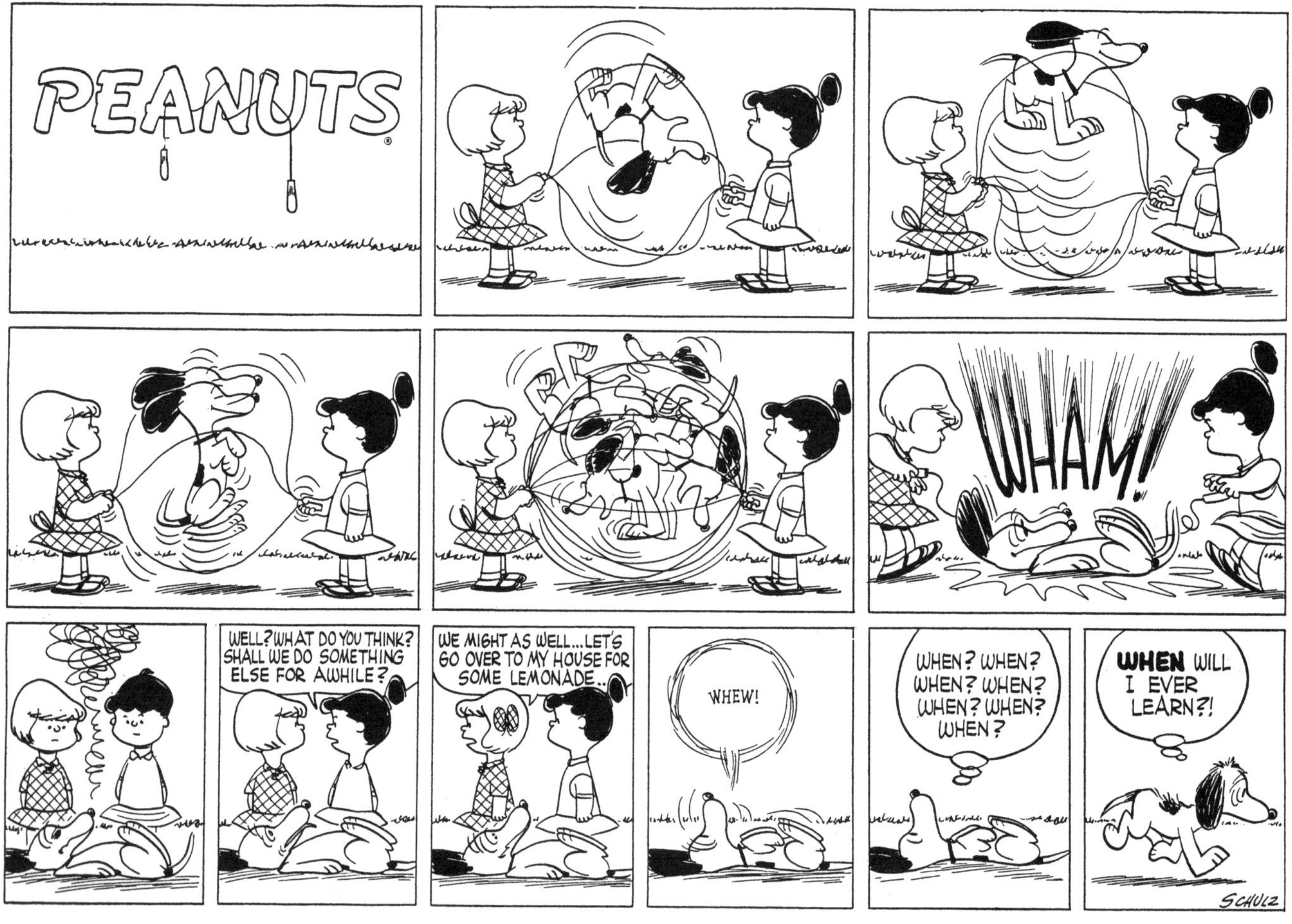

PEANUTS
WHAM!
WELL? WHAT DO YOU THINK? SHALL WE DO SOMETHING ELSE FOR AWHILE?
WE MIGHT AS WELL...LET'S GO OVER TO MY HOUSE FOR SOME LEMONADE..
WHEW!
WHEN? WHEN? WHEN? WHEN? WHEN? WHEN? WHEN?
WHEN WILL I EVER LEARN?!
SCHULZ

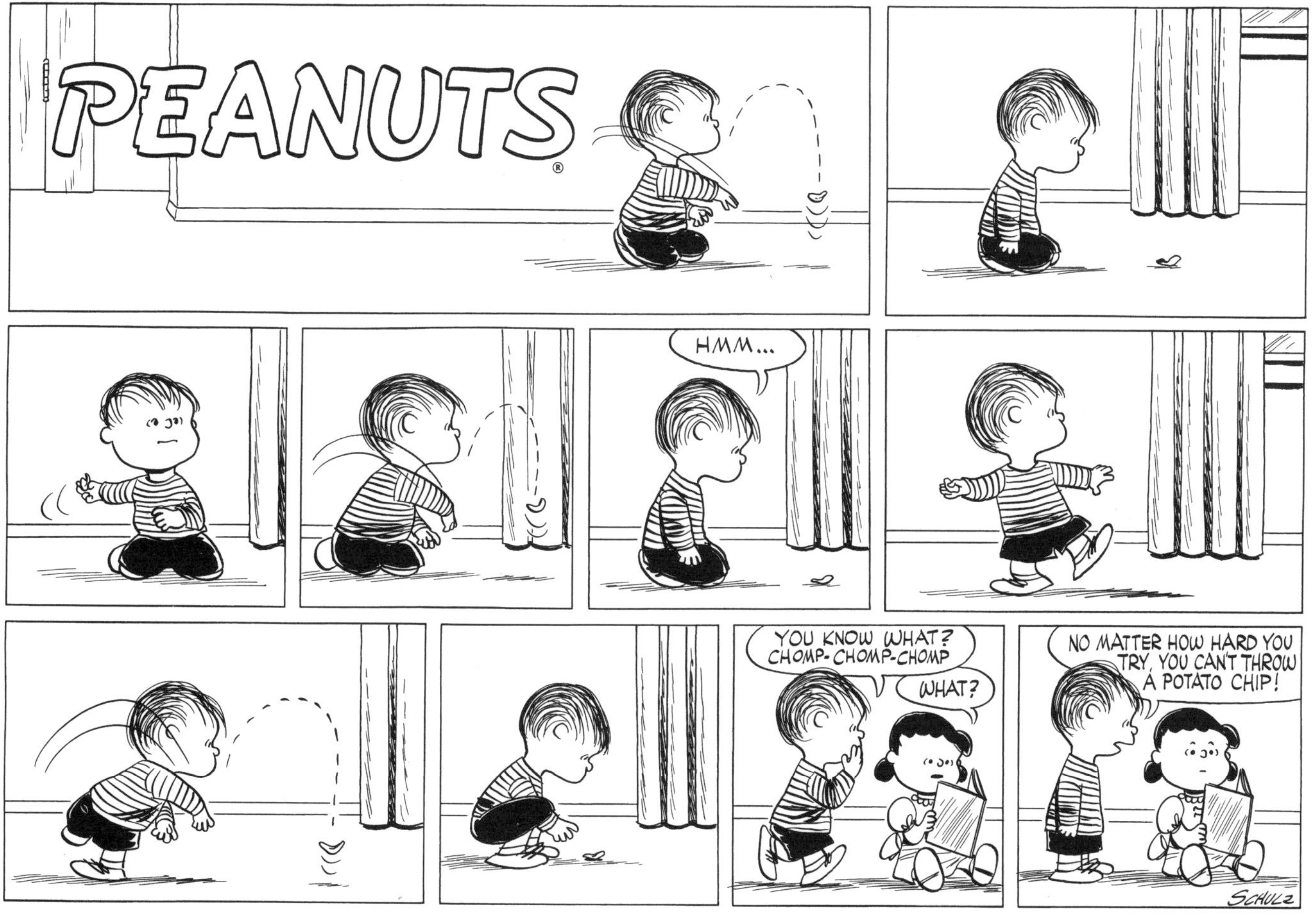
PEANUTS
HMM...
YOU KNOW WHAT? CHOMP-CHOMP-CHOMP
WHAT?
NO MATTER HOW HARD YOU TRY, YOU CAN'T THROW A POTATO CHIP!
SCHULZ

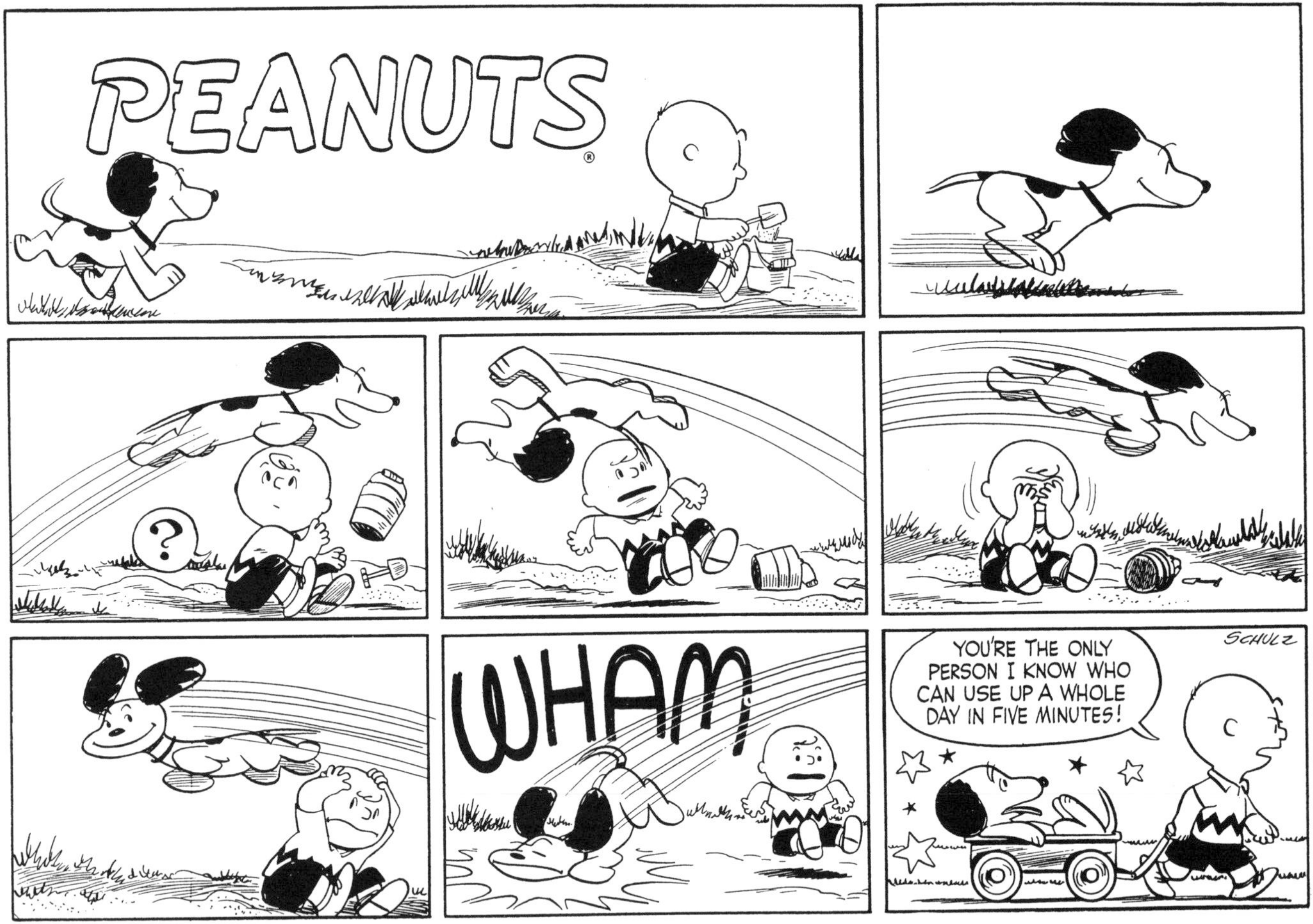
PEANUTS
WHAM
SCHULZ
YOU'RE THE ONLY PERSON I KNOW WHO CAN USE UP A WHOLE DAY IN FIVE MINUTES!

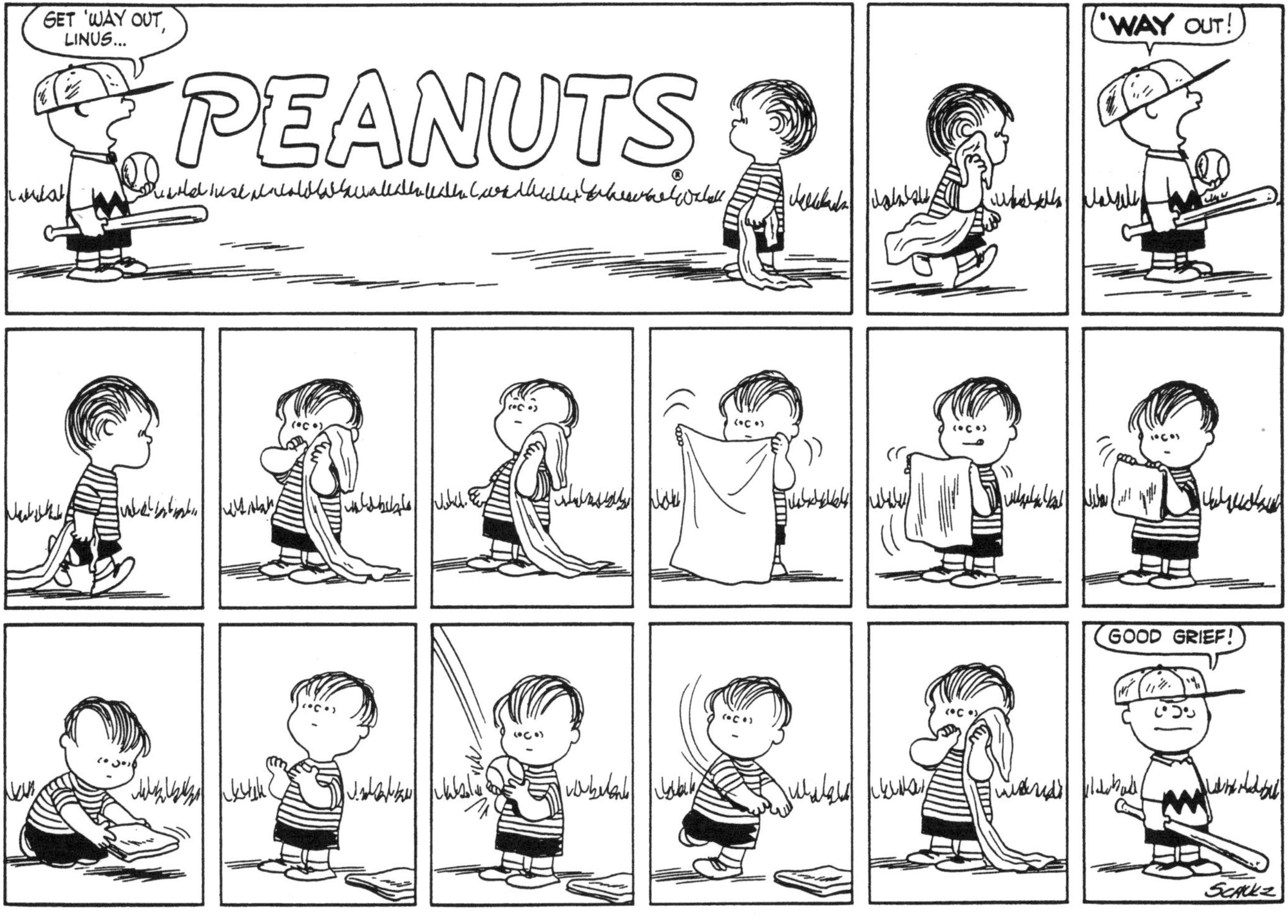
GET 'WAY OUT, LINUS...
PEANUTS
'WAY OUT!
GOOD GRIEF!
SCHULZ

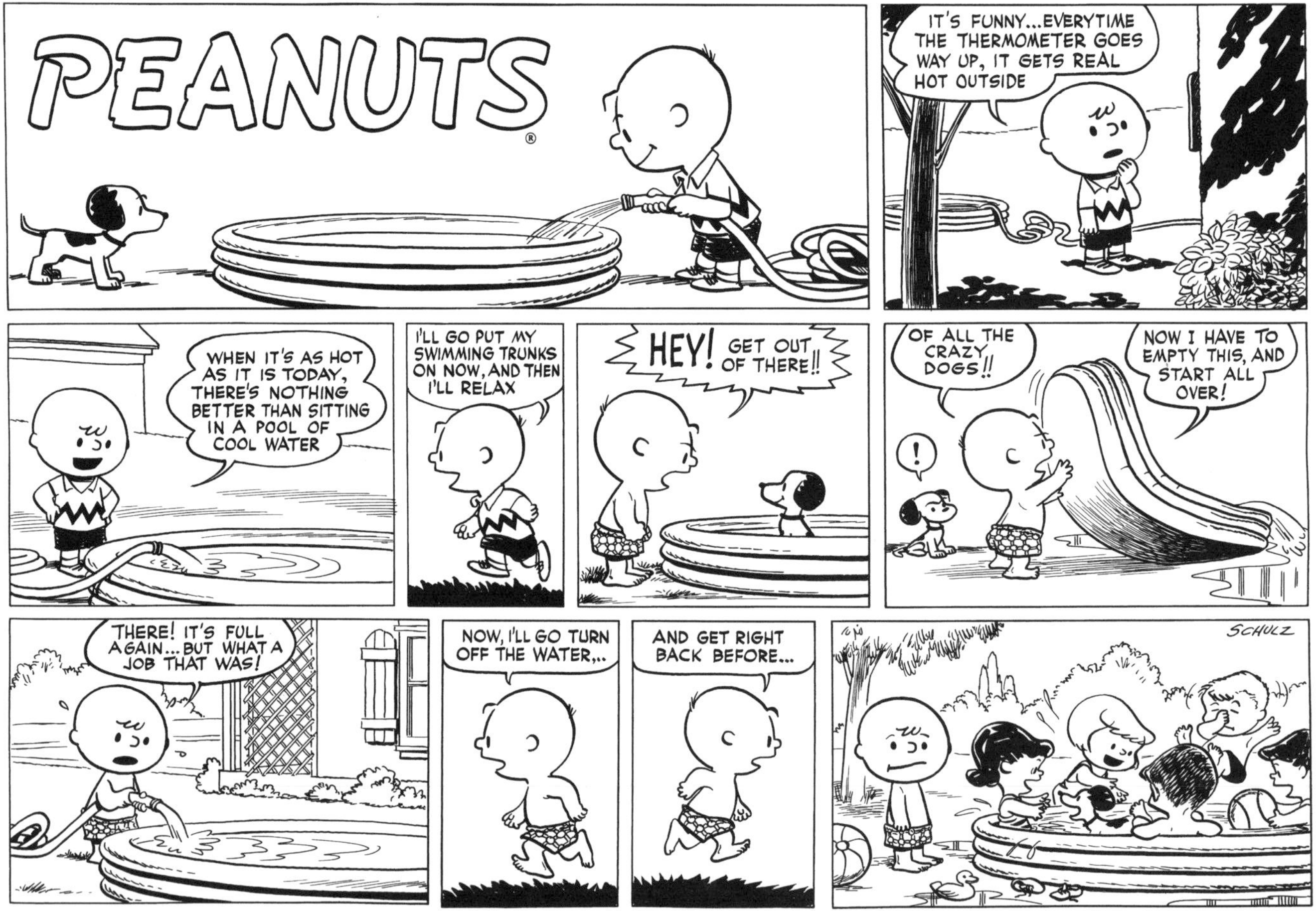
PEANUTS®
IT'S FUNNY...EVERYTIME THE THERMOMETER GOES WAY UP, IT GETS REAL HOT OUTSIDE
WHEN IT'S AS HOT AS IT IS TODAY, THERE'S NOTHING BETTER THAN SITTING IN A POOL OF COOL WATER
I'LL GO PUT MY SWIMMING TRUNKS ON NOW, AND THEN I'LL RELAX
HEY! GET OUT OF THERE!!
OF ALL THE CRAZY DOGS!!
!
NOW I HAVE TO EMPTY THIS, AND START ALL OVER!
THERE! IT'S FULL AGAIN... BUT WHAT A JOB THAT WAS!
NOW, I'LL GO TURN OFF THE WATER,..
AND GET RIGHT BACK BEFORE...
SCHULZ

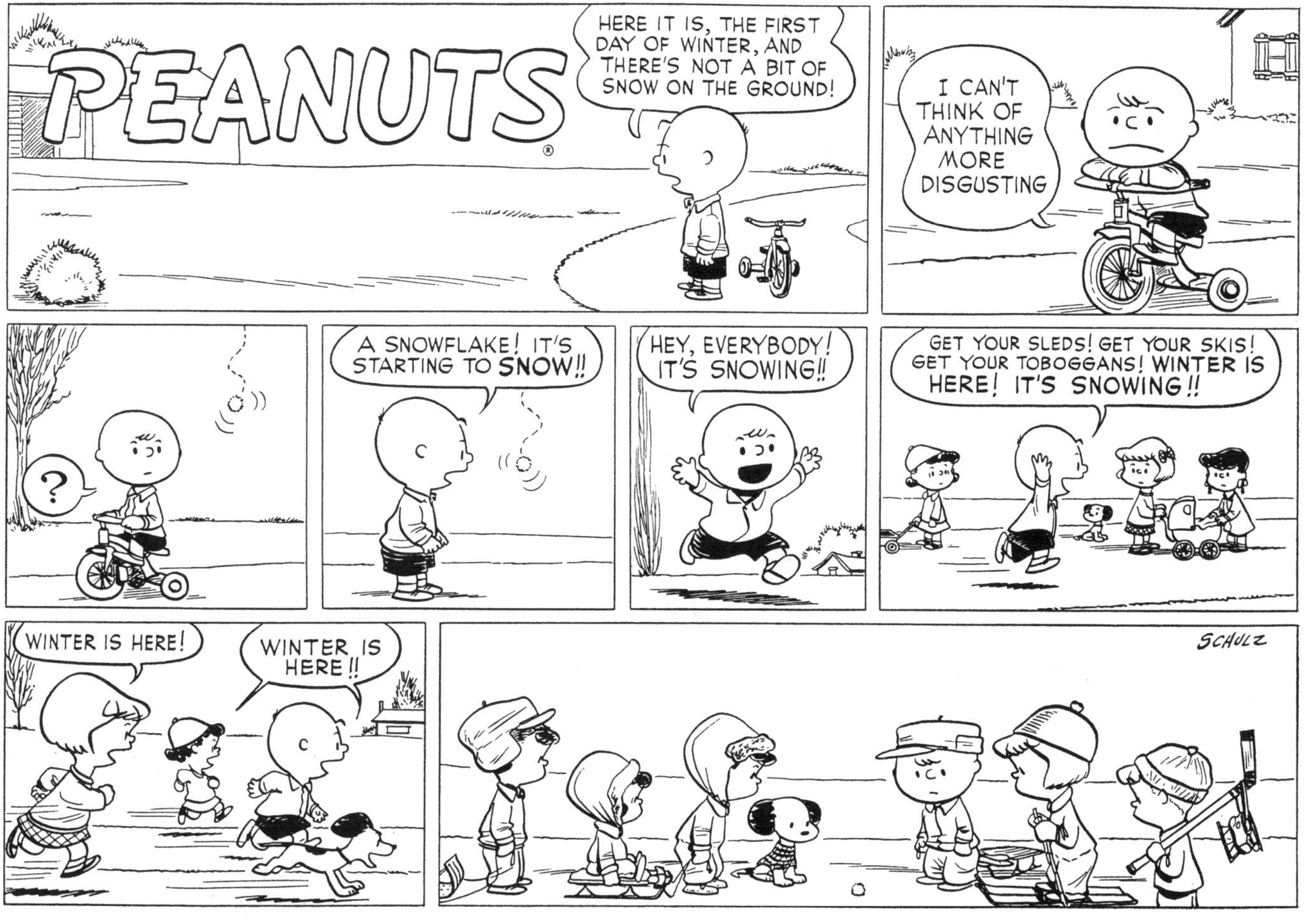
PEANUTS
HERE IT IS, THE FIRST DAY OF WINTER, AND THERE'S NOT A BIT OF SNOW ON THE GROUND!
I CAN'T THINK OF ANYTHING MORE DISGUSTING
?
A SNOWFLAKE! IT'S STARTING TO SNOW!!
HEY, EVERYBODY! IT'S SNOWING!!
GET YOUR SLEDS! GET YOUR SKIS! GET YOUR TOBOGGANS! WINTER IS HERE! IT'S SNOWING!!
WINTER IS HERE!
WINTER IS HERE!!
SCHULZ

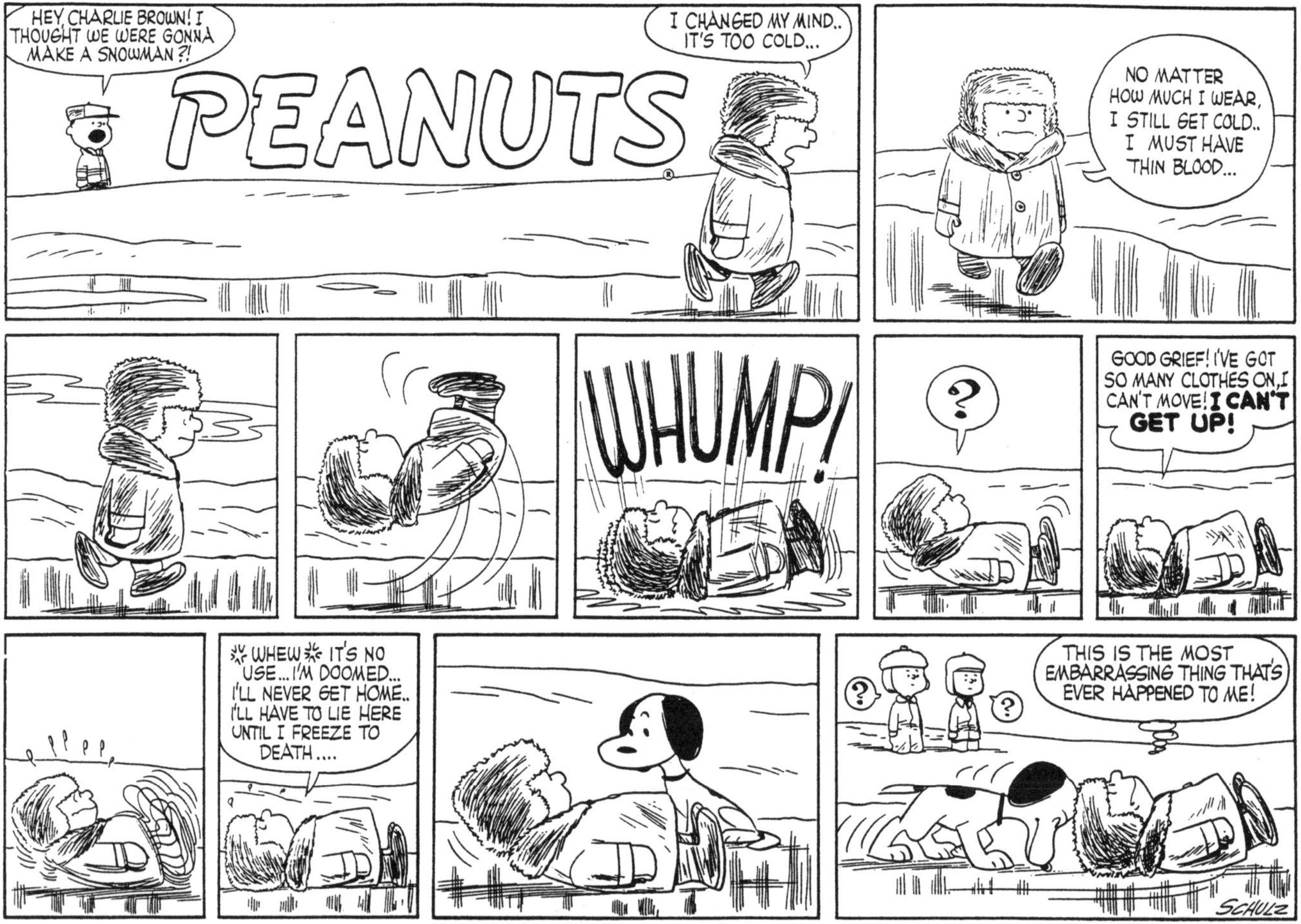
PEANUTS
HEY, CHARLIE BROWN! I THOUGHT WE WERE GONNA MAKE A SNOWMAN ?!
I CHANGED MY MIND.. IT'S TOO COLD...
NO MATTER HOW MUCH I WEAR, I STILL GET COLD.. I MUST HAVE THIN BLOOD...
WHUMP!
?
GOOD GRIEF! I'VE GOT SO MANY CLOTHES ON, I CAN'T MOVE! **I CAN'T GET UP!**
WHEW IT'S NO USE... I'M DOOMED... I'LL NEVER GET HOME.. I'LL HAVE TO LIE HERE UNTIL I FREEZE TO DEATH....
?
?
THIS IS THE MOST EMBARRASSING THING THAT'S EVER HAPPENED TO ME!
SCHULZ

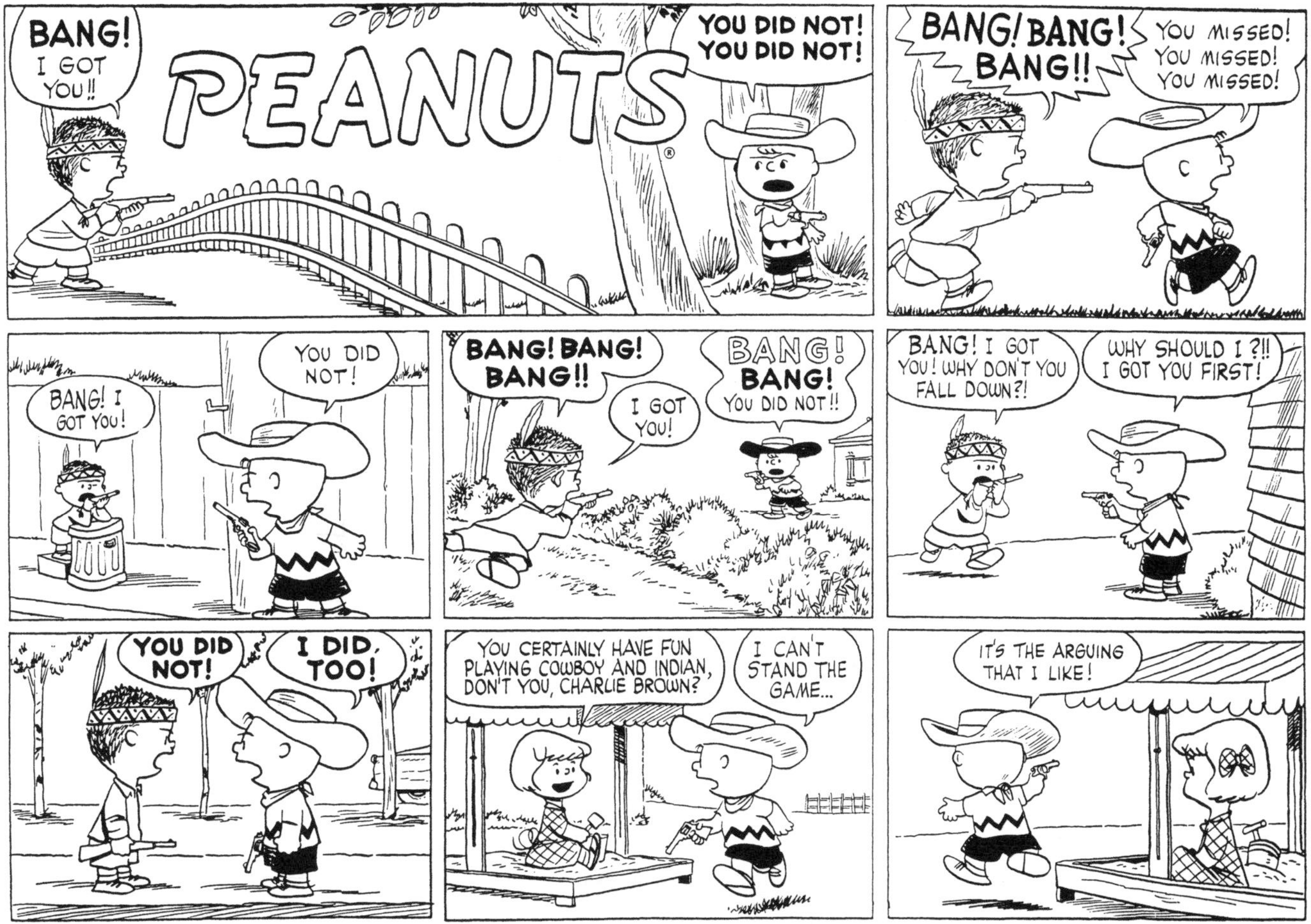

PEANUTS
BANG! I GOT YOU!!
YOU DID NOT! YOU DID NOT!
BANG! BANG! BANG!!
YOU MISSED! YOU MISSED! YOU MISSED!
BANG! I GOT YOU!
YOU DID NOT!
BANG! BANG! BANG!!
I GOT YOU!
BANG! BANG! YOU DID NOT!!
BANG! I GOT YOU! WHY DON'T YOU FALL DOWN?!
WHY SHOULD I ?!! I GOT YOU FIRST!
YOU DID NOT!
I DID, TOO!
YOU CERTAINLY HAVE FUN PLAYING COWBOY AND INDIAN, DON'T YOU, CHARLIE BROWN?
I CAN'T STAND THE GAME...
IT'S THE ARGUING THAT I LIKE!

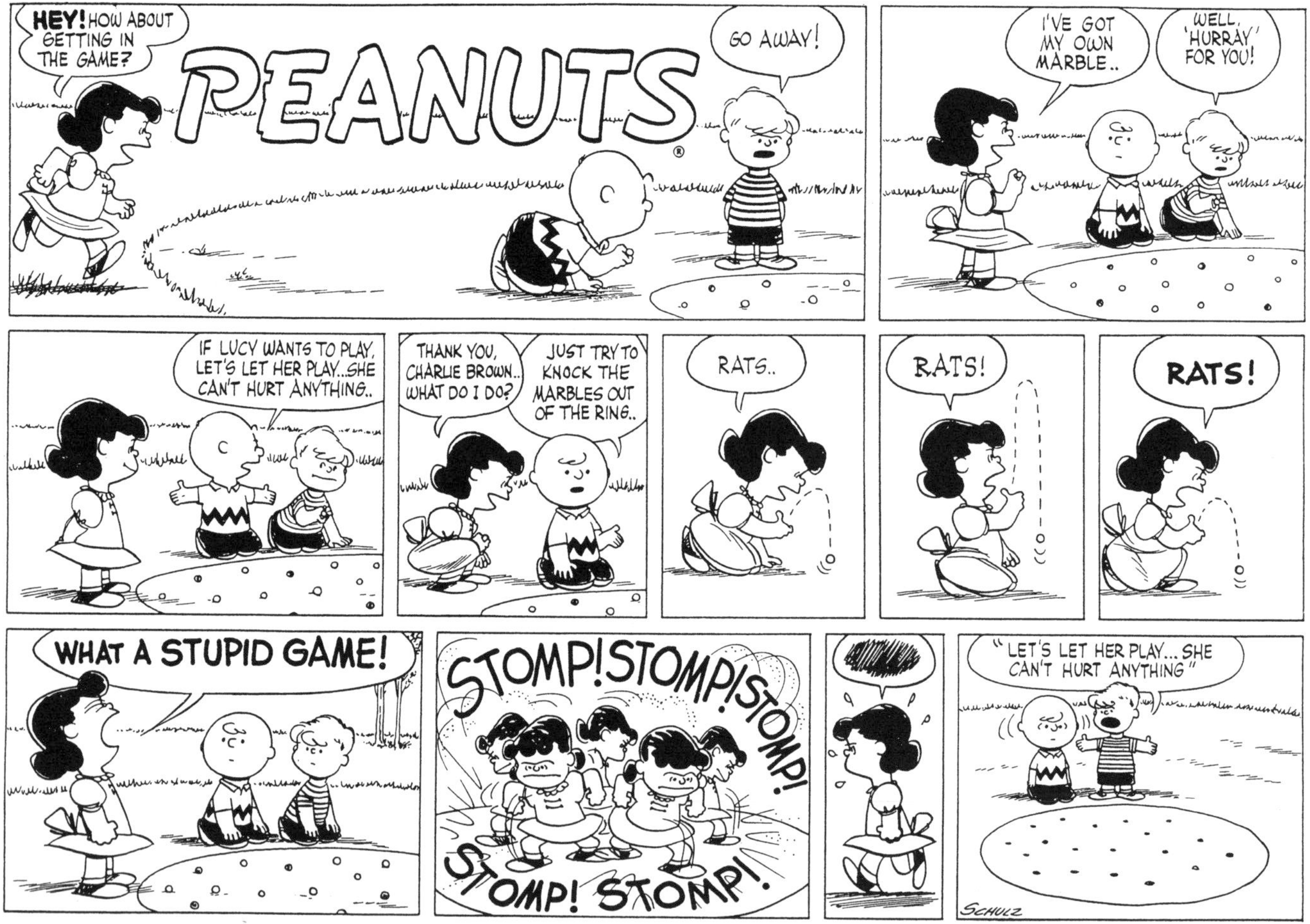
HEY! HOW ABOUT GETTING IN THE GAME?
PEANUTS
GO AWAY!
I'VE GOT MY OWN MARBLE..
WELL, 'HURRAY' FOR YOU!
IF LUCY WANTS TO PLAY, LET'S LET HER PLAY...SHE CAN'T HURT ANYTHING..
THANK YOU, CHARLIE BROWN.. WHAT DO I DO?
JUST TRY TO KNOCK THE MARBLES OUT OF THE RING..
RATS..
RATS!
RATS!
WHAT A STUPID GAME!
STOMP! STOMP! STOMP! STOMP!
STOMP! STOMP!
"LET'S LET HER PLAY... SHE CAN'T HURT ANYTHING"
SCHULZ

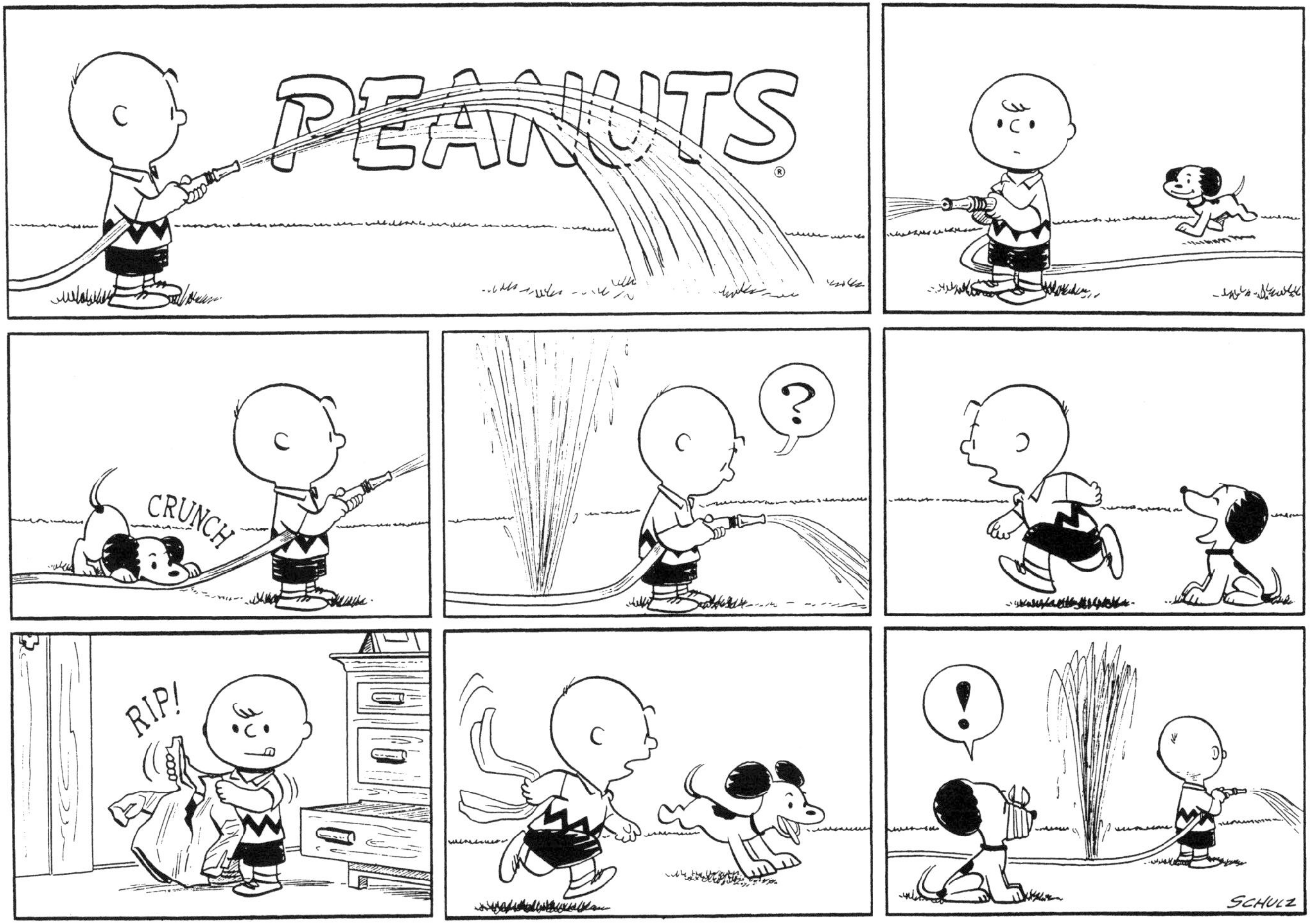

PEANUTS
CRUNCH
?
RIP!
!
SCHULZ

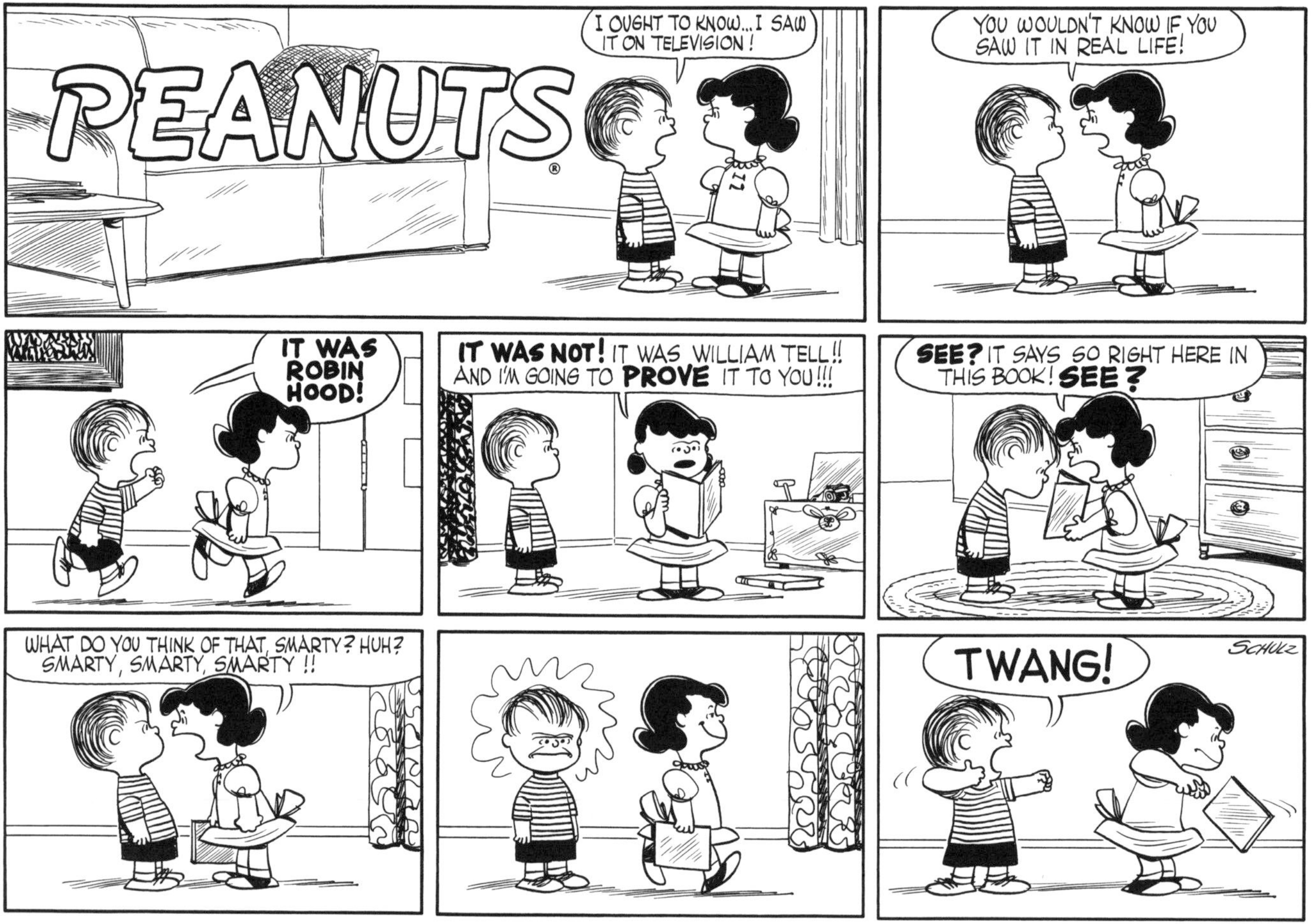
PEANUTS®
I OUGHT TO KNOW... I SAW IT ON TELEVISION!
YOU WOULDN'T KNOW IF YOU SAW IT IN REAL LIFE!
IT WAS ROBIN HOOD!
IT WAS NOT! IT WAS WILLIAM TELL!! AND I'M GOING TO PROVE IT TO YOU!!!
SEE? IT SAYS SO RIGHT HERE IN THIS BOOK! SEE?
WHAT DO YOU THINK OF THAT, SMARTY? HUH? SMARTY, SMARTY, SMARTY!!
TWANG!
SCHULZ

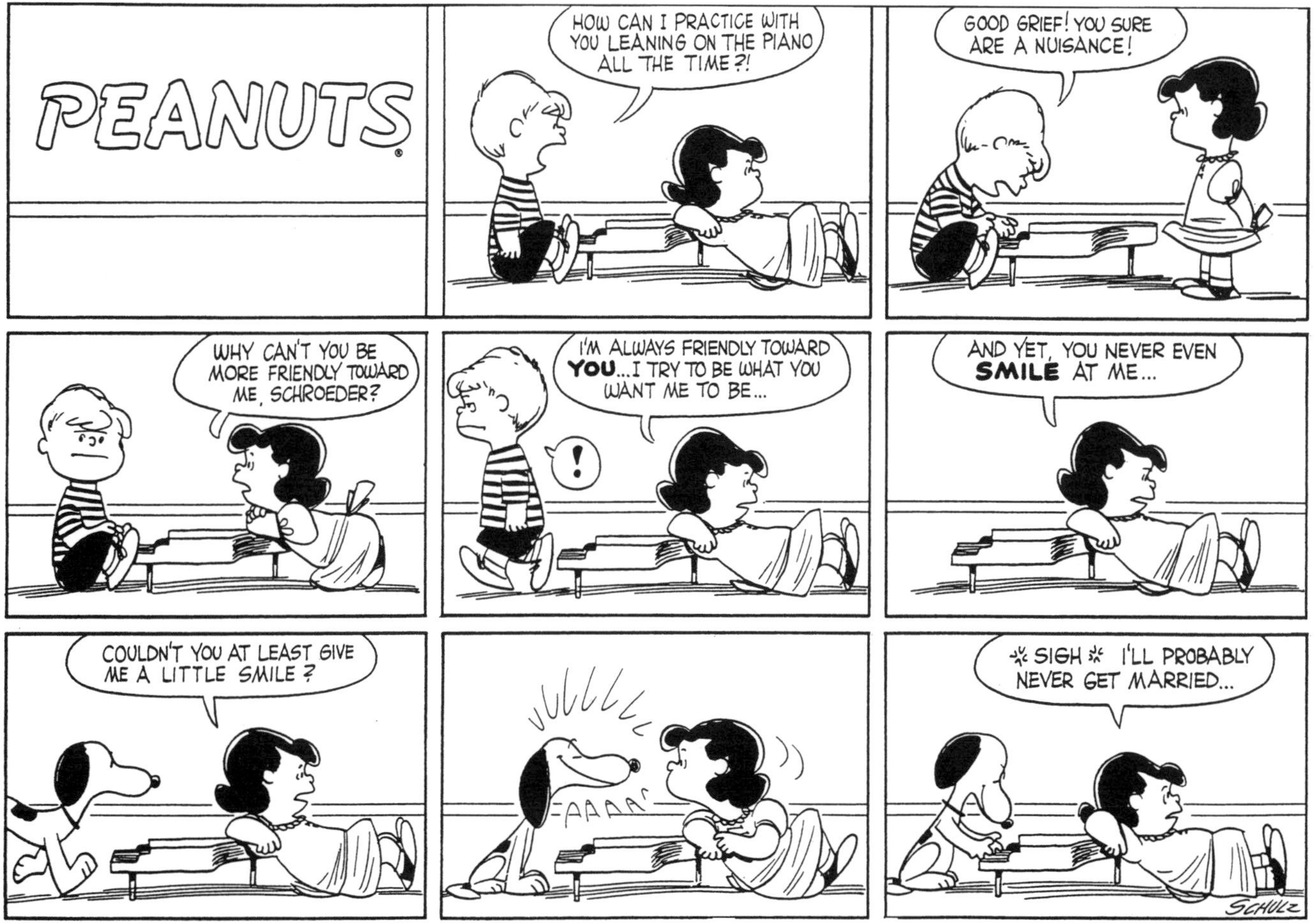
PEANUTS
HOW CAN I PRACTICE WITH YOU LEANING ON THE PIANO ALL THE TIME?!
GOOD GRIEF! YOU SURE ARE A NUISANCE!
WHY CAN'T YOU BE MORE FRIENDLY TOWARD ME, SCHROEDER?
I'M ALWAYS FRIENDLY TOWARD YOU...I TRY TO BE WHAT YOU WANT ME TO BE...
!
AND YET, YOU NEVER EVEN SMILE AT ME...
COULDN'T YOU AT LEAST GIVE ME A LITTLE SMILE?
SIGH I'LL PROBABLY NEVER GET MARRIED...
SCHULZ

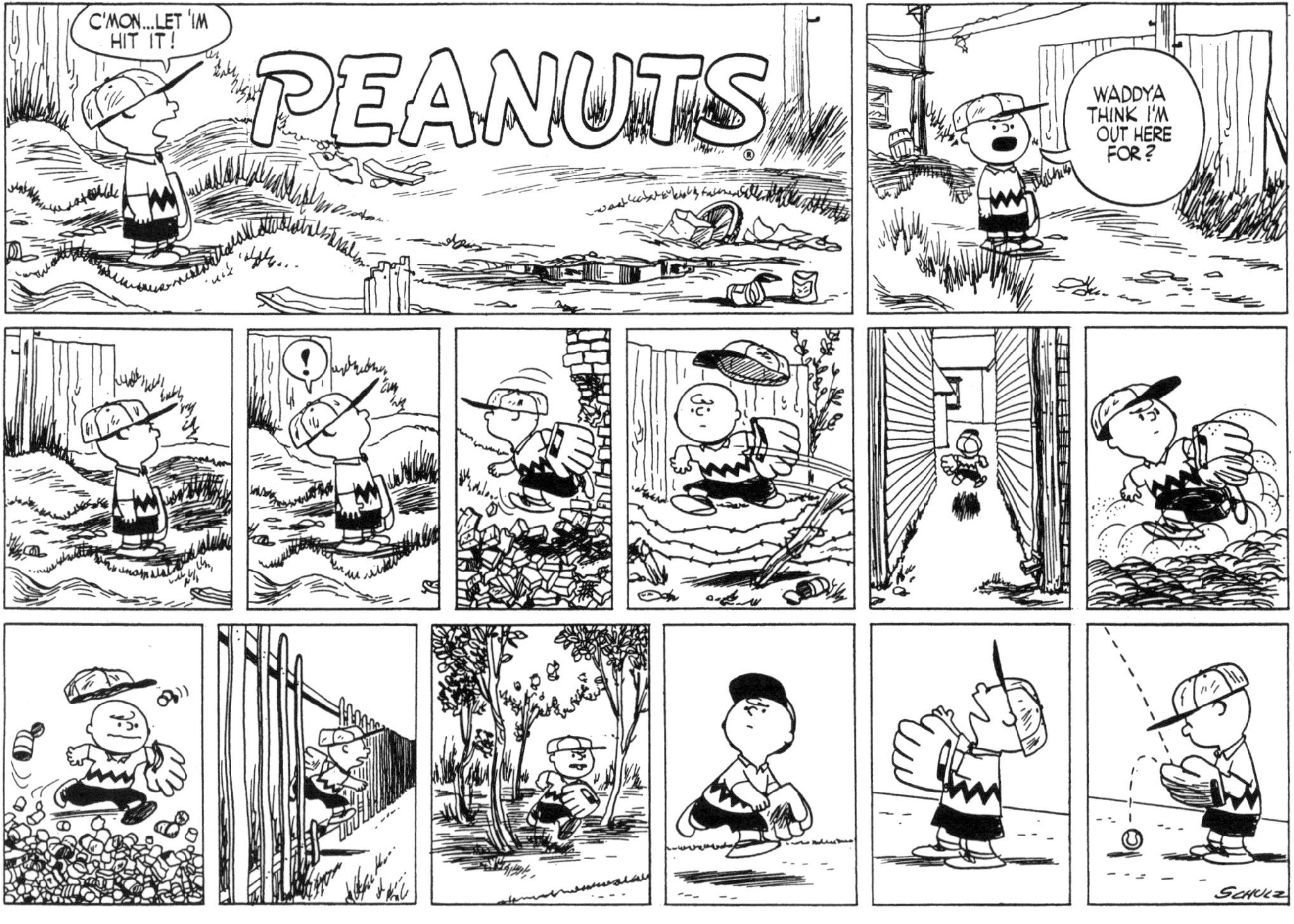
C'MON...LET 'IM HIT IT!
PEANUTS
WADDYA THINK I'M OUT HERE FOR?
!
SCHULZ

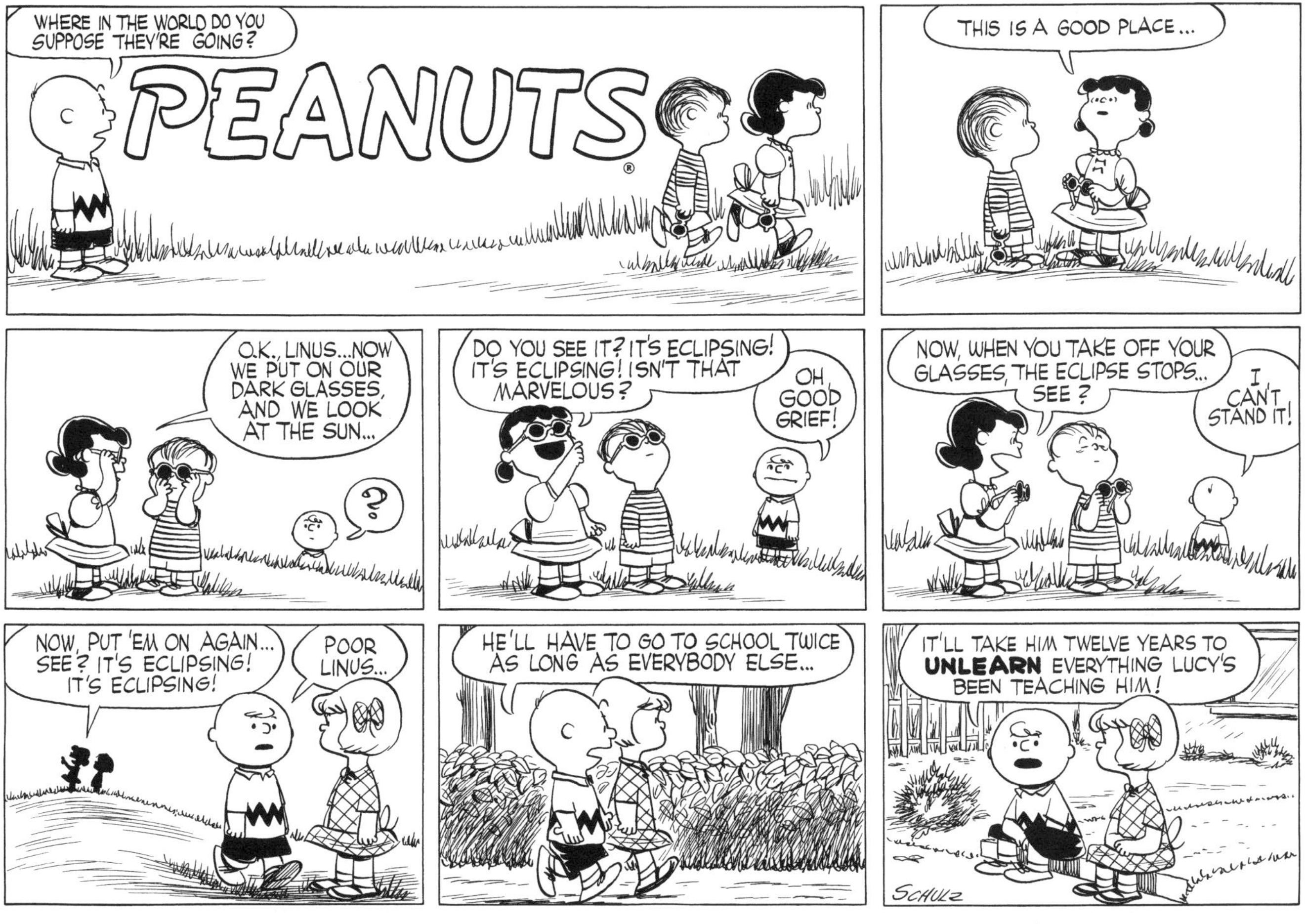
WHERE IN THE WORLD DO YOU SUPPOSE THEY'RE GOING?
PEANUTS®
THIS IS A GOOD PLACE...
O.K., LINUS...NOW WE PUT ON OUR DARK GLASSES, AND WE LOOK AT THE SUN...
?
DO YOU SEE IT? IT'S ECLIPSING! IT'S ECLIPSING! ISN'T THAT MARVELOUS?
OH GOOD GRIEF!
NOW, WHEN YOU TAKE OFF YOUR GLASSES, THE ECLIPSE STOPS... SEE?
I CAN'T STAND IT!
NOW, PUT 'EM ON AGAIN... SEE? IT'S ECLIPSING! IT'S ECLIPSING!
POOR LINUS...
HE'LL HAVE TO GO TO SCHOOL TWICE AS LONG AS EVERYBODY ELSE...
IT'LL TAKE HIM TWELVE YEARS TO **UNLEARN** EVERYTHING LUCY'S BEEN TEACHING HIM!
SCHULZ

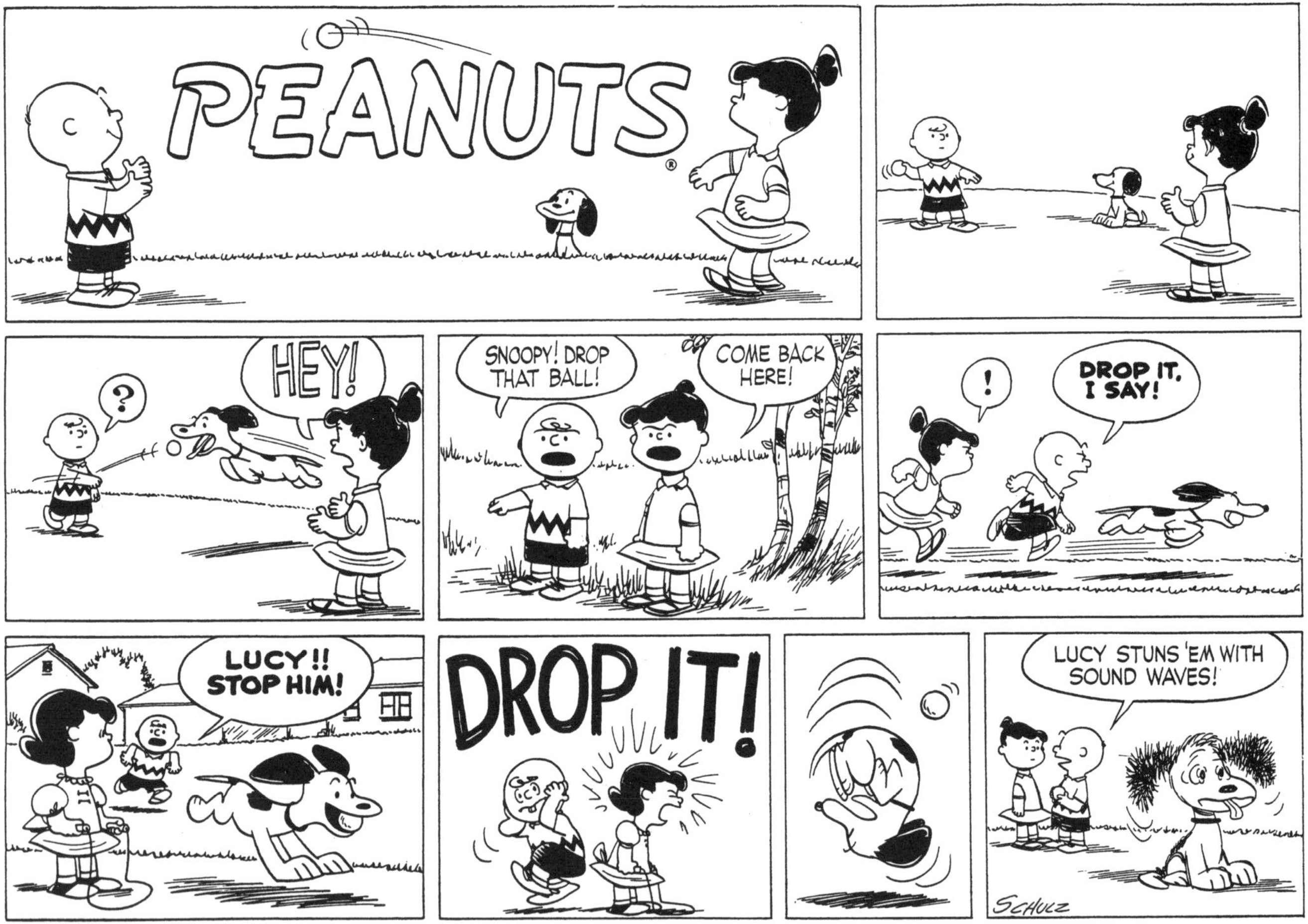
PEANUTS
HEY!
?
SNOOPY! DROP THAT BALL!
COME BACK HERE!
!
DROP IT, I SAY!
LUCY!! STOP HIM!
DROP IT!
LUCY STUNS 'EM WITH SOUND WAVES!
SCHULZ

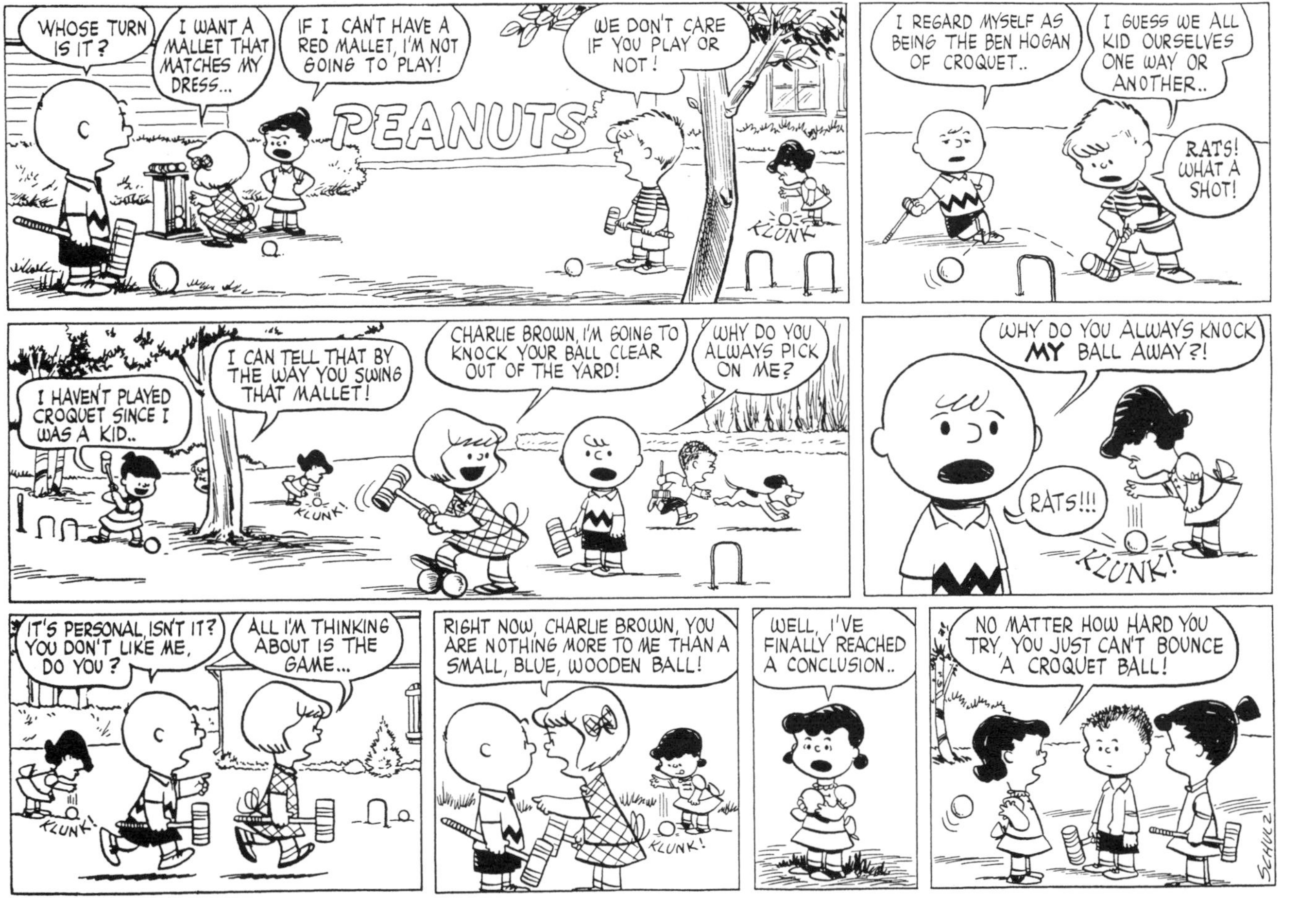
WHOSE TURN IS IT?
I WANT A MALLET THAT MATCHES MY DRESS...
IF I CAN'T HAVE A RED MALLET, I'M NOT GOING TO PLAY!
PEANUTS
WE DON'T CARE IF YOU PLAY OR NOT!
KLUNK
I REGARD MYSELF AS BEING THE BEN HOGAN OF CROQUET..
I GUESS WE ALL KID OURSELVES ONE WAY OR ANOTHER..
RATS! WHAT A SHOT!
I HAVEN'T PLAYED CROQUET SINCE I WAS A KID..
I CAN TELL THAT BY THE WAY YOU SWING THAT MALLET!
CHARLIE BROWN, I'M GOING TO KNOCK YOUR BALL CLEAR OUT OF THE YARD!
WHY DO YOU ALWAYS PICK ON ME?
KLUNK!
WHY DO YOU ALWAYS KNOCK **MY** BALL AWAY?!
RATS!!!
KLUNK!
IT'S PERSONAL, ISN'T IT? YOU DON'T LIKE ME, DO YOU?
ALL I'M THINKING ABOUT IS THE GAME...
KLUNK!
RIGHT NOW, CHARLIE BROWN, YOU ARE NOTHING MORE TO ME THAN A SMALL, BLUE, WOODEN BALL!
KLUNK!
WELL, I'VE FINALLY REACHED A CONCLUSION..
NO MATTER HOW HARD YOU TRY, YOU JUST CAN'T BOUNCE A CROQUET BALL!
SCHULZ

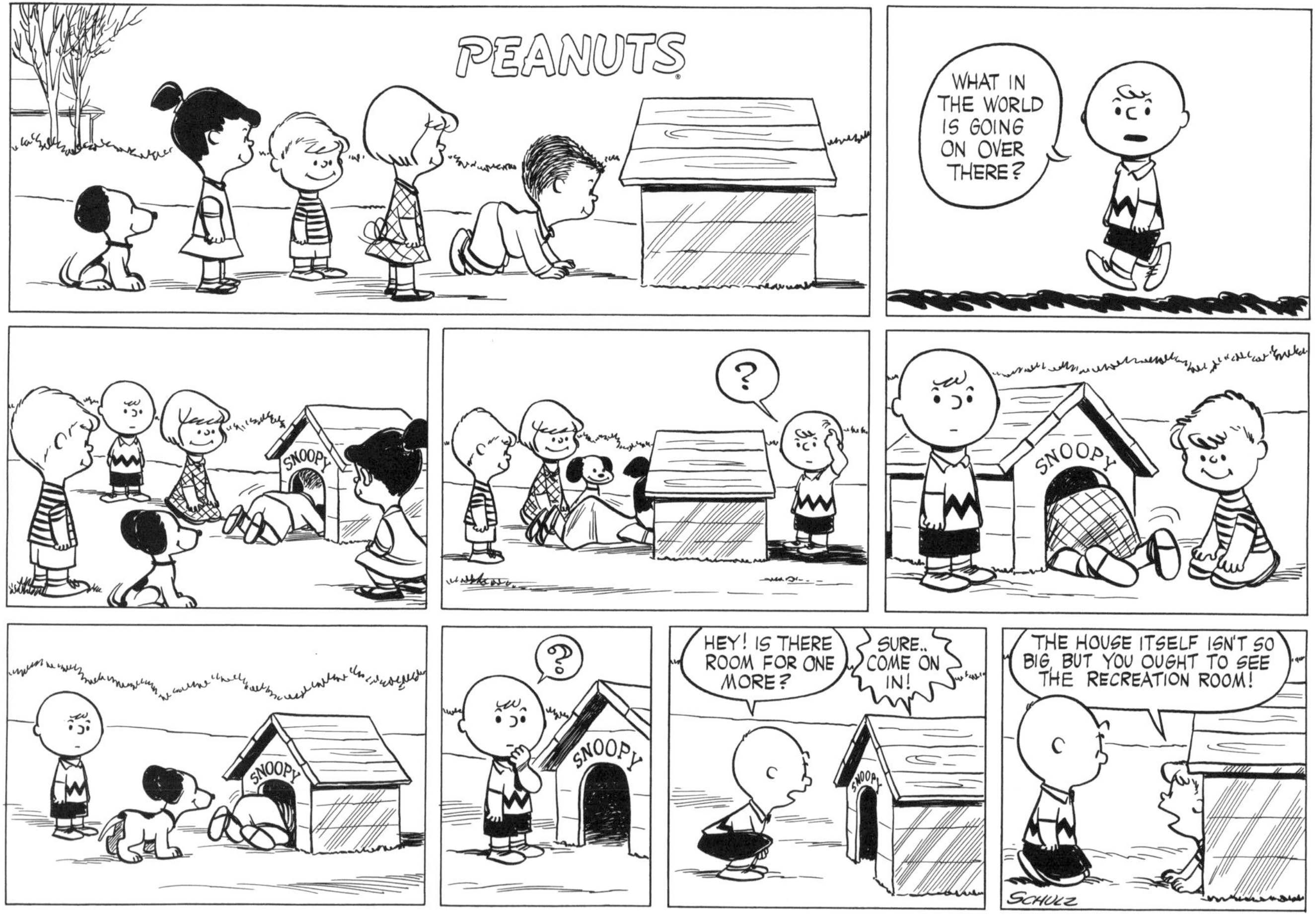
PEANUTS
WHAT IN THE WORLD IS GOING ON OVER THERE?
SNOOPY
?
SNOOPY
SNOOPY
?
SNOOPY
HEY! IS THERE ROOM FOR ONE MORE?
SURE.. COME ON IN!
SNOOPY
THE HOUSE ITSELF ISN'T SO BIG, BUT YOU OUGHT TO SEE THE RECREATION ROOM!
SCHULZ

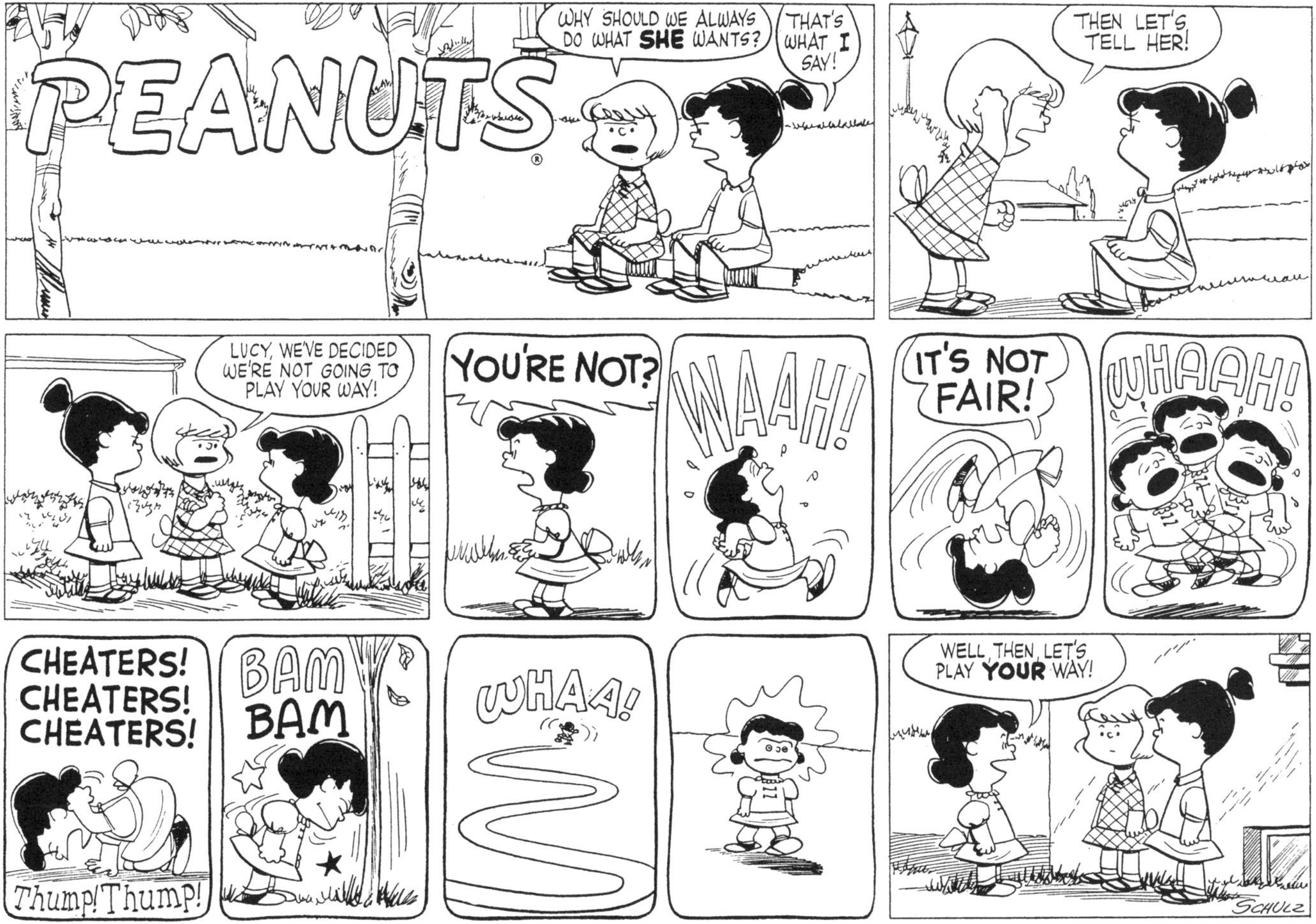
PEANUTS
WHY SHOULD WE ALWAYS DO WHAT SHE WANTS?
THAT'S WHAT I SAY!
THEN LET'S TELL HER!
LUCY, WE'VE DECIDED WE'RE NOT GOING TO PLAY YOUR WAY!
YOU'RE NOT?
WAAAH!
IT'S NOT FAIR!
WHAAAH!
CHEATERS! CHEATERS! CHEATERS!
Thump! Thump!
BAM BAM
WHAA!
WELL THEN, LET'S PLAY YOUR WAY!
SCHULZ

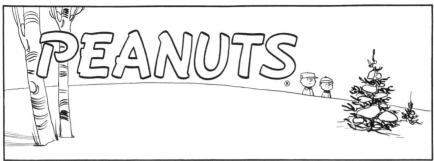

PEANUTS

THIS LOOKS LIKE A GOOD SPOT..

YOU BUILD YOUR SNOW FORT 'WAY OVER THERE LINUS, AND I'LL BUILD MINE HERE..

LET ME KNOW WHEN YOU'RE READY, AND WE'LL HAVE A BIG BATTLE..

♪

AH! AN IMPREGNABLE FORTRESS OF SNOW!

THAT POOR LITTLE KID WILL BE SICK WITH JEALOUSY WHEN HE SEES WHAT I'VE BUILT...

I'M NOT READY..

SCHULZ

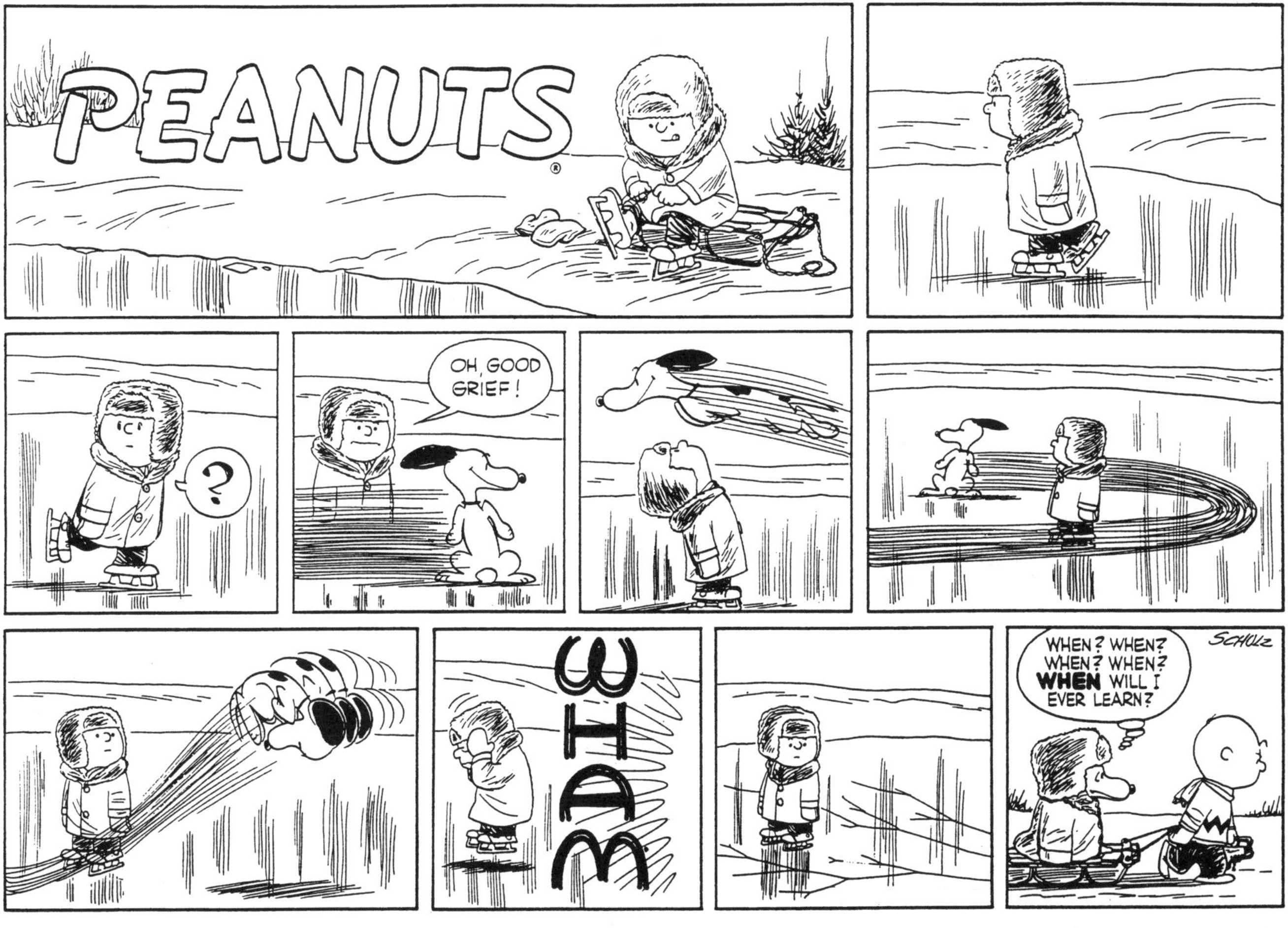
PEANUTS®
?
OH, GOOD GRIEF!
SCHULZ
WHEN? WHEN? WHEN? WHEN? **WHEN** WILL I EVER LEARN?

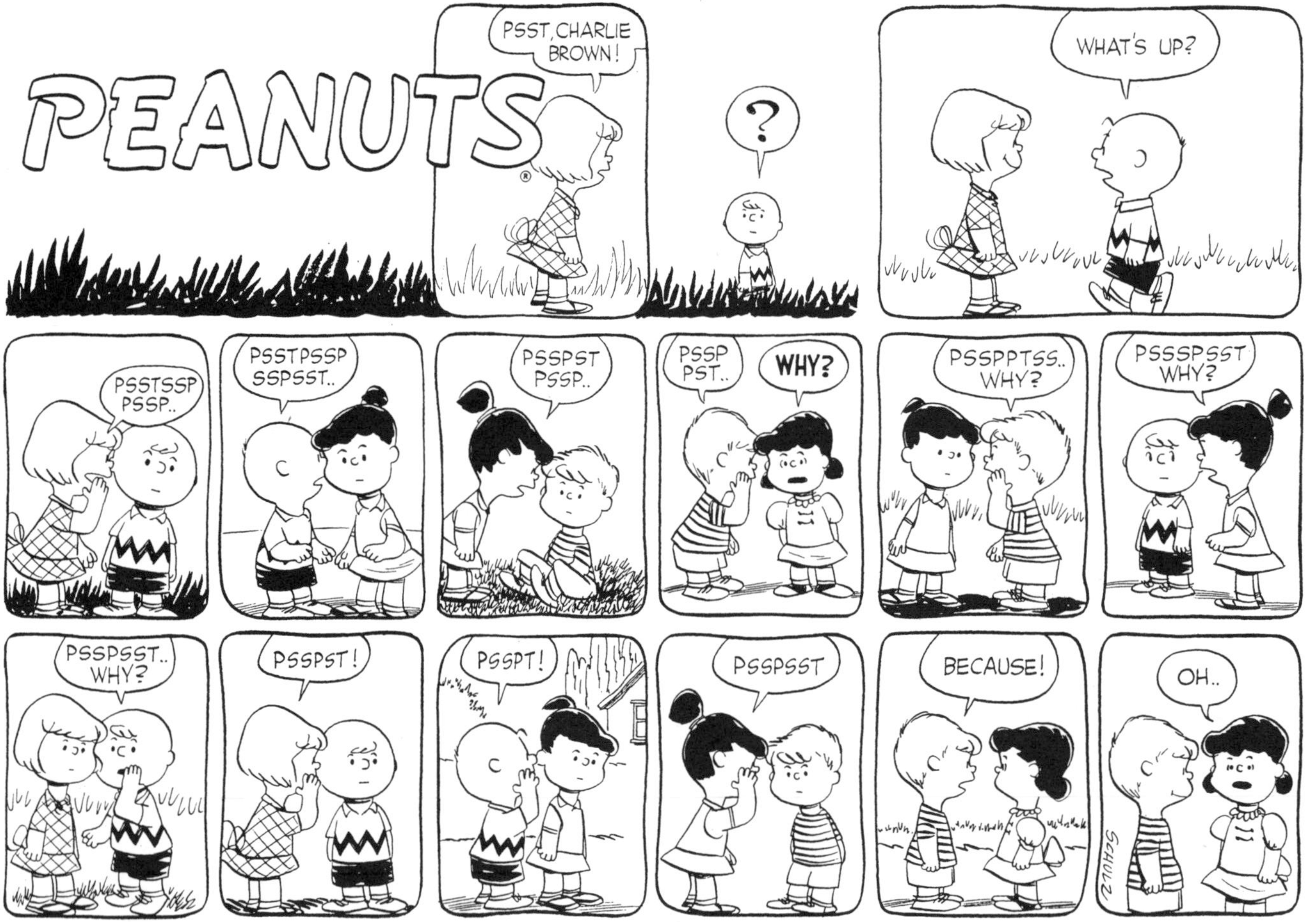
PEANUTS
PSST, CHARLIE BROWN!
?
WHAT'S UP?
PSSTSSP PSSP..
PSSTPSSP SSPSST..
PSSPST PSSP..
PSSP PST..
WHY?
PSSPPTSS.. WHY?
PSSSPSST WHY?
PSSPSST.. WHY?
PSSPST!
PSSPT!
PSSPSST
BECAUSE!
OH..
SCHULZ

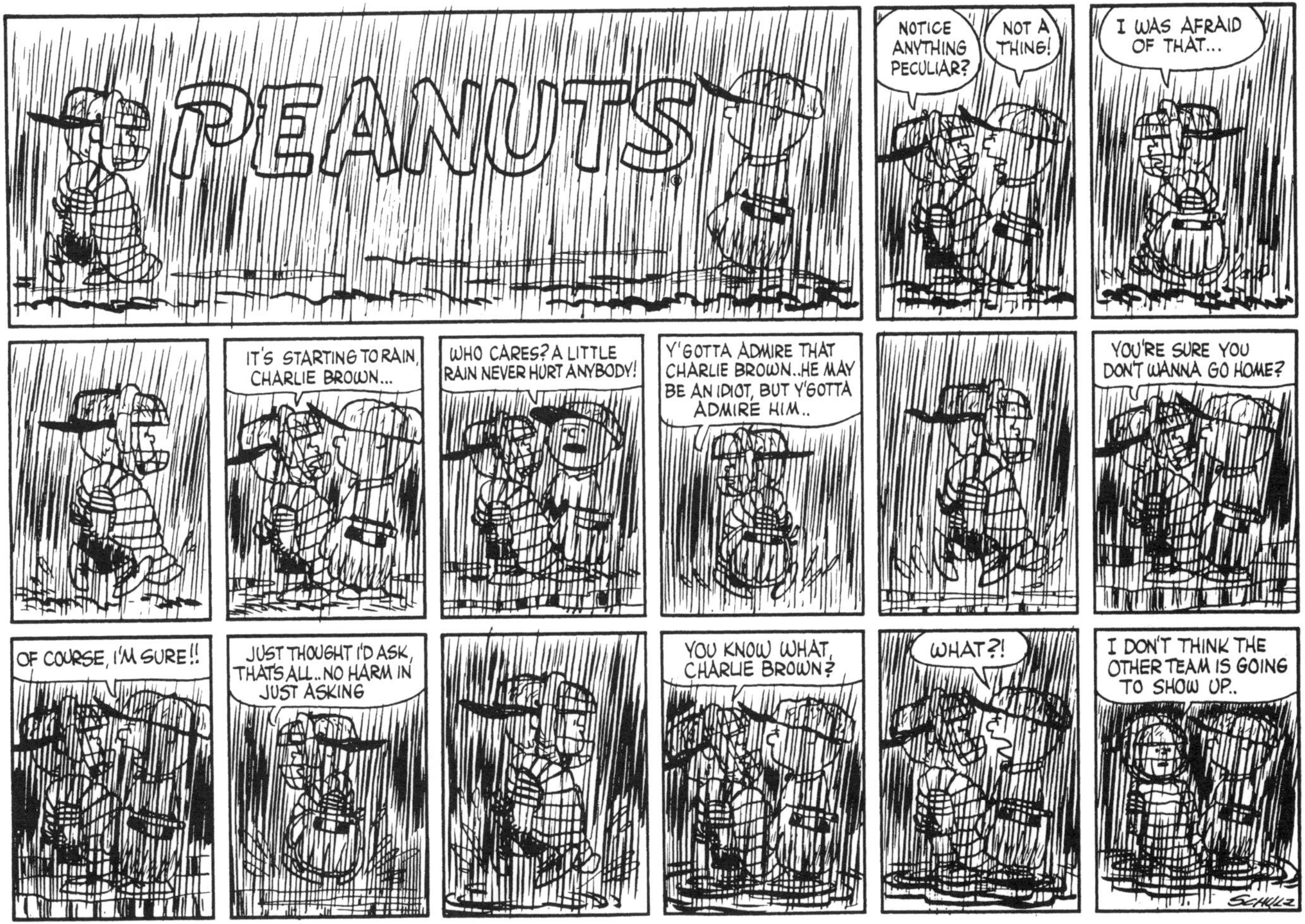
PEANUTS
NOTICE ANYTHING PECULIAR?
NOT A THING!
I WAS AFRAID OF THAT...
IT'S STARTING TO RAIN, CHARLIE BROWN...
WHO CARES? A LITTLE RAIN NEVER HURT ANYBODY!
Y'GOTTA ADMIRE THAT CHARLIE BROWN..HE MAY BE AN IDIOT, BUT Y'GOTTA ADMIRE HIM..
YOU'RE SURE YOU DON'T WANNA GO HOME?
OF COURSE, I'M SURE!!
JUST THOUGHT I'D ASK, THAT'S ALL..NO HARM IN JUST ASKING
YOU KNOW WHAT, CHARLIE BROWN?
WHAT?!
I DON'T THINK THE OTHER TEAM IS GOING TO SHOW UP..
SCHULZ

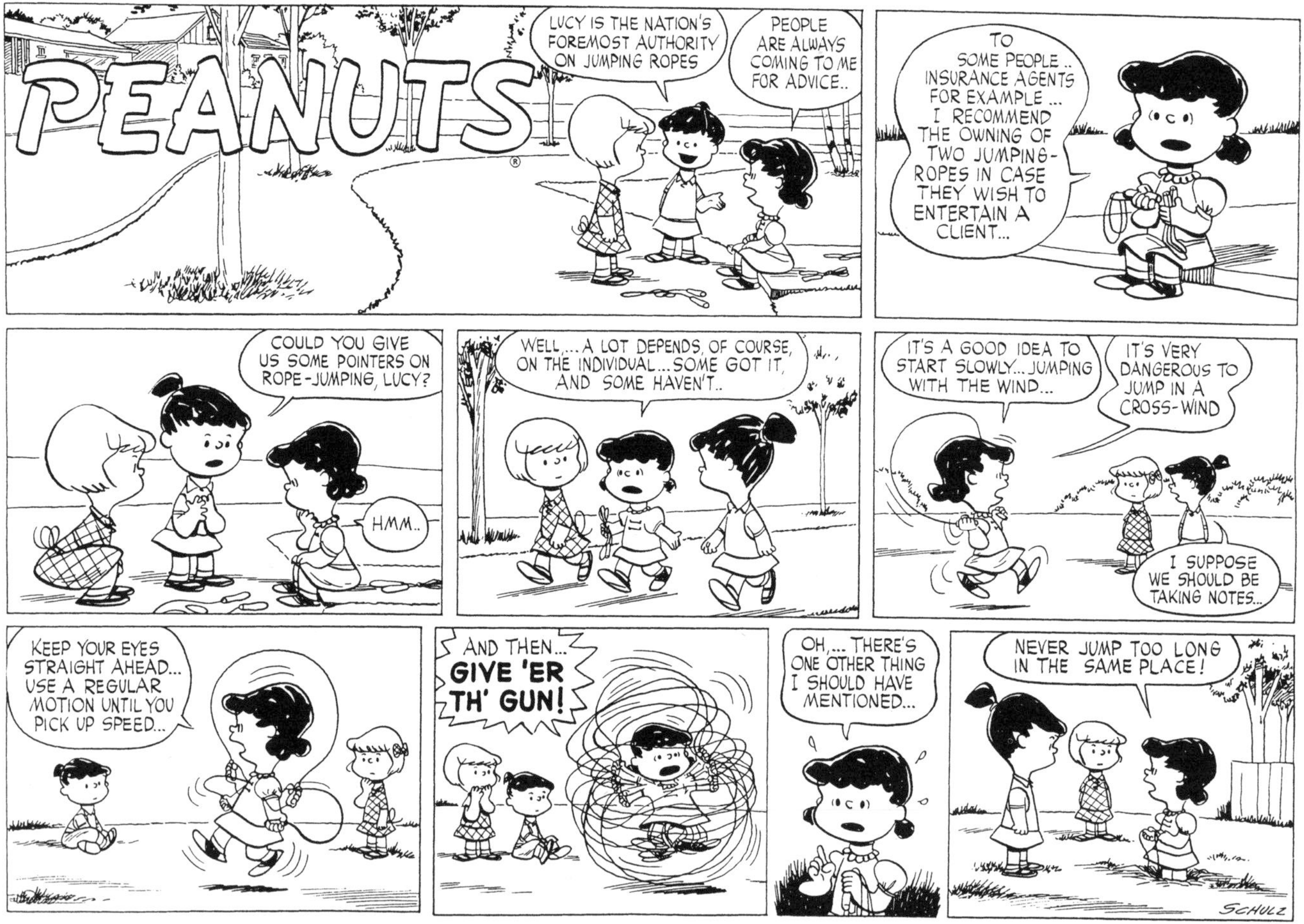
PEANUTS
LUCY IS THE NATION'S FOREMOST AUTHORITY ON JUMPING ROPES
PEOPLE ARE ALWAYS COMING TO ME FOR ADVICE..
TO SOME PEOPLE.. INSURANCE AGENTS FOR EXAMPLE ... I RECOMMEND THE OWNING OF TWO JUMPING-ROPES IN CASE THEY WISH TO ENTERTAIN A CLIENT...
COULD YOU GIVE US SOME POINTERS ON ROPE-JUMPING, LUCY?
HMM..
WELL,... A LOT DEPENDS, OF COURSE, ON THE INDIVIDUAL... SOME GOT IT, AND SOME HAVEN'T..
IT'S A GOOD IDEA TO START SLOWLY... JUMPING WITH THE WIND...
IT'S VERY DANGEROUS TO JUMP IN A CROSS-WIND
I SUPPOSE WE SHOULD BE TAKING NOTES...
KEEP YOUR EYES STRAIGHT AHEAD... USE A REGULAR MOTION UNTIL YOU PICK UP SPEED...
AND THEN... GIVE 'ER TH' GUN!
OH,... THERE'S ONE OTHER THING I SHOULD HAVE MENTIONED...
NEVER JUMP TOO LONG IN THE SAME PLACE!
SCHULZ

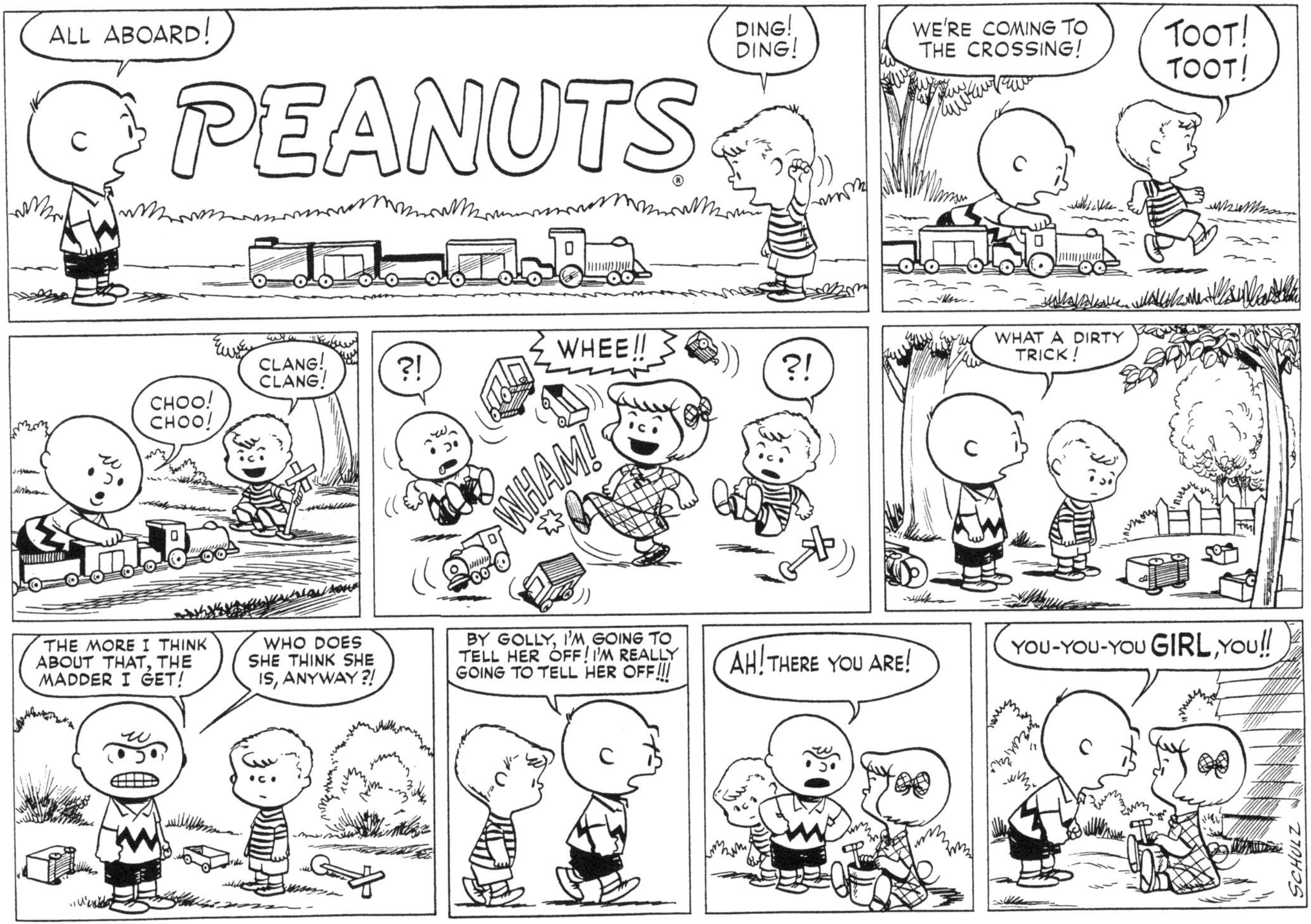

ALL ABOARD!
PEANUTS
DING! DING!
WE'RE COMING TO THE CROSSING!
TOOT! TOOT!
CHOO! CHOO!
CLANG! CLANG!
?!
WHEE!!
?!
WHAM!
WHAT A DIRTY TRICK!
THE MORE I THINK ABOUT THAT, THE MADDER I GET!
WHO DOES SHE THINK SHE IS, ANYWAY?!
BY GOLLY, I'M GOING TO TELL HER OFF! I'M REALLY GOING TO TELL HER OFF!!!
AH! THERE YOU ARE!
YOU-YOU-YOU GIRL, YOU!!
SCHULZ

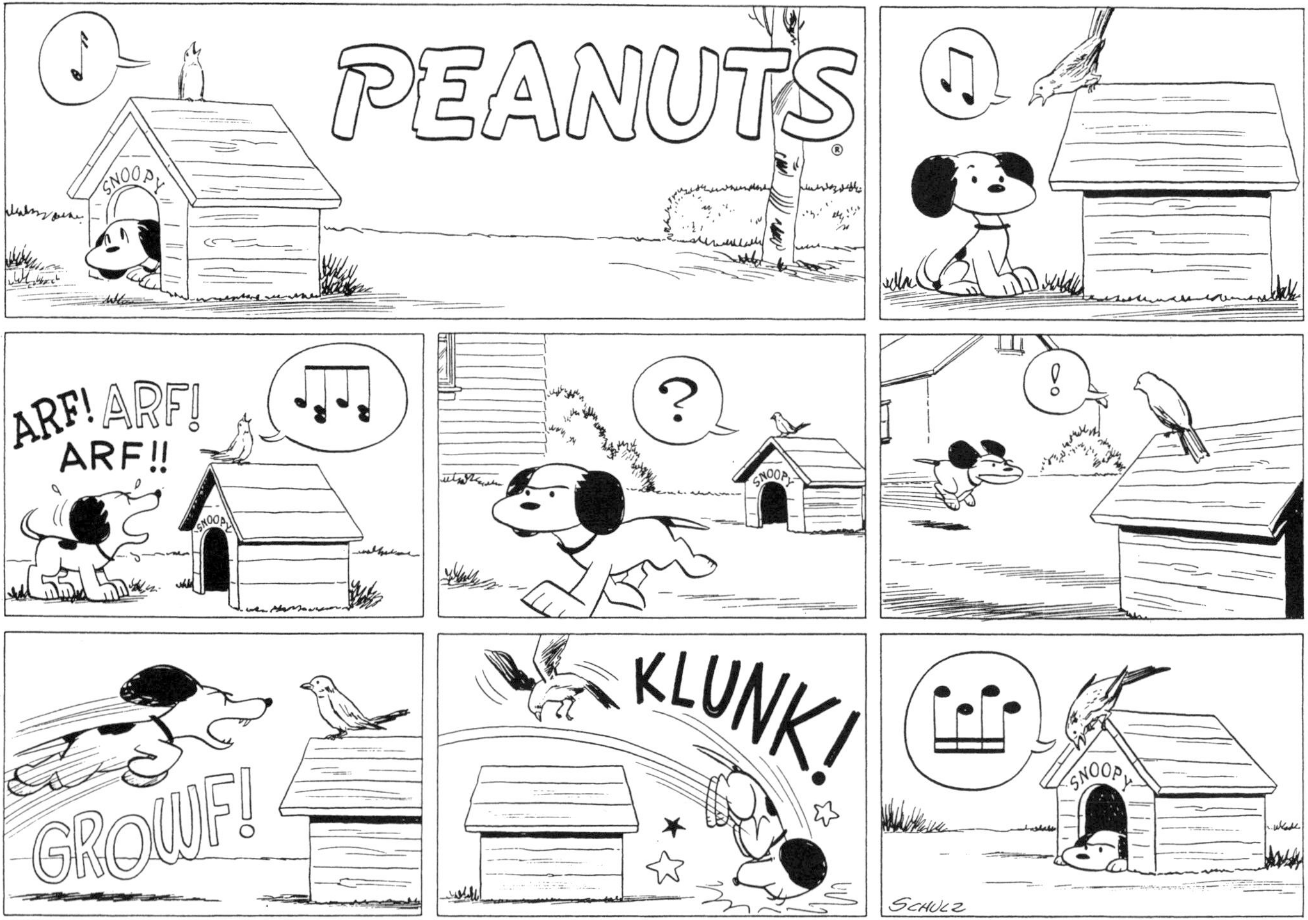

PEANUTS
SNOOPY
ARF! ARF!
ARF!!
SNOOPY
?
SNOOPY
!
GROWF!
KLUNK!
SNOOPY
SCHULZ

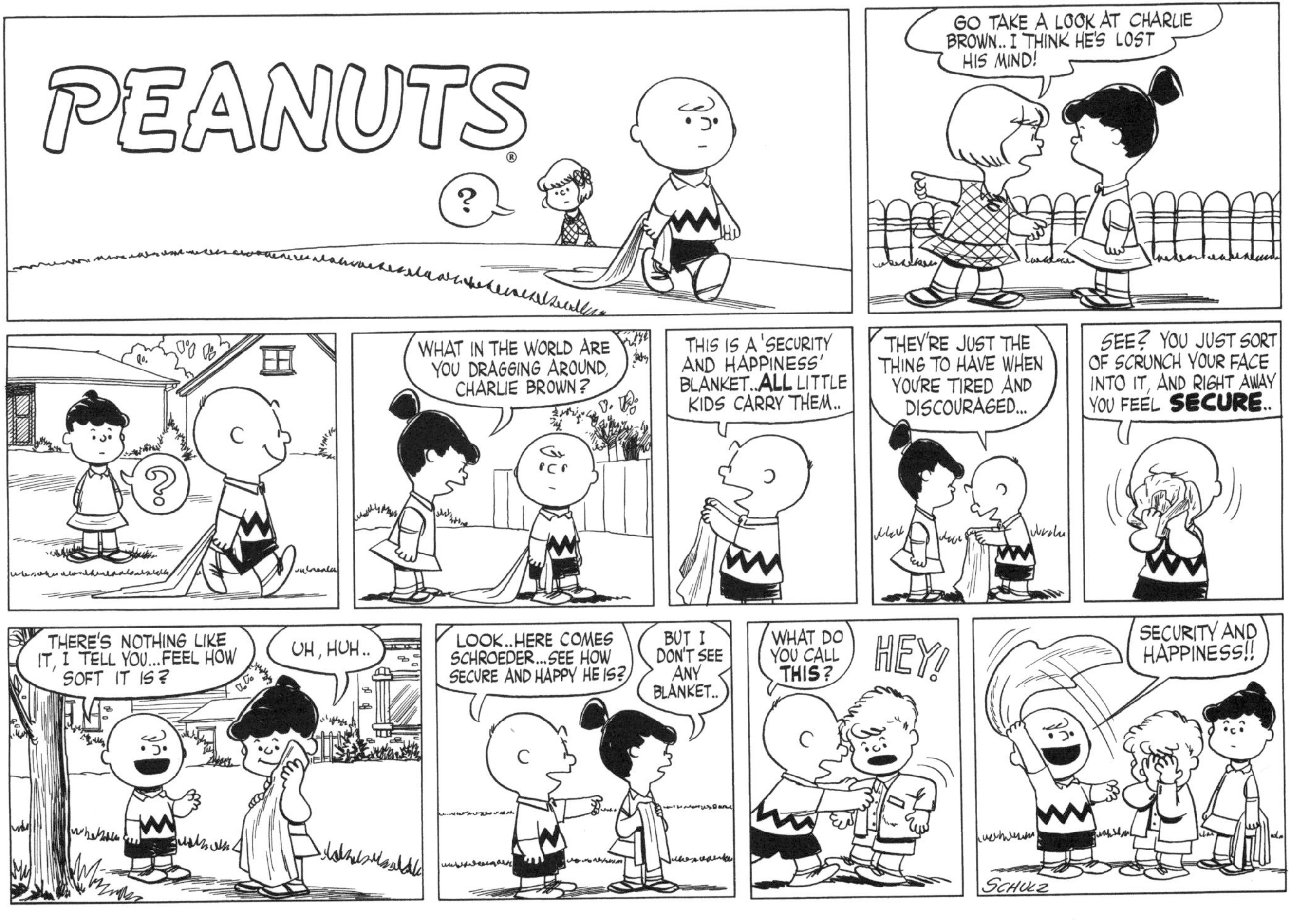
PEANUTS
?
GO TAKE A LOOK AT CHARLIE BROWN.. I THINK HE'S LOST HIS MIND!
?
WHAT IN THE WORLD ARE YOU DRAGGING AROUND, CHARLIE BROWN?
THIS IS A 'SECURITY AND HAPPINESS' BLANKET..ALL LITTLE KIDS CARRY THEM..
THEY'RE JUST THE THING TO HAVE WHEN YOU'RE TIRED AND DISCOURAGED...
SEE? YOU JUST SORT OF SCRUNCH YOUR FACE INTO IT, AND RIGHT AWAY YOU FEEL SECURE..
THERE'S NOTHING LIKE IT, I TELL YOU...FEEL HOW SOFT IT IS?
UH, HUH..
LOOK..HERE COMES SCHROEDER...SEE HOW SECURE AND HAPPY HE IS?
BUT I DON'T SEE ANY BLANKET..
WHAT DO YOU CALL THIS?
HEY!
SECURITY AND HAPPINESS!!
SCHULZ

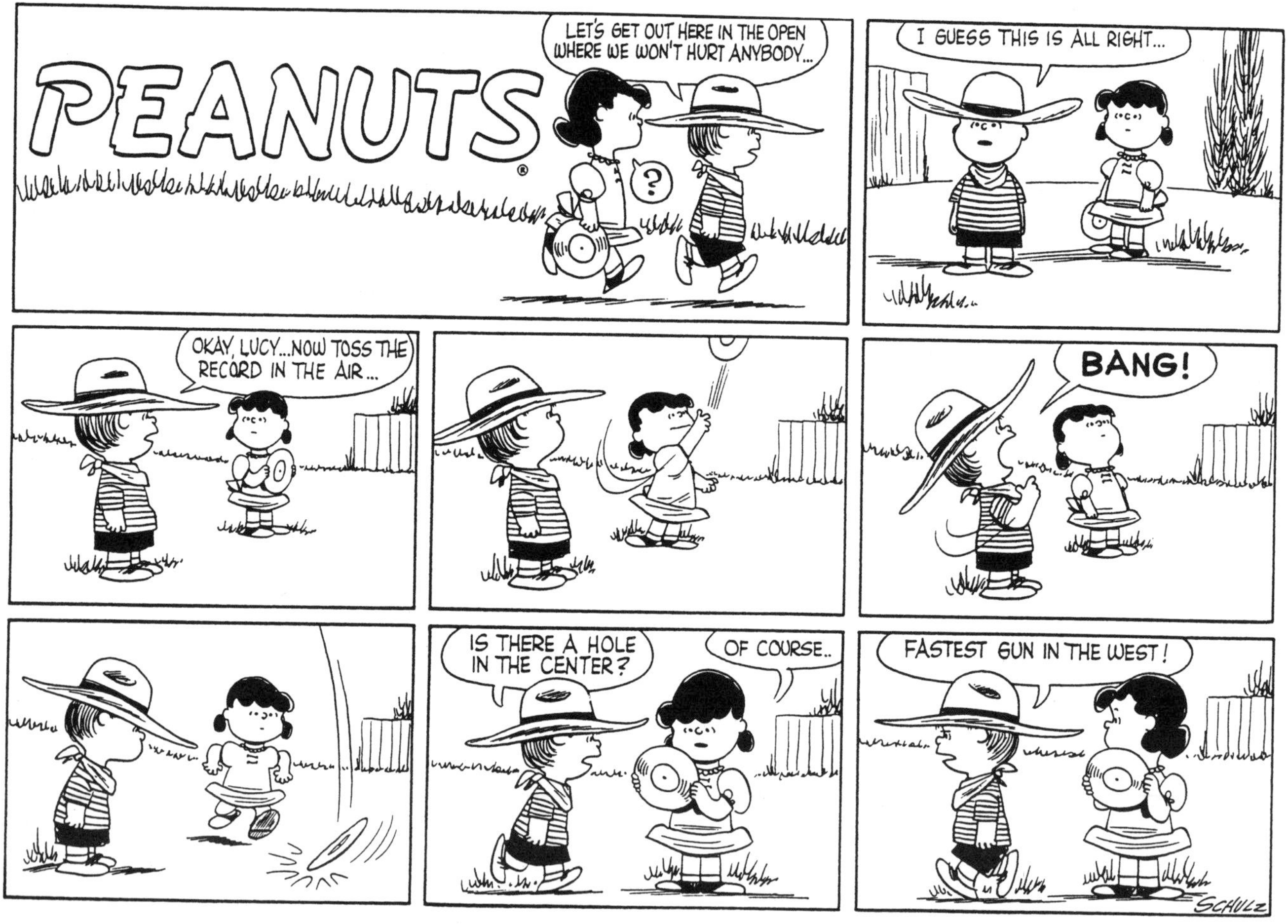
PEANUTS
LET'S GET OUT HERE IN THE OPEN WHERE WE WON'T HURT ANYBODY...
?
I GUESS THIS IS ALL RIGHT...
OKAY, LUCY...NOW TOSS THE RECORD IN THE AIR...
BANG!
IS THERE A HOLE IN THE CENTER?
OF COURSE..
FASTEST GUN IN THE WEST!
SCHULZ

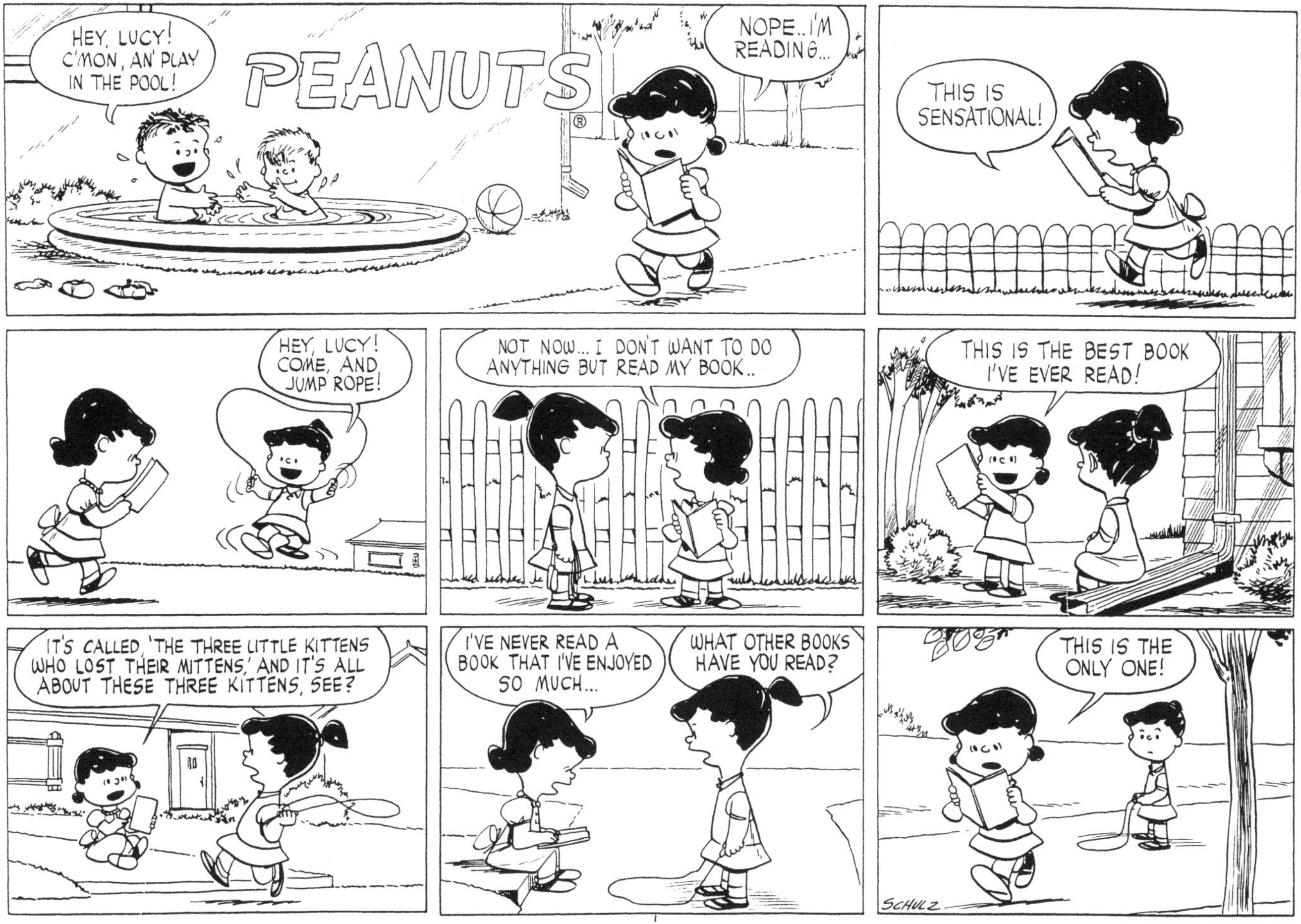
HEY, LUCY! C'MON, AN' PLAY IN THE POOL!
PEANUTS®
NOPE.. I'M READING...
THIS IS SENSATIONAL!
HEY, LUCY! COME, AND JUMP ROPE!
NOT NOW... I DON'T WANT TO DO ANYTHING BUT READ MY BOOK..
THIS IS THE BEST BOOK I'VE EVER READ!
IT'S CALLED, 'THE THREE LITTLE KITTENS WHO LOST THEIR MITTENS,' AND IT'S ALL ABOUT THESE THREE KITTENS, SEE?
I'VE NEVER READ A BOOK THAT I'VE ENJOYED SO MUCH...
WHAT OTHER BOOKS HAVE YOU READ?
THIS IS THE ONLY ONE!
SCHULZ

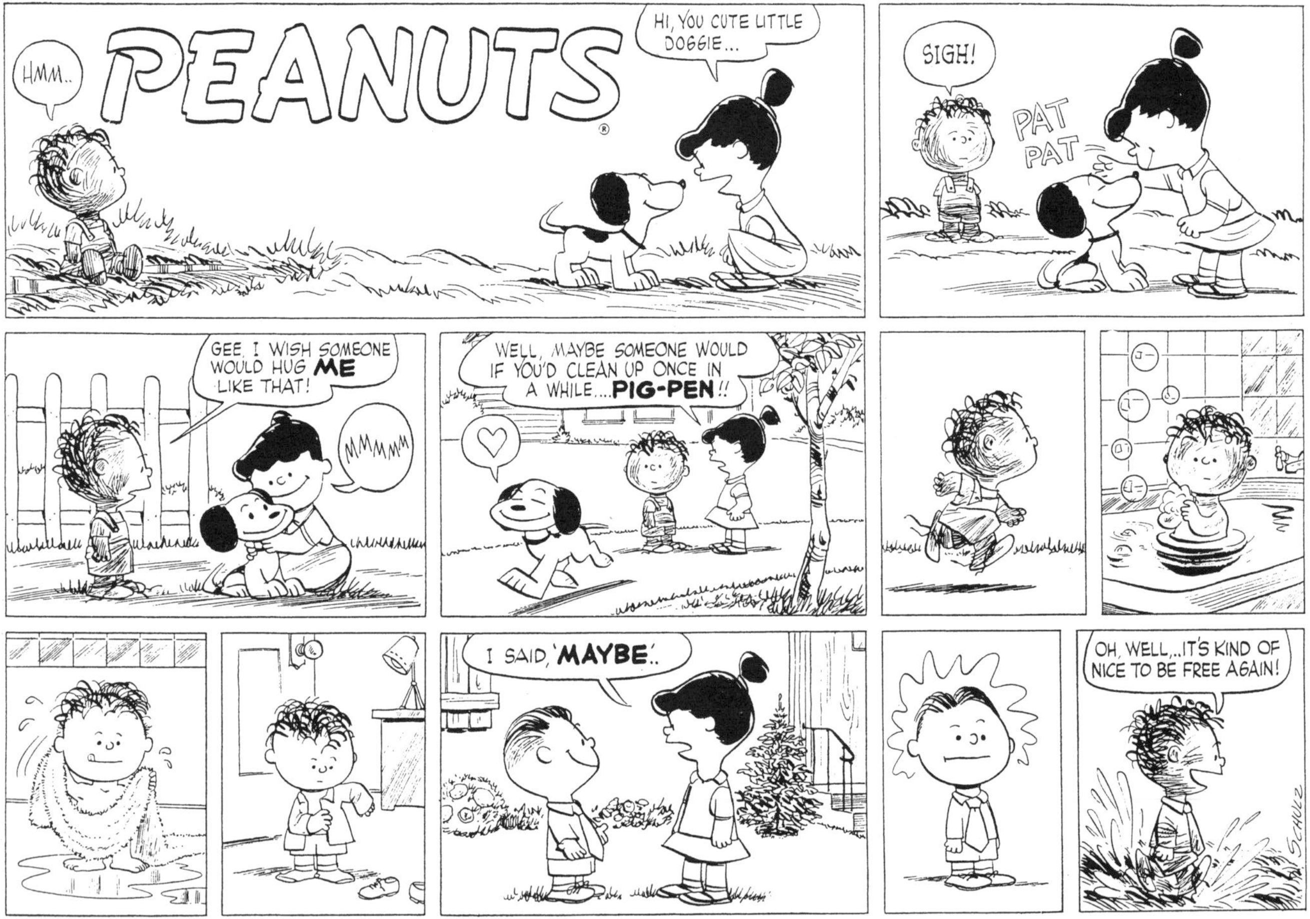
PEANUTS
HMM..
HI, YOU CUTE LITTLE DOGGIE...
SIGH!
PAT PAT
GEE, I WISH SOMEONE WOULD HUG **ME** LIKE THAT!
MMMMM
WELL, MAYBE SOMEONE WOULD IF YOU'D CLEAN UP ONCE IN A WHILE....**PIG-PEN**!!
I SAID, '**MAYBE**'..
OH, WELL...IT'S KIND OF NICE TO BE FREE AGAIN!
SCHULZ

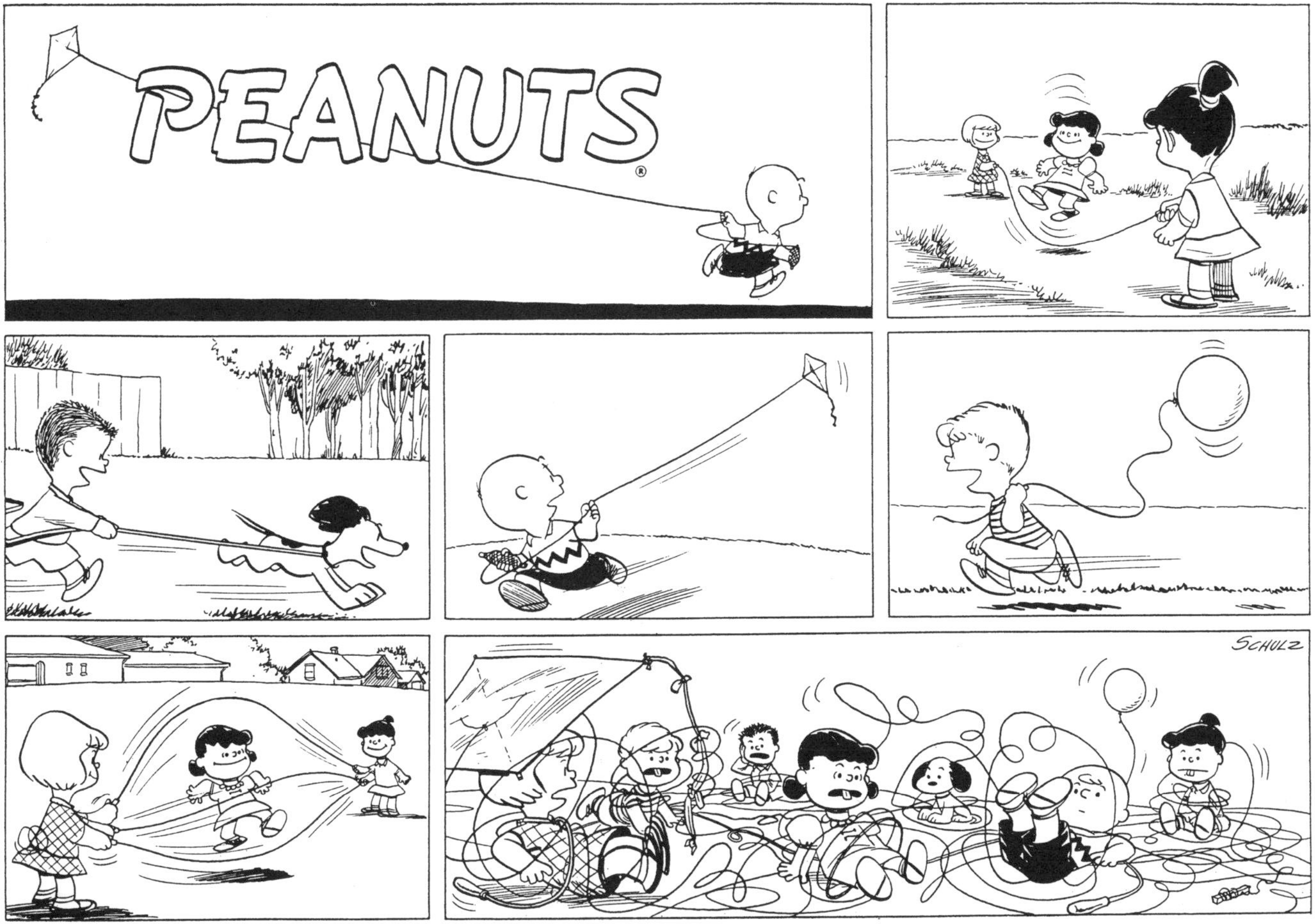
PEANUTS
SCHULZ

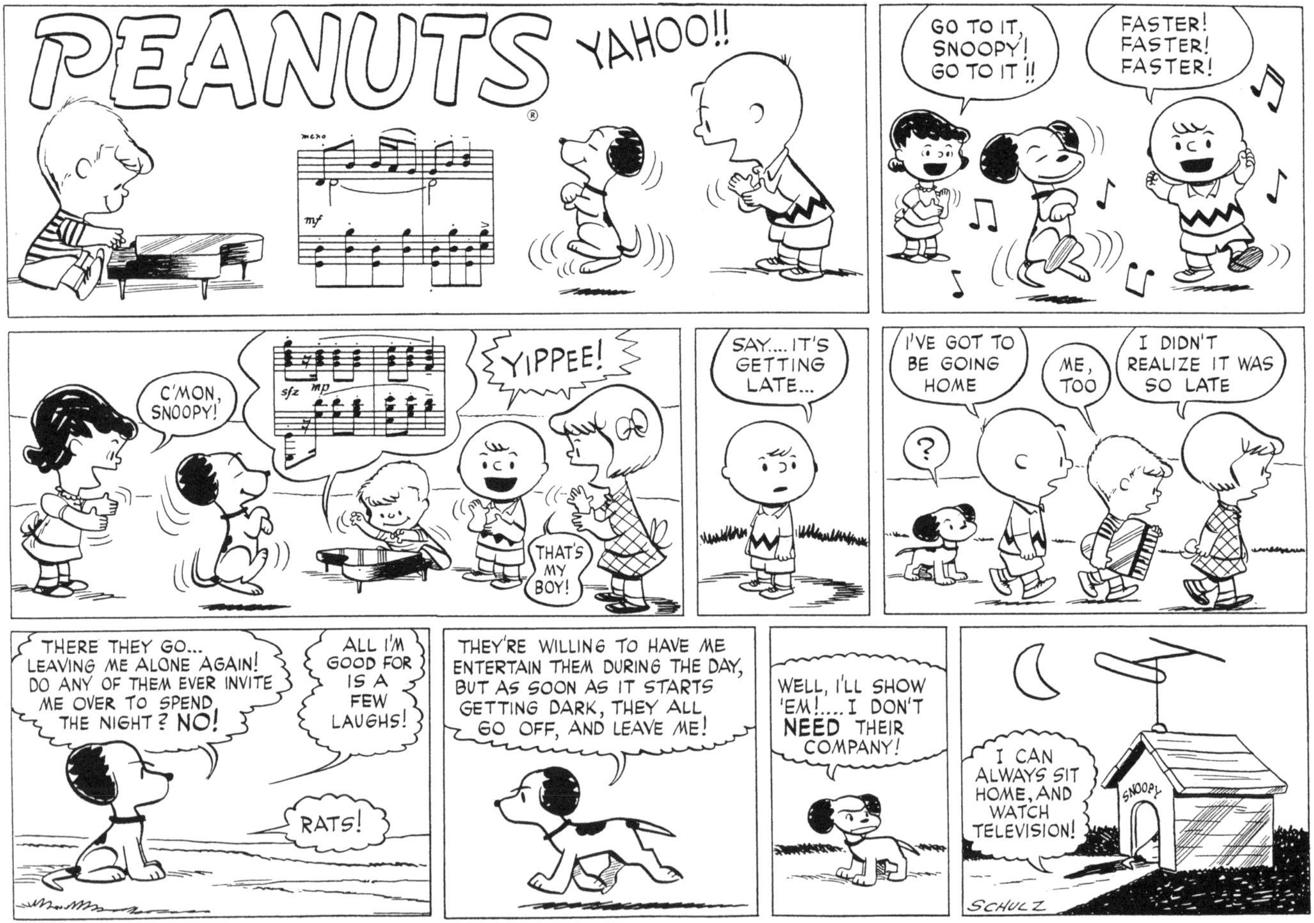
PEANUTS
YAHOO!!
GO TO IT, SNOOPY! GO TO IT!!
FASTER! FASTER! FASTER!
C'MON, SNOOPY!
YIPPEE!
THAT'S MY BOY!
SAY.... IT'S GETTING LATE...
I'VE GOT TO BE GOING HOME
ME, TOO
I DIDN'T REALIZE IT WAS SO LATE
?
THERE THEY GO... LEAVING ME ALONE AGAIN! DO ANY OF THEM EVER INVITE ME OVER TO SPEND THE NIGHT? NO!
ALL I'M GOOD FOR IS A FEW LAUGHS!
RATS!
THEY'RE WILLING TO HAVE ME ENTERTAIN THEM DURING THE DAY, BUT AS SOON AS IT STARTS GETTING DARK, THEY ALL GO OFF, AND LEAVE ME!
WELL, I'LL SHOW 'EM!.... I DON'T NEED THEIR COMPANY!
I CAN ALWAYS SIT HOME, AND WATCH TELEVISION!
SNOOPY
SCHULZ

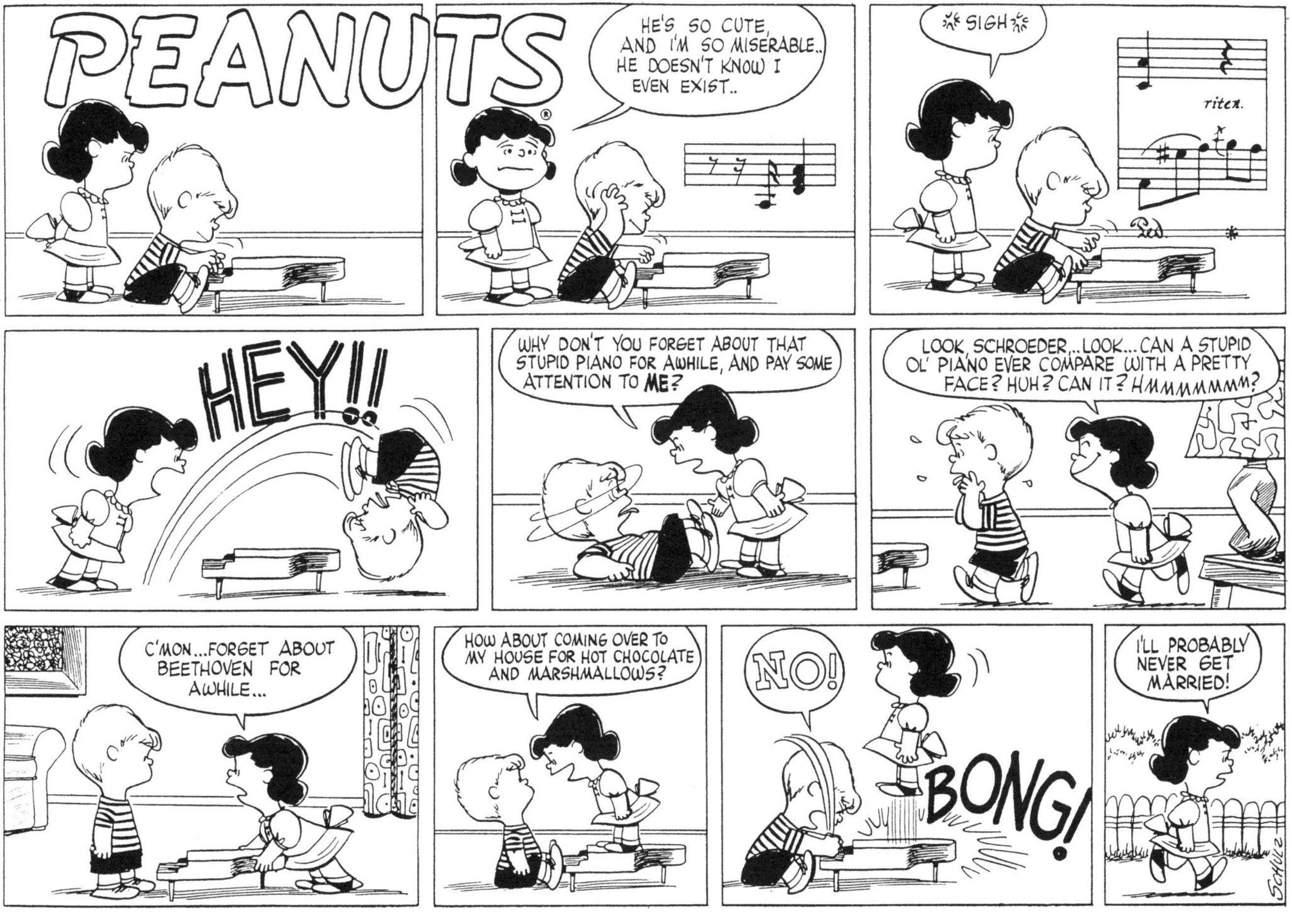
PEANUTS
HE'S SO CUTE, AND I'M SO MISERABLE.. HE DOESN'T KNOW I EVEN EXIST..
SIGH
riten.
HEY!!!
WHY DON'T YOU FORGET ABOUT THAT STUPID PIANO FOR AWHILE, AND PAY SOME ATTENTION TO ME?
LOOK, SCHROEDER...LOOK...CAN A STUPID OL' PIANO EVER COMPARE WITH A PRETTY FACE? HUH? CAN IT? HMMMMMMM?
C'MON...FORGET ABOUT BEETHOVEN FOR AWHILE...
HOW ABOUT COMING OVER TO MY HOUSE FOR HOT CHOCOLATE AND MARSHMALLOWS?
NO!
BONG!
I'LL PROBABLY NEVER GET MARRIED!
SCHULZ

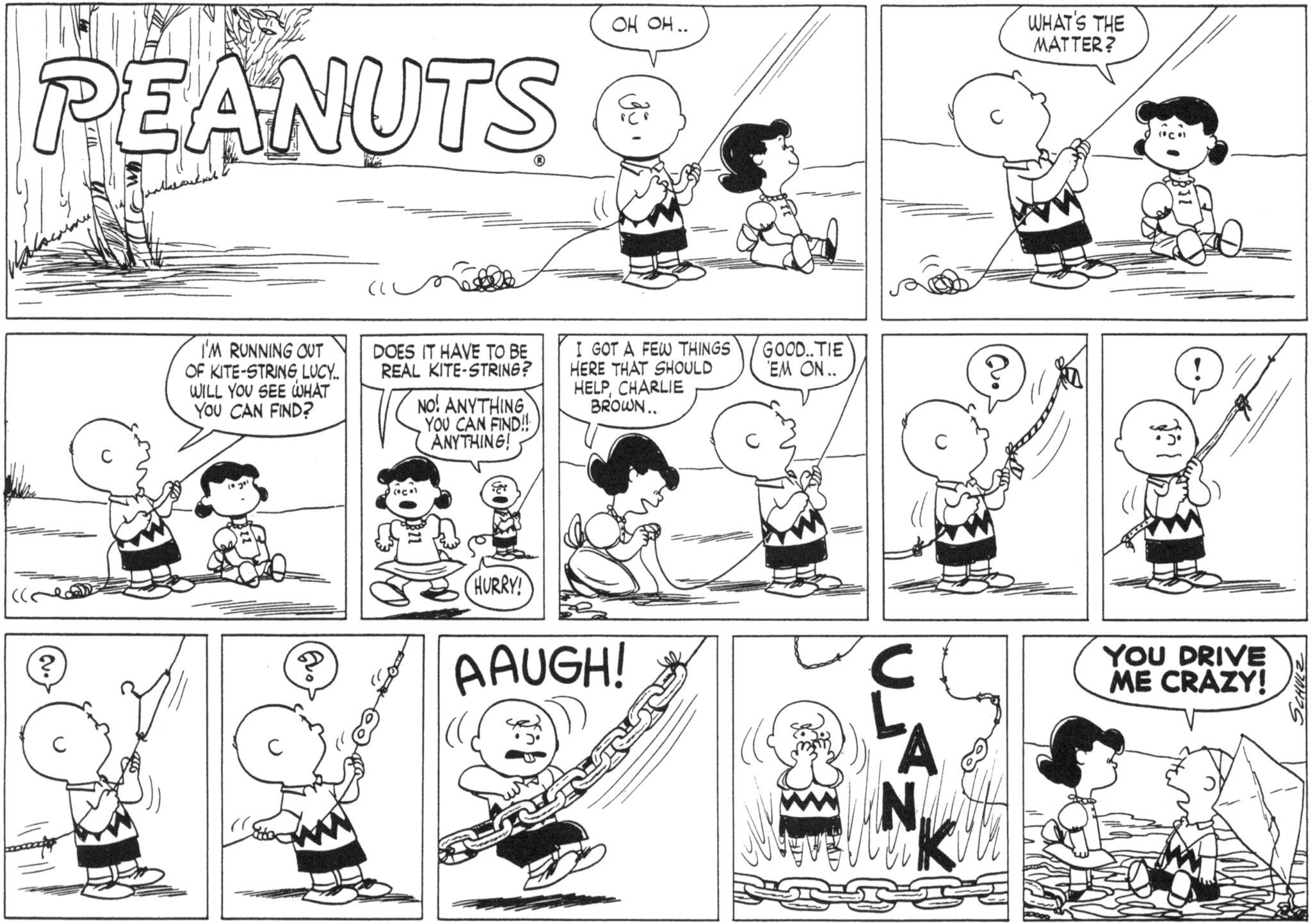
PEANUTS
OH OH..
WHAT'S THE MATTER?
I'M RUNNING OUT OF KITE-STRING LUCY.. WILL YOU SEE WHAT YOU CAN FIND?
DOES IT HAVE TO BE REAL KITE-STRING?
NO! ANYTHING YOU CAN FIND!! ANYTHING!
HURRY!
I GOT A FEW THINGS HERE THAT SHOULD HELP, CHARLIE BROWN..
GOOD..TIE 'EM ON..
?
!
?
?
AAUGH!
CLANK
YOU DRIVE ME CRAZY!
SCHULZ

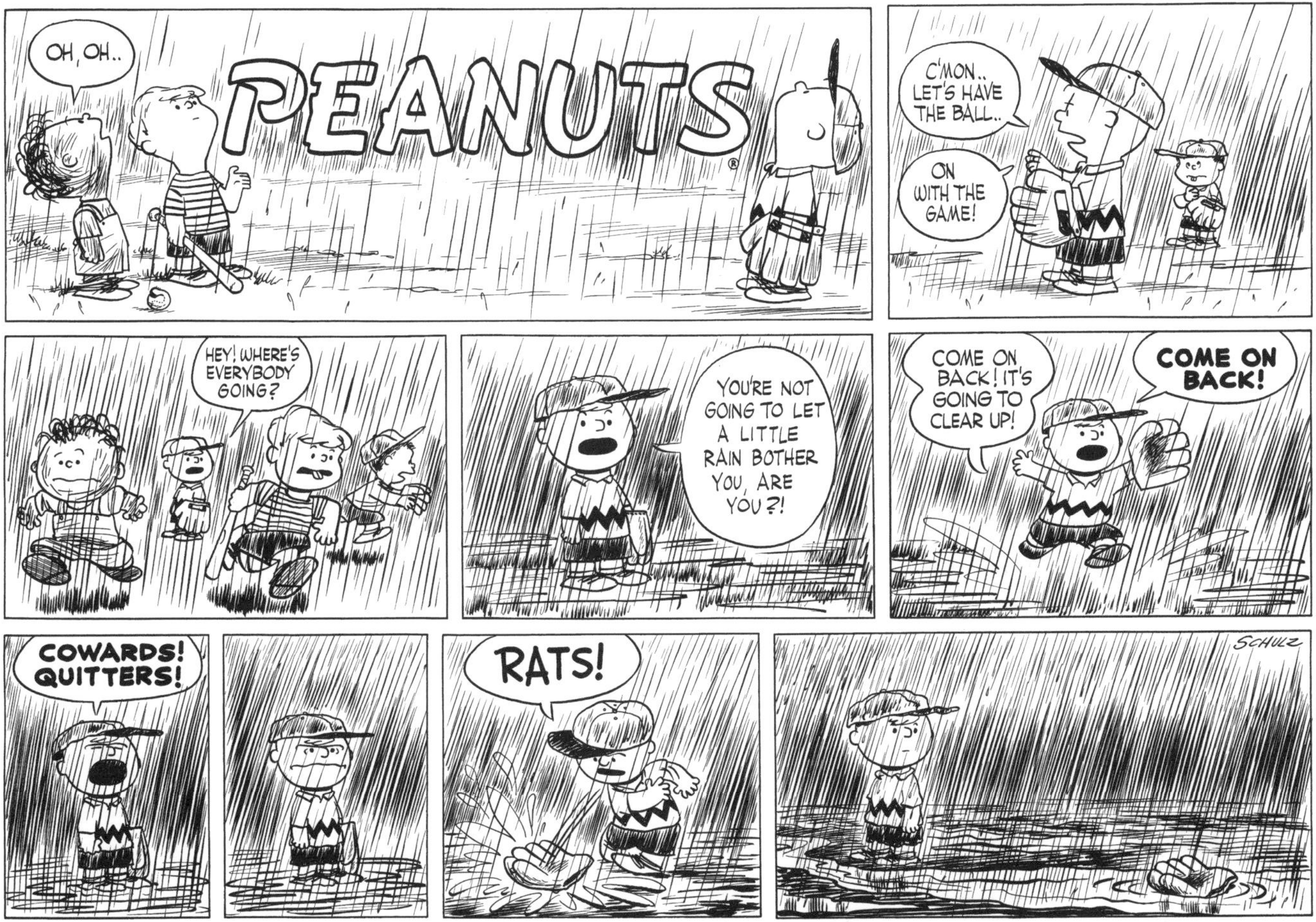

OH, OH..
PEANUTS®
C'MON.. LET'S HAVE THE BALL..
ON WITH THE GAME!
HEY! WHERE'S EVERYBODY GOING?
YOU'RE NOT GOING TO LET A LITTLE RAIN BOTHER YOU, ARE YOU?!
COME ON BACK! IT'S GOING TO CLEAR UP!
COME ON BACK!
COWARDS! QUITTERS!
RATS!
SCHULZ

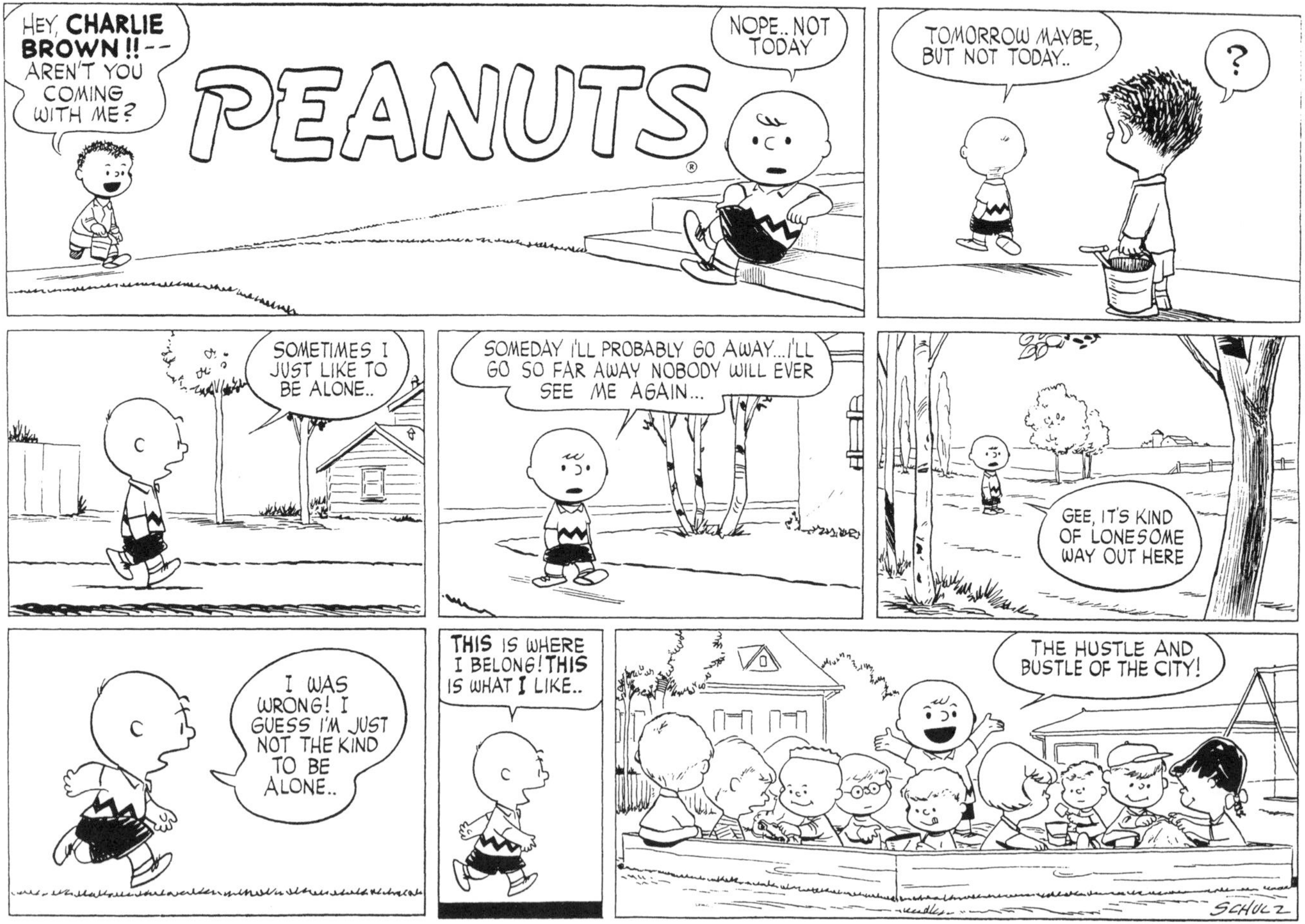
HEY, CHARLIE BROWN!! -- AREN'T YOU COMING WITH ME?
PEANUTS
NOPE.. NOT TODAY
TOMORROW MAYBE, BUT NOT TODAY..
?
SOMETIMES I JUST LIKE TO BE ALONE..
SOMEDAY I'LL PROBABLY GO AWAY...I'LL GO SO FAR AWAY NOBODY WILL EVER SEE ME AGAIN...
GEE, IT'S KIND OF LONESOME WAY OUT HERE
I WAS WRONG! I GUESS I'M JUST NOT THE KIND TO BE ALONE..
THIS IS WHERE I BELONG! THIS IS WHAT I LIKE..
THE HUSTLE AND BUSTLE OF THE CITY!
SCHULZ